COMMUNICATION THEORY

Racially Diverse and Inclusive Perspectives

EDITORS

JASMINE T. AUSTIN
Texas State University

MARK P. ORBE
Western Michigan University

JEANETTA D. SIMS
University of Central Oklahoma

SAN DIEGO

Bassim Hamadeh, CEO and Publisher
Todd R. Armstrong, Publisher
Michelle Piehl, Senior Project Editor
Sara Watkins, Developmental Editor
Alia Bales, Production Editor
Emely Villavicencio, Senior Graphic Designer
Trey Soto, Licensing Specialist
Stephanie Adams, Senior Marketing Program Manager
Natalie Piccotti, Director of Marketing
Kassie Graves, Senior Vice President, Editorial
Jamie Giganti, Director of Academic Publishing

3970 Sorrento Valley Blvd., Ste. 500, San Diego, CA 9212

CONTENTS

STORIED REFLECTIONS

PREFACE

Teaching communication theory can be a challenge; the content is often perceived as abstract, obsolete, unnecessarily complex, or irrelevant to daily experiences, particularly to students with salient racial, ethnic, and cultural identities who find difficulty connecting with scholarly inquiry in which they are not represented. They are being taught theories from a white-colonial-normative core that does not provide a holistic understanding of communication theory. Recent turmoils in the communication studies discipline highlight this major hurdle. Thus, the need exists for a text that scholars and students alike will find engaging, accessible, and relevant to the racial, ethnic, and cultural diversity in today's world.

Communication Theory: Diverse and Inclusive Perspectives has the explicit mission of decentering traditional views of communication by highlighting perspectives from the global majority. We aim for readers to learn many of the same foundational theories, including diverse perspectives from marginalized racial and ethnic groups, and we seek for communication theorizing and practice to more fully represent non-white-colonial-normative theoretical frameworks. This textbook is an intervention and radical upheaval of "traditional" communication thought and theorizing, and it imbeds a diversity of racial, cultural, physical, and gendered standpoints.

Our Mission

Communication Theory: Diverse and Inclusive Perspectives tracks the state of theory and theorizing in the communication studies discipline, while decentering whiteness and normative identities and (re)centering the identities, experiences, and perspectives of marginalized groups by featuring seasoned, established, and emerging theorists. It facilitates an understanding of how the communicative experiences of marginalized groups fit in previously conceived theoretical frameworks, and it offers innovative conceptions of communication theorizing centered in/through the perspectives of African American/Black, Latinx, Asian American, and Indigenous/First Nations people—individuals who are regarded as multidimensional and intersectional in terms of their identities.

Communication Theory: Diverse and Inclusive Perspectives benchmarks the different sections consistent with best-selling undergraduate communication theory textbooks so that this text can be used alongside of, or as a replacement to, an existing communication theory textbook to approach communication theories from historical *and* contemporary perspectives. Two key motivations that can inform use of the book in a communication theory course are: (1) a desire to teach many of the same, foundational theories and include diverse perspectives from marginalized racial and ethnic groups, and (2) a desire to centralize nonwhite-colonial-normative theoretical frameworks as more fully representative of contemporary communication theorizing and practice.

Benefits and Features of This Text

Communication Theory: Diverse and Inclusive Perspectives is accessible, engaging, and centers diverse voices at the content's core. This book reflects the highest academic quality given that the featured contributors are theorists writing about their own work, established scholars who offer summaries from peer-reviewed publications and rising scholars who offer new perspectives through previously published scholarship. In this regard, readers benefit from a targeted group of scholars of color who have the academic credentials, commitment to diversifying existing curriculum, and passion for this project. In addition to this distinctive group of contributors, we offer additional benefits and features of this book.

Introductory Part Overviews

Communication Theory: Diverse and Inclusive Perspectives is organized into the following six parts: (1) The Self and Identity; (2) Interpersonal Messages; (3) Relating and Relationships; (4) Leadership and Organizations; (5) Rhetoric and Influence; and (6) Media and Technology. We set the tone for each part with an introduction that offers a discussion of existing canonized theories, an overview of each featured theoretical contribution, and a glimpse of what to expect from the storied reflections. By introducing existing canonized theories, the reader benefits from a balance of established communication theories overwhelmingly reflective of white and western perspectives paired with an elaboration on oft-times lesser-known theories from a decolonized perspective. These individual part introductions are beneficial to the instructor and students as a transitional pedagogical tool to prepare the students for what is to come and to review before moving forward.

Insightful and Diverse Theoretical Contributions

The group of diverse scholars featured throughout this book lends well to a revolutionary combination of theoretical frameworks. Many of these chapters stem from and extend existing canonized theories, while others are a direct result of theorists not seeing their identities, experiences, and/or perspectives represented in communication scholarship and theorizing. These extensions are beneficial as they link past, well-established theories with integral, unconventional, and decolonized theories. The aim is not to discredit established communication theories; instead, our objective is to expand and enhance how we see, use, and apply communication theory, including contemporary culturally centric theoretical frameworks. The content of the theoretical contributions place emphasis on centralizing diverse perspectives.

Novel and Distinctive Storied Reflections

A unique feature of this book is the 18 storied reflections embedded in every part. Storied reflections are personal narratives that offer something often missed and taken for granted in the broader composition of our developing and vibrant theory-building enterprise—a glimpse of diverse scholars at various stages of their careers ruminating on their own experiences with theory. These storied reflections breathe life into theory and help readers make personal connections to how scholarship can inform life and how ethnic and racialized standpoints can inform scholarship. The purpose of the storied reflections is to aid in contextualizing theory, gaining a critical understanding of the connectedness between scholarship and personal experiences, and to move the reader towards seeing themselves in theorizing by centering real scholars amidst theory. Contributors range from accomplished professors to early career doctoral students—all are scholars from racial and ethnically diverse backgrounds. The storied reflections share the maturation of scholars as they navigate doubts, engage with mentors, and face mental triggers, among other personal experiences; these reflections and turning points are typically unseen in the pages of communication theory texts. Through the storied reflections, readers benefit from seeing the personal development of scholars alongside the progression of theory.

Special Pedagogical Features

Apparent in each chapter are special pedagogical aids and high-interest features. Readers will note that each chapter is structured similarly; this organizational format allows individuals to engage in each theoretical framework in similar ways (e.g., intellectual traditions, main features and concepts, etc.). Every chapter also includes a practical application section, in which the theory is applied to a recent example. We are proud of our chapter authors for making these examples engaging, relevant, and accessible for our readers. Finally, each chapter concludes with a list of four to seven questions for further thought and reflection. These questions aid readers in processing theoretical underpinnings and help foster lively and meaningful discussion.

Acknowledgments

As editors of this volume, we first thank Cognella Academic Publishing for the opportunity to collaborate on such a timely and needed text on communication theory. We thank our chapter authors, who graciously agreed to lend their time, talents, and expertise while following a rigorous publication schedule amid a global pandemic and protests against racialized police brutality. Also, we express heartfelt gratitude to our storied reflection contributors for their willingness to offer authentic, brave, and illuminating accounts of their experiences in academia.

We also gratefully acknowledge those racially and ethnically diverse people who have experienced educational spaces on the margins. This includes family members who blamed themselves for their lack of success in schools that failed to provide learning environments that were inclusive, relevant, and welcoming. It also includes generations of students, scholars, and theorists of the global majority whose ideas were muted, marginalized, or ignored by dominant group scholars who were invested in sustaining a status quo from which they inherently benefitted.

Finally, we wish to especially say thank you to our pillars of strength in the form of our angels (ancestors and loved ones), family, friends, mentors, mentees, colleagues, and one and all who, directly or indirectly, lent their hand in this venture.

Dumela,
Jasmine T. Austin
Mark P. Orbe
Jeanetta D. Sims

Diversifying the Communication Discipline

Communication Theory: Diverse and Inclusive Perspectives, at its core, is about communication theorizing with a particular emphasis on including those whose identities reflect the global majority. The pandemic and protests in recent years, combined with calls for change in the communication discipline, have fueled a reexamination of communication theory—with a specific focus on featuring diverse racial, ethnic, and cultural voices. Through giving attention to theory, this text invites a critical exploration of what we know, how we have come to know it, and who has contributed to our knowing.

Why Communication Theory?

"Why do I need to know theory?"

"Theories are too irrelevant, abstract, and complicated—they're just too theoretical."

"What's the connection between communication theory and my personal life?"

"Theory is boring and detached from the personal, lived experience."

"How does learning about theory make me an effective communicator?"

"Theory is nonessential for addressing contemporary problems."

These are a few of the statements and questions we often hear from students upon the mention of the word *theory*. And among students who are Black, Indigenous, or People of Color (BIPOC), a prevalent criticism is that communication theory offers a limited view, if any view at all, of their daily, lived experiences—theory is seen as void of their cultural, racial, and ethnic backgrounds. Indeed, it appears "to most people, theories seem to be of little use" (Shoemaker et al., 2004, p. 6).

Yet, the study of communication is theory-infused, and simply put, theory is vital to the strength and vitality of the communication discipline. It is impossible to be a serious student of communication without being a learner of communication theory. The state of theorizing in our discipline is vibrant with greater levels of breadth, depth, and scope in our ways of knowing, particularly among scholars from diverse racial and cultural backgrounds. For this reason, *Communication Theory: Diverse and Inclusive Perspectives* has the explicit goal of decentering traditional views of communication by highlighting nonwhite perspectives as we revisit, critique, reimagine, and reconstruct communication theories and concepts.

Understanding and Defining Communication Theory

Theory is mystifying to some people. The word *theory* stems from the Greek word *theoria*, which translates to mean contemplation or speculation. "Theories are a human creation" (Kaplan, 1964, p. 296). Theory and communication inquiry are inseparable since theory provides us a way of looking at communicative interactions. Consider the following brief phrases we associate with theory as:

- an untested hypothesis
- a way of seeing the world
- a lens for viewing phenomena
- a set of statements connected by logic
- a description of a piece of reality
- an exercise of hard work coupled with imagination

Consistent with these descriptions, theory is one's understanding of how communication processes function, operate, and work (Shoemaker et al., 2004). Additional words often associated with theory include perspective, guidepost, pointer, description, set of ideas, and relationships. Every examination of communication involves a lens guided by theoretical underpinnings. One cannot probe the communication process without assuming a stance or taking up an argument on theory. As demonstrated in the following storied reflection, understanding theory helps us better understand ourselves and others; "the 'need' for theories lies in the human behavior of wanting to impose order on unordered experiences" (Dubin, 1969, p. 6).

STORIED REFLECTION
Living for This Stuff!

Mark P. Orbe
Western Michigan University

As an undergraduate student majoring in organizational communication and minoring in sociology/psychology, my relationship to theory was best characterized as unenthusiastic disconnection. Some theories made sense and facilitated some general understanding of human behavior. However, the vast majority seemed unnecessarily complicated with little relevance to my everyday life. Shortly after undergrad, I completed a master's degree in higher education; my program was designed for student affairs professionals and focused on practical considerations. I would describe it as "light on theory and research and heavy on practical application." Again, theory was situated as separate from, and in many ways, less important than effective practice.

In 1990, motivated by a passion to teach on the university level, I began a doctoral program in interpersonal communication with a desire to focus on culture. Initially, I struggled with much of the material, which seemed so very removed from my own lived experiences. The little bit of research related to my scholarly interests that I did locate offered problematically stereotypical representations (e.g., interracial romantic alliances as pathologically based). On a rural Appalachian campus studying with predominately white faculty and peers, the imposter complex for a biracial, inner-city, first-generation high school graduate student like myself was crippling.

One of my very first doctoral classes focused on communication theory, and a core assignment was a collaborative presentation on a theory of our choosing. As the assignment was announced, I sat quietly observing other students pairing up and discussing their theory selections. In the end, there were two of us without partners, so by default, I partnered with a young white woman. After perusing the list of theories in our book, we settled on muted group theory, a framework that we both found interesting and engaging. We decided to meet our white male professor during office hours to notify him of our choice and get some additional guidance on how to approach the assignment.

As we began to share our desire to present on muted group theory, the professor quickly interrupted and advised, "You don't want to waste your time and present on that theory—no one in the field of communication uses it." Immediately, my home training kicked in, and I found myself thanking the professor for his wise advice, which would save us from wasting our time on an irrelevant theory. My presentation partner and I didn't think twice about challenging his statement, and we were grateful for his guidance in selecting a "better, more relevant" social scientific theory.

In retrospect, I now fully recognize how this brief interaction was illustrative of the powerful ways in which graduate students are socialized to understand the importance of learning some theories over others. I've learned and relearned this lesson time and time again. Some concepts, methods, and theories are at the core of the discipline. Others only have tangential relevance and value.

An important shift in school occurred when I took my first ever, and only, qualitative research methods class. I was able to read research and theory that centralized culture in ways that were healing as I worked to comprehend "what was happening around and within me" (hooks, 1991, p. 1). This was empowering and cultivated a sense of agency in my attempts to navigate communication research and theory. It also allowed me to understand my problematic relationship with empirical research that treated one's cultural identity as a variable that could be measured, manipulated, and correlated to produce generalizable findings—which seemed a lot like promoting stereotypes to me.

Over time, I learned to understand muted group theory as a valuable resource as I sought out theoretical frameworks that would provide a productive lens to the complex ways in which underrepresented group members strategically communicate in spaces where their bodies and voices are marginalized. In the end, my own lived experiences and commitment to learn about the experiences of others prompted a series of research projects that helped to build co-cultural theory that extends from the foundations of muted group and standpoint theories (Orbe, 1998). I never set out to create a theory; I just wanted to understand myself and others better. Over the past two decades, I've come to appreciate the value of communication theory, especially how frameworks provide a lens into the mysteries of communication that otherwise would remain unsolvable. I bring that appreciative energy and passion for theory into the communication theory mass lecture course that I teach each year. As a student once wrote in an online evaluation: "He loves what he's teaching. I mean he LIVES for this stuff!"

Communication theory is different than our daily use of commonsense, guesses, and hunches. Instead of mere informal reasoning, communication theory has attributes and characteristics that are more thoughtful and systematic—all of which employ some form of logic. The logic involves the use of arguments aimed at providing explanation, understanding, or prediction about focal phenomena. Theory represents the best thinking within a discipline and is a scholar's best response to the questions posed about human interaction. A body of theories is required for scholars in the communication discipline to address human problems or make distinctive contributions (Gerbner, 1983). Understanding and contributing to the discipline involves having a key grasp of communication theory.

The Importance of
Communication Theory

As building blocks for understanding the communication discipline, theories are important. In the communication discipline, individuals often associate communication scholars with the theories they have constructed or that they tend to employ. Thus, theory is vital, because it makes our knowledge both of communication scholarship and of communication scholars more robust.

The more theories you understand, the greater you are equipped for probing communication across contexts, situations, and cultures. Communication occurs virtually everywhere—families, organizations, romantic relationships, friendships, health, public speaking, mass media, intercultural, leadership, teams—and many more fields of communication study abound. When students understand the vast array of communication theory, they become more highly skilled, increasing their relevance, research, and areas of expertise.

A limited view (or no view at all) of theory is detrimental. Imagine attempting to capture the full essence of a sporting event as a photographer when only using a standard camera lens. What is missed? For instance, if one sits in the nosebleed section of the baseball stadium, photographing players near the dugout with a standard lens will be impossible; one would need a super telephoto or 300mm+ lens to take photos from a distance. On the other hand, capturing home run high fives and slides into second base would be best accomplished with a lens fit for action rather than with the 300mm+ lens. Just like some views of the action in the stadium are omitted when a particular camera lens is used, aspects of the communication process and components of lived experiences are uncaptured in some theoretical frameworks.

In the same way that a camera without a lens is useless to a photographer, a student of communication not knowing theory is inadequate. Much like using a single camera lens, understanding a single communication theory can be beneficial. However, grasping multiple theories—similar to using multiple camera lenses—enhances our abilities to work skillfully across contexts, situations, and fields of communication study.

Racial Controversies and Communication Theory

Limited representations in theory also lead to limited ways of knowing. The extant research (e.g., Rogers, 1994; Schramm, 1983; Schramm, 1997) on the beginnings of communication study in the United States emphasize the contributions of a prolific four—political scientist Harold Lasswell, social psychologist Kurt Lewin, experimental psychologist Carl Hovland, and sociologist Paul Lazarsfeld—with Wilbur Schramm as the founder of U.S. communication study. Schramm (1983) credits the four scholars as forefathers in the historical development of the discipline. He asserts that each contributed to what we know about the communication discipline in at least four ways: (1) all emphasized an empirical approach more than their predecessors; (2) all borrowed from the intellectual traditions of the hard and social sciences; (3)

all studied human communication; and (4) all were keenly aware of and interested in examining the effects of communication in life as well as in a laboratory or in books.

"Communication study is probably the most widely accepted new field in American universities" (Rogers, 1994, p. 445) over the past century. Certainly, each of the forerunners contributed to shaping this new field of communication study. Yet, who else, in addition to these men, contributed to communication scholarship, research, and theorizing? How do Indigenous ways of knowing influence the development of communication thought? And what might be the early influences of current theorizing related to the scholarship of People of Color? This underrepresentation of nonwhite scholars has proven controversial in the communication discipline (Flaherty, 2019). #CommunicationSoWhite, the forum on #RhetoricSoWhite, the viral hashtag #BlackInTheIvory, and the teach-in for #ScholarStrike all underscore the racialized experiences of communication scholars and draw attention to the theoretical contributions of BIPOC. We agree with Chakravartty et al.'s (2018, p. 262) assertion—"knowledge production that reinforces Whiteness as its undisputed, unexamined frame is incapable of asking what we might learn from the experiences" of others with salient racial, ethnic, and cultural identities. This next storied reflection is an example of how this lack of representation prompts theorizing, informs scholarship, and contributes to this text.

STORIED REFLECTION
"Humph, But Not For Long!"

Jasmine T. Austin
Texas State University

My mom is the smartest person I know. While growing up, I vividly remember watching her at the breakfast table drinking a large cup of coffee and completing a crossword puzzle or scrabble board. With all this expertise, my mom could not help but be a wordsmith. She is the CEO for my brothers and me—our chief editing officer. There isn't a paper that I have written that my mom has not read and conducted word-sorcery upon. She delighted in finding synonyms to help us sound as well-read as she was. She enjoyed making a murky sentence clear by fixing grammatical errors. And I remember the moment when her satisfaction was gone. ...

I was in the second year of my doctoral program, taking a course about communication in organizations. We discussed organizational theories and were given writing assignments to summarize and reflect upon. As per usual, I completed the assignment and requested my CEO's assistance to proofread my work. Upon returning the review, my mom took a deep breath and said to me, "Jazzy, I'm getting tired of reading about these theories that have nothing to do with you." My mom, who was never a graduate student and who never took a theory course in her life, was keen to the lack of BIPOC representations in the theories and readings I had been assigned. Even my mom knew there had to be *more* representation out there. There had to be *me* out there. To my surprise, she followed with a comment that changed the trajectory of how I see myself as a scholar. She said, "Humph, but not for long!" She expected *me* to change this. I took that comment as my *calling*. I felt a responsibility, in the most energizing way, to change representation in the theories and topics I was taught—that *we* were taught. This defining moment led to three important missions that influenced my identity as a scholar-activist.

Questioning Authority

That next week, I met with my professor to discuss assigned readings. He, a white male, was oblivious to the lack of racial and ethnic representation of the authors he assigned as readings. We had a productive conversation about how a lack of representation in authorship can, quite literally, erase me and other BIPOC experiences. I exclaimed that if I do not see myself in the theories and theorizing, this space must not be made for me. I, then, am the impostor. I, then, must not have any contribution of value. I, then, was reminded of my mom's comment, "Humph, but not for long!"

Owning My Learning Experience

After speaking to my professor and him being open to my questions and challenges to his course material selections, I felt empowered to have courses designed for my specific interests. With nine hours remaining in my degree plan, I requested that three of my Black mentors— faculty members in different departments on campus—create independent study courses that center Black scholarship. One course was a Black organizational communication theory-centric course, where we studied the likes of Drs. Patricia Parker, Brenda Allen, and Patricia Hill Collins. Another course was a university-wide Black women's reading group about Black experiences on predominately white campuses. The final course was one that centered the Black experience and human relations in organizations. Before taking these courses, I had no idea the impact Black women scholars had on the communication field. Their contributions were hidden from me—"Humph, but not for long!"

Organizing for Change

In September of 2020, I served as the lead organizer of the first African American Communication & Culture (AACC) #ScholarStrike Conference. With the guidance of Drs. Mark Orbe, Jeanetta Sims, and Ronald Jackson, this was a phenomenally successful virtual event with over 4,000 in attendance for the synchronous and asynchronous presentations. This conference directly addressed an issue I had been dealing with since graduate school—the lack of representation of diverse perspectives in the communication discipline. Stemming from the momentum of the #ScholarStrike, I was inspired to put activism on paper, and with Drs. Orbe and Sims, produce *this* text. This text (re)centers difference and the identities of marginalized and underrepresented groups. Before this text, I had minimal knowledge on the theoretical contributions of BIPOC—you guessed it—"Humph, but not for long!"

Though this narrative does not apply a specific theory to my experiences, the lack of representation of BIPOC in theorizing has influenced my identity as a scholar-activist. It is because I did not see myself represented in theories that were taught in classes that I make it my calling—my responsibility to change that. So, I pose this question to you: what is a certain way now—"but not for long?"

Why This Book?

Though we do not all view communication phenomena through the same theoretical lens and may not agree on the primary group of pioneers as the key contributors to our focal areas of study, we all employ some form of communication theory. This book will be beneficial for you in the following ways:

- *It shares examples of models, theories, and theoretical frameworks:* You will be presented with a range of theorizing that is rich in prediction, explanation, and description of communication processes.

- *It shares the work of scholars from diverse racial, ethnic, and cultural identities:* You will see their contributions amid canonized theories with the development of communication scholarship.

- *It shares theorizing across contextual areas of communication study:* You will be introduced to the utility of communication theory in fields of study connected to your preexisting interests or that may expand your primary areas of interest.

- *It shares established and emerging communication theory:* You will learn many foundational theories along with theorizing that is newly developed and evolving.

- *It shares evidence of a thriving discipline:* You will appreciate the vibrancy and vitality of thought within the communication discipline with hopefully a greater desire to assume a role in it.

To accomplish these aims, the text is organized into six parts that feature 20 theoretical contributions and include 21 storied reflections. As seen in the two preceding storied reflections, these are personal narratives that reflect the experiences of established and emerging scholars with theory. In each part of the book, your understanding will be advanced through a review of canonized theories and a preview of the theoretical contributions and storied reflections to come. Every chapter contains a theory overview, the theory's intellectual tradition, practical examples, and questions to prompt your further thought—all designed for you to have an easy, accessible presentation of diverse theoretical frameworks. Our hope is that you understand the value of communication theory and have success in employing theory to assume your place in the discipline.

Join the Movement

In the pages of this text, you will find more fascinations, frameworks, and knowledge pauses like those shared in the next storied reflection. In reading each theoretical contribution and reliving each storied reflection, you too have an opportunity to join the movement. Now more than ever, the discipline is at a crossroads. As you stand at the intersection, we hope you will join us on the path to diversifying the communication studies discipline.

STORIED REFLECTION

Fascinations, Frameworks, and Knowledge Pauses

Jeanetta D. Sims
University of Central Oklahoma

Recalling my first exposure to communication theory is difficult. It might have been through undergraduate or master's level studies using Stephen Littlejohn's classic text. What I do remember is first being obsessed with the construct of credibility. In particular, I had early interest in understanding the differential impact of credibility when communicators were white, Black, and Brown. I waded through journal articles that asserted the dimensionality of the construct and enjoyed reading disagreements laid out in the extant literature across decades. The summation of credibility dimensions and later the reconsideration of a lost dimension provided examples of what I have come to call *knowledge pauses*—times where scholars pause to account for what we think we know. I did not realize it then, but I have always been interested in persuasion and influence. I am drawn to probing contextual areas, which usually include organizational and business settings.

With Dubin (1969) and Chaffee (1991) as fundamental readings for understanding communication theory, I began tracing the historical development of communication theory as well as teasing out metatheoretical assumptions in further training. We spent class time debating the relative drawbacks and advantages of the various ways of knowing and chronicling the forerunners of communication inquiry. Forerunners, in this case, were synonymous with forefathers (see Schramm, 1997) since the individuals studied were primarily men, and none were Black women scholars like my aspirational self.

Despite not seeing myself in communication theory, my fascination continued with inoculation theory. The theory originated as an explanation for why the attitudes of U.S. prisoners of war collapsed when captured and for why two-sided messages are more persuasive than their one-sided counterparts. Researching the scholar while examining the origins of inoculation theory permitted me to see the evolution of a scholar's interests. One scholar's example gave me insight on how to study, pivot, and move on to new areas of communication inquiry. Another scholar's example affirmed the acceptability of examining theory for theory improvement, refinement, and nuance as well as for applying theory across relevant contexts of diversity, stealth campaigns, public relations, and public opinion. Additionally, I witnessed how reading research, while observing phenomena in real life, can impact what I research. Eventually, I too had a growing interest in understanding why previously favorable attitudes might collapse when faced with value-in-diversity messages.

While teaching and working in public relations, I had further fascinations with theories and frameworks related to deception and issues management. Seminars and conference sessions where scholars shared their knowledge pauses in person are most memorable. I found it intriguing to hear the real-time reflections of their research and theory development. The dialogue among seasoned and aspiring scholars seemed to remove the mystique of research. The conversations revealed their obsessions and simultaneously encouraged me to discover my own.

Now as a mid-career scholar, I remain fascinated with how communication theory continues to offer a lens to probe matters of race and relevancy. The bulk of my career has been spent translating communication theory to business students in a College of Business department of marketing. Through Diverse Student Scholars, my interdisciplinary program of undergraduate research engagement founded in 2007, students in marketing, management, and communication have benefited from the fertile ground of communication scholarship. Communication theory has sufficiently supported the varied interests of students who have conducted research in sports marketing, entrepreneurship, campaigns, branding, leadership, and a host of other areas.

Along with student research mentorship, I have continued research related to credibility, inoculation theory, and deception. Like my early training as a student of communication, dialectics has been a useful theoretical framework for unpacking my own (e.g., Sims, 2011) and others' experiences (e.g., Anderson et al., 2015). When models appear to be missing or remiss in offering explanatory power, I have enjoyed conceptualizing and conducting investigations to create new frameworks. Each observation enables me to engage in the same knowledge pauses I witnessed among other scholars. And I continue to be fascinated with understanding and applying communication theory to phenomena typically in business and organizational settings.

PART I

The Self and Identity

O ne constant in all forms of communication is the presence of self. In fact, the concept of self—or more aptly described as identity—is inextricably linked to how we communicate with others. We bring our identities to each and every communication interaction we have, regardless if it is a one-on-one interaction, small group discussion, or large meeting. This remains true whether we are doing so in-person or through virtual channels.

Theorizing identity, in communication and related fields, has largely focused on individual identity rather than shared collective identity (Yin, 2018). This focus reflects a traditional Western perspective which centers individualism as a core value. Consider, for an instance, the famous René Descartes adage, "I think, therefore I am." Now compare that statement with the African (Ubuntu) philosophy of "I am because we are." The former focuses on an individualistic sense of self, whereas the latter highlights how one's identity cannot be separated from relationships with others.

Conceptualizing self, and how it is situated with other aspects central to understanding the communication process, can take different forms. For instance, Wilmot (1995) explains three different paradigmatic views of the related concepts of self, other, and relationship. These reflect a variety of perspectives. First is *individual selves loosely connected*, which emphasizes the self and other as separate units attached through a fragile relational thread. This paradigm is common in individualistic cultures, like in the United States where the self is regarded as more important than the other person or the relationship. *Embedded self* is a second paradigm. This one reflects that self is best understood within the context of relationships, and the relationship itself is viewed as a separate identity. This paradigm makes a fundamental shift because that self cannot be seen as a separate identity. Instead, the self is always understood within the context of relationships with others. This paradigm focuses on the self being created through interconnections with others. The third and final paradigm described by Wilmot is the *nonseparable self/other/relationship*. This paradigm explicitly challenges the very notion of a separate, identifiable self. Instead, this perspective believes that we come into being through our interactions with others so much so that discussing any one of the concepts (i.e., self, other, relationships) necessitates talking about all of them collectively. The core idea here is that we cannot separate self, other, and relationships from one another; any change to one concept necessarily changes the other concepts. The distinctions between these three paradigms are important as we differentiate the chapters featured in Part 1 with existing canonized theories typically found in communication theory books. As you will see in the next section, many of the existing canonized theories were situated within Wilmot's first paradigm. The three theories in this section, like those throughout the rest of the book, reflect the second and third paradigms.

Existing Canonized Theories

The field of communication, by its nature, is an interdisciplinary discipline. The earliest theories destined to understand human interaction were created by scholars trained in psychology, sociology, linguistics, anthropology, and the like. Many theories, within this realm, represent a sociopsychological tradition where individual differences preexist before social relationships. In comparison, theories reflecting a sociocultural tradition situate social relationships as predating individual differences, a key aspect of Wilmot's second and third paradigms as described earlier. As such, several sociocultural theories embrace the idea that individuals (communicators) come to understand themselves as unique persons based on socially constructed differences—not fixed psychological or biological differences.

Symbolic interactionism and self-presentation theory are two examples of sociocultural theories focused on identity. The core idea of symbolic interactionism is that individuals gain a sense of who they are through their interactions with others (Mead, 1934). Generated in the field of sociology, symbolic interactionism provides an understanding as to how people interact with one another, and over time, develop a shared sense of self and others. It remains as one of the most significant and influential theoretical frameworks on communication theorizing of identity. Self presentation theory (Goffman, 1959) is another often-cited framework for communication scholars. Goffman utilizes the theatre as a metaphor to describe how individuals ("actors") communicate their sense of self ("play the part") to others ("supporting cast") in particular settings ("scenes"). This theory highlights how, within any situation, individuals present—or perform—a certain role on different stages and for different audiences. Both theories demonstrate how individuals communicate in ways that create and/or maintain a sense of self to others.

Within the field of communication, scholars have made significant contributions to how identity is negotiated in our interactions with others, especially across cultures

(Ting-Toomey, 2005). Of note is the work of Hecht and colleagues (2005) who have conceptualized a communication theory of identity (CTI). This theory centers the role of communication in identity matters, and highlights the ways in which self-identity is multifaceted, holistic, and interdependent with others. According to this theory, identity is a naturally communicative *and* relational phenomenon—one that exists within different locations or frames: personal (self-concept), enacted (self-expression), relational (self as coconstructed with others) and communal (self as bonded by larger collective memory). In many ways, CTI provides a theoretical framework that acknowledges the importance of self as situated within other relational constellations. So while it does not center racially and ethnically lived experiences explicitly, it offers a framework to do so if scholars are committed to doing so (e.g., Drummond & Orbe, 2009).

As discussed in the Introduction of this book, the vast majority of existing canonized theories in the field of communication have been criticized for their implicit centering of whiteness and marginalization of people of the global majority. The theories included in Part 1, as summarized in the next section, help to rectify this problem by centralizing Black, Indigenous, or People of Color (BIPOC) experiences within their conceptual frameworks.

Overview of Chapters

Within Part 1, we embrace a *culture-as-living-tradition approach* (Yin, 2018). Within this framework, cultural traditions of marginalized peoples are regarded as resources for self-understanding, self-expression, and self-assertion. Self, however, is not understood as the singular focus. Instead, it is situated within larger relational contexts, something akin to Wilmot's (1995) nonseparable self/other/relationship paradigm. Through an examination of Kemetic (ancient Egyptian) and Confucian modes of selfhood, Yin describes the self as a center of relationships, a perspective characterized by five common dimensions of being human: (1) collectivity or community, (2) moral reasoning, (3) sensitivity and responsiveness to others, (4) transformability and human agency, and (5) inclusivity and interconnection.

The first three chapters of this book reflect the culture-as-living tradition. Each of the theoretical frameworks highlighted in this introductory part features a productive lens to understanding the relationship between self, identity, and communication—as embedded in the experiences, knowledge, and perspectives of racially diverse people. As such, they draw attention to the limitations of existing theories that fail to address issues of privilege, power dynamics, and culture.

Chapter 1 focuses on undocumented critical theory, known as UnDocuCrit for short. We are especially excited to include this chapter, written by Carlos Aguilar and Daniela Juarez, in Part I for a couple of reasons. First, it highlights the utility of critical race theory (CRT)—a theoretical framework so powerful that some 21st-century politicians are working to prohibit its use in educational classrooms and professional development workshops. Second, UnDocuCrit embodies the essential value of this book: Focusing on racially and ethnically diverse and inclusive perspectives is crucial to the ultimate value of theorizing. Like other emerging CRTs (e.g., Latinx critical theory, Tribal critical race theory), it centers the role that racism plays in U.S. society. More specifically, the chapter presents four principal tenets that guide the readers toward a deeper understanding of the communicative experiences of undocumented individuals and communities across the United States. Ultimately, the chapter's authors push all of us to think about "illegality" in a new light—one that centralizes the lived experiences of undocumented people to understand human communication more fully in the 21st century. Written from the vantage point of both undocumented immigrants and emerging scholars, Aguilar and Juarez offer a chapter that embodies a scholar-activist approach to engaging current sociopolitical issues that typically are presented and consumed in polarizing ways. Their chapter on UnDocuCrit provides a framework that allows for a more multidimensional and nuanced understanding—something crucial to greater acknowledging the consequences of U.S. racism and white supremacy.

Marnel Niles Goins and Jasmine T. Austin describe Black feminist thought in Chapter 2. Regarded as one of several frameworks under the umbrella of feminist standpoint theory, the chapter highlights the contributions of Patricia Hill Collins and other scholar-activists in advancing a body of work that centralizes the experiences, knowledge, and agency of African American women. The core idea of standpoint theories is that sociogroup membership creates a vantage point, or cultural location, from which individuals view the world. Cultural locations inform one's perspective of world as well as knowledge creation. Black feminist thought has been instrumental in demonstrating the central importance of studying the intersections of gender, race, and class simultaneously. Throughout the chapter, Niles Goins and Austin highlight a variety of Black women who have fought, and continue to fight, for gender and racial equality. These examples range from legendary activists, rhetors, and authors to more contemporary community and political leaders. In doing so, they demonstrate how Black feminist thought rejects the marginalization that exists within white feminist and black masculinist ideologies and, instead, highlights the ways in which Black women are well-positioned to lead social and political movements.

Chapter 3, written by Ronald Jackson and Gina Castle Bell, describes cultural contracts theory. This author team is a productive fit for this chapter, as Jackson is the primary creator of the theory and Castle Bell has utilized the theory in some of her recent work. The core idea of cultural contracts theory is that all of our everyday daily communication encounters are informed by a preverbal state of un/consciously accepted social conditions. According to the authors, these social conditions can be best understood through the concept of cultural contracts: those that are ready to sign, quasicompleted, and/or cocreated. The theory's ability to help us understand how individuals negotiate their racial and ethnic identities in different contexts is noteworthy, especially as it reveals how identity negotiation is a process through which individuals sustain, manage, and/or protect their sense of self—something that intensifies when interactions are not coordinated and subsequently pose a threat to one's identity. Jackson and Castle

Bell demonstrate the value of cultural contracts theory through a number of examples taken from national and global headlines (e.g., George Floyd and Derek Chauvin), everyday interactions pertaining to different sociocultural issues, as well as recent research projects focused on race. In the end, they challenge all of us to critically reexamine the preverbal conditions that often unconsciously inform our interactions with racially and ethnically diverse individuals.

Overview of Storied Reflections

Within each part of the book, we also feature different storied reflections that speak to the relationships of BIPOC and communication theorizing. Britney N. Gilmore, assistant professor at Texas Christian University, writes about how her relationship with theorizing is centered around questions of fit for diverse groups. She reflects back on her experiences as a K–12 educator and describes the harm that occurs when theory-based decisions are adopted and the theories themselves problematically mute and/or marginalize minoritized people. Mark C. Hopson, professor of communication and senior director of ethnic studies at Chapman University, describes his relationship with theory by focusing on his engagement with theorizing Black masculinities. Within his storied reflection, he identifies key books, writers, and scholars who have informed the work of his academic career, including his current focus on the U.S. phenomenon of killing Black bodies. Our final storied reflection in Part I is by Ashlee Lambert, a doctoral student at Arizona State University. Within her storied reflection, she describes how her relationship with communication theorizing has been less than ideal, recounting how her earlier exposure to theory was disappointing—failing to fit hers and others' lived experiences. While she has identified a couple of engaging theories that speak to her sense of communicative self, she articulates the crucial importance of racially diverse and inclusive theories in the field of communication.

CHAPTER 1

Undocumented Critical Theory

Carlos Aguilar

University of Pennsylvania

Daniela Juarez

University of Texas at Dallas

W riting about illegalized communities is not an easy feat. The writing process, whomever the writer, is filled with a number of questions related to its practical, theoretical, ethical, and representational implications, to mention a few. When it is conducted by those directly impacted by "illegality," writing can also be perceived as a luxury, given the immediate needs, lived experiences, and (lack of) opportunities that the writers and their communities encounter (Abrego & Negrón-Gonzales, 2020). Books such as *We Are Not Dreamers* have been carefully curated to demonstrate critical research done by those who are or at one point were impacted by juridical illegality, highlighting that writing and theorizing are also necessary political statements and tools for illuminating alternative ways of knowing, being, and thinking about the world (Santos, 2006). For us, the same applies here.

In this chapter, we introduce you to undocumented critical theory (UndocuCrit), a theoretical intervention that advances four tenets or guiding principles to understand some of the experiences and (lack of) opportunities that undocumented communities encounter (Aguilar, 2019). This is an introductory piece but one that we hope can push some of you to think about "illegality," experiences, and [lack of] opportunities in a new light. We begin by providing a brief introduction to critical race theory (CRT), the framework from which UndocuCrit emerges. The chapter then continues with a summary of UndocuCrit and some of its theoretical and practical applications to date. We then close the piece by exploring some of its strengths, weaknesses, and future directions. Situated within Santos's (2006) ecology of knowledges, we are aware that the pragmatism, utility, or even attractiveness of UndocuCrit is to be determined in the context of specific conditions, such as theoretical or practical needs, as well as epistemological approaches. By epistemological approaches, we mean that what we know and how we come to know vary both across individuals and time. As a result, the utility of this writing is dependent, to a large extent, on what an individual knows, how they came to know it, and what they are looking to do with such knowledge.

To engage with undocumented communities, in research and otherwise, goes beyond the adoption of this theory. We invite you, the reader, to engage with the reading critically, cognizant that undocumentedness is not a homogenous experience and is many times difficult to capture on paper.

Intellectual Traditions of UndocuCrit Theory

As a theoretical piece, UndocuCrit was inspired both from lived experiences as well as emergent themes in the literature on undocumented immigrants in the United States. But because experiential knowledge tends to be devalued and perceived as inferior knowledge, UndocuCrit was to emerge from a tradition that respects and honors the knowledge accumulated through lived and embodied experiences. Critical race theory (CRT) creates such space (Cabrera, 2019). While at times imaginary habitats, Latina/o critical legal theory (LatCrit) theorist Margaret Montoya (2019) reminds us that theories are nonetheless sustaining intellectual habits, allowing us to make sense of current circumstances that ultimately facilitate the opportunity to engage in action and solidarity.

As a critical theory, CRT centers the role that racism plays in U.S. society, positing that racism is endemic in our society, given the constitutive role that the concept of race played in the foundation of our societies (Delgado & Stefancic, 2017). Although disagreements exist as to a definitive list, some of the most referenced CRT tenets highlight: (1) the permanence of racism; (2) the existence of interest convergence; (3) intersectionality; (4) the power of storytelling/lived experiences; and (5) critiques of liberalism. Initially focused on a Black and white binary, off-shoots have emerged to theorize on the experiences of other racialized and marginalized communities. Off-shoots like Latinx critical theory and Tribal critical race theory, for example, have pushed CRT to examine how assimilation, white settler colonialism, sexuality, skin color, identity, culture, class, language, and immigration status, to name a few, remain important in racializing and marginalizing these communities (Brayboy, 2005; Delgado & Stefancic, 2017). In the specific case of TribalCrit (Brayboy, 2005), for example, tenets that highlight colonization, imperialism, the many policies directed to appropriate and assimilate lands and Indigenous peoples, as well as the importance of stories and knowledges are introduced. LatCrit, on the other hand, explores issues related to immigration, language, culture, and skin color, among others.

Overall, CRT has provided academic scholars the foundation to analyze and scrutinize the role that racism plays. Off-shoots like Tribal critical race theory (TribalCrit) has further analyzed the relationship between white-settler colonialism and racism.

Through this lens, Indigenous scholars can use TribalCrit to theorize the lived experiences that their community has and continues to experience. Similarly, Latinx critical theory has attended more accurately to the lived experiences of Chicanxs and Latinx individuals. We hold that UndocuCrit builds on these off-shoots given that while many of the undocumented experiences can be analyzed through these lenses, we also saw it necessary to introduce tenets that spoke more faithfully to some of these experiences.

Ultimately, CRT presents tools to investigate white supremacy, the role of racism in society, the subordination of racialized people, as well as ways to change these power relations—in other words, to engage in praxis. While important to understand race and racism in the United States, Cabrera (2018) stresses that tenets advanced by CRT do not present a theory of race and racism but rather delineate the outcomes of racism. Similar to CRT, UndocuCrit also focuses on outcomes; in doing so, it delineates some of the experiences that some (undocumented) immigrant communities encounter.

Main Goals and Features of UndocuCrit Theory

Augmenting on the various tenets introduced by CRT and its many extensions, UndocuCrit presents four tenets, principles, or guiding posts to better understand some of the experiences that undocumented individuals or communities encounter in the United States. The tenets introduced posit that (1) fear is endemic among (undocumented) immigrant communities; (2) different experiences of liminality translate into a different experience of reality; (3) parental *sacrificios* become a form of capital; and (4) *acompañamiento* is the embodiment of mentorship, academic redemption, and community engagement. While many of these tenets might be considered "common sense" to undocumented and other racialized and marginalized communities, we ought to be aware that in the same way that experiences foster some knowledges, experiences too hinder others.

With the first tenet, fear is endemic among (undocumented) immigrant communities, UndocuCrit seeks to highlight a sociopolitical context created by the state that infuses fear in the lives of undocumented immigrants. Such sociopolitical context is created through anti-immigrant rhetoric, policies and practices that negatively impact the lived experiences and opportunities of undocumented immigrants and their families. For example, former president Donald Trump attempted to end the Deferred Action for Childhood Arrivals (DACA) that benefited over 800,000 undocumented immigrants. Because of his administration's attempts to discontinue an already unstable program, many DACA beneficiaries and their families became fearful over their future as the possibility of returning to an even more precarious legal condition, or even deportation, became a potential outcome. This, without even considering the lack of action at a federal level to include an undocumented community that is believed to make up approximately 11 million in the United States. Through (in)actions like these, increased border and interior immigration enforcement, and discourses that paint the undocumented as inherently criminal, illegality is constructed not only at a sociopolitical level but also at an embodied and lived one. It is one that has been documented to foster fear among undocumented communities.

UndocuCrit's second tenet acknowledges that different legal statuses exist within our immigration system and that these expose individuals and families to varying levels of uncertainty and persecution but also possibilities. For instance, even though some young undocumented immigrants qualified for DACA and were able to reap its benefits, others were not, creating a diverse set of experiences across the United States for both DACA and unDACAmented individuals. Other designations such as Temporary Protected Status (TPS) have also fostered new opportunities that differ from those with and without any legal status. Given that these individuals are oftentimes members of mixed-status families, their experiences and (lack of) opportunities are also likely to impact their families' conditions. This is especially evident for those without documentation. But even for those with citizenship status, their experiences are also often impacted by racialized anti-immigrant rhetoric, policies, and practices, though the consequences and occurrences might not be as drastic or frequent. Ultimately, even within statuses, experiences are not homogenous when living in a racist, classist, patriarchal, heteronormative, and ableist society, to name a few other axes of oppression.

UndocuCrit also highlights that parental *sacrificios* become a form of capital. With this third tenet, UndocuCrit does not seek to ignore the conditions leading to the need for parental sacrifices in the first place. However, it is important to highlight the sacrifices in which many parents and family members engage to provide a better life for their children and families. Despite literature on the educational experiences of (undocumented) immigrants that describe the actions and behaviors of their parents as reflective of a culture in opposition to education, UndocuCrit highlights the decisions and behaviors in which undocumented parents engage to support their children and the impact these have on their children's lives (Cuevas, 2019). For example, undocumented parents make the decision of leaving their home country and families to provide a better future, in a country where they are not only faced with new customs, language, and culture but that also deems them as unworthy and criminals. Without some of the protections that a legal status might provide, many undocumented parents are forced to work in manual labor for long hours and in harsh conditions. Despite this, works like that of Cuevas (2018) have documented the behaviors and actions in which undocumented parents engage to procure a better future, such as driving their children to school functions without a license or prioritizing school-related financial needs at the expense of other responsibilities. This is what she has described as concerted migration and emotional, day-to-day *sacrificios* (Cuevas, 2018), actions and behaviors oftentimes ineligible to a system created to privilege certain ways of being and knowing. Additionally, when DACA was created, political leaders placed DACA beneficiaries on a pedestal, creating a binary that demonized and criminalized those outside the program, including their parents. This rhetoric continued as political leaders, such as former president Trump, denounced that undocumented parents were careless for bringing their children without documentation. When read from a White-supremacist logic, the *sacrificios* that undocumented parents are forced to make are not only ignored but also criminalized. We differ.

The last tenet highlights *acompañamiento,* which is the embodiment of mentorship, academic redemption, and community engagement. This tenet serves as an invitation to accompany undocumented immigrants and others with different legal statuses through their journeys, educational and otherwise. To accompany, however, can take many forms. To support and protect individuals and communities who are subject to state violence, to include and reach out to parents in ways that work for them, and to continue the search for humane and comprehensive solutions to the immigration system are, among others, important ways to *acompañar* (undocumented) immigrants. For instance, across the country and in response to immigrants' efforts, Dream Centers have been created at universities to provide support for undocumented students. Dream Centers are critical to address the needs of undocumented students, provide emotional and academic support, and create a community for undocumented immigrants. Within the Dream Centers, non-immigrants are able to advocate and help secure the success of undocumented college students. *Acompañamiento* and allyship are fundamental components to uplift and support undocumented immigrants.

These four tenets introduced by UndocuCrit extend the initial framework of CRT by further examining some of the experiences that many undocumented immigrants might experience in the United States. While they are not exhaustive, we nonetheless believe these might have important research and practical implications. In what follows, we present some of these opportunities.

Research and Practical Applications of UndocuCrit Theory

UndocuCrit is a relatively new theoretical framework. Yet it has already been adopted by a few practitioners, scholars, and students interested in the topic of immigration. For example, Daniela, one of the authors of this chapter, employed UndocuCrit to explore the challenges that undocumented students face after graduating from universities. Throughout her undergraduate research, the first tenet of UndocuCrit emerged as an important theme, highlighting the fear that undocumented graduates experience as they navigate challenges created by the lack of a legal status. Having graduated and exited an institution that often served as a safe haven, at least in terms of a legal status, undocumented graduates were often faced with limited opportunities for employment and increased levels of anxiety. Employing UndocuCrit in their research was critical to understand the complexities of living in the United States while undocumented. When Daniela was conducting research, she noticed that one of her participants was in a constant fear of their future upon their college graduation. When the participant graduated, they realized that their immigration status prevented them from working. Their university provided career services, but those were not tailored towards undocumented immigrants, forcing many undocumented students to navigate an already overwhelming labor market alone.

The sociopolitical context fostered by the state creates negative repercussions in the lived experiences and opportunities faced by undocumented immigrants and their families. Thus, as students, professionals, or whatever role we occupy, it is essential to be cognizant of such realities so that our practices account for the experiences of the most marginalized. Right before its publication and as UndocuCrit had begun to circulate around a very small circle of people, Carlos received an email from an obstetrician and gynecologist (OB/GYN) with a specialty in family planning from New Mexico. During one of her keynote speeches in South Texas with medical providers, she adopted the first tenet of UndocuCrit to underscore the need for medical providers to adopt trauma-informed care as required to work with immigrant communities, especially along the U.S.-Mexico border. In such a context, providing services to undocumented women must take into consideration the role that surveillance and immigration enforcement play in limiting their spatial mobility and ability to access such services. Being aware of these conditions and fear, if taken seriously, can thus facilitate a better implementation of support systems in search of improving the lived experiences and opportunities of undocumented immigrants and their families.

Also employing UndocuCrit in a study at a California University, Rosas (2020) demonstrates how both the fear of disclosing their status and a potential deportation kept some respondents from seeking or maximizing services at their disposal. Despite the many barriers encountered, however, the *acompañamiento*—support, encouragement, and a sense of belonging—provided by their peers and the Undocumented Student Resource Center (USRC) facilitated their educational experiences. Ultimately, Rosas (2020) highlights the different experiences encountered by undocumented students (Villegas, 2020), as well as the *sacrificios* their parents made to attend important events such as orientation programs and parent engagement sessions. Building on UndocuCrit, Rosas's (2020) work ultimately delineates recommendations to improve the impact that USRCs can have in the educational trajectories of undocumented students.

Continuing the Conversation

Following the tradition of CRT, UndocuCrit examines some of the consequences of decades of racism and white supremacy on undocumented communities. While important to pair it with a theory of racism for a better understanding of processes leading to these outcomes (Cabrera, 2019), this nonetheless provides an important framework that accounts for some of the experiences that many undocumented immigrants face in the United States. As it is also the case with other CRT pieces, UndocuCrit emerges from situated knowledge. As such, given that the author's positionality can be seen throughout the piece (Aguilar 2019), some might argue that UndocuCrit is neither a representative nor exhaustive rendering of the history and experiences of all (undocumented) immigrants in the United States. And this is true. UndocuCrit does not appeal to generalizability but rather identification, which can sometimes go beyond racial lines, geographies, and time. For this reason, UndocuCrit does not claim to be *the* theory. Situated within Santos's (2006) ecology of knowledges, the utility of UndocuCrit should not be considered a priori but rather determined in the context of specific conditions. This means walking away from a dichotomous understanding of the world and towards a rationality that underscores knowledges as part of a totality (Santos, 2006). To argue otherwise, that UndocuCrit covers it all or is *the* way to go, even if from a marginalized position, would be to reproduce Eurocentric logics.

The positionality within the piece should not disqualify its contributions, however. That is, while it is true that our voices and experiences are visible throughout the writing, UndocuCrit relies on a plethora of research that allows us to locate experiences within a larger social context, going beyond an anecdotal piece. Ultimately, evaluating UndocuCrit presents a difficult feat, as its insights, provocativeness, ethics, and/or social change depend on who is conducting the evaluation. Due to published (Cabrera, 2019) and informal critiques, we believe that while UndocuCrit might serve as an important, illuminating, or motivating piece for some (undocumented) students and others alike, many more might find it as inadequate, biased, or lacking.

Faithful to our way of thinking, we do not feel that we have the authority, or that even such authority should exist, to map future directions. Nonetheless, as an increasing number of undocumented and formerly documented immigrants go through the education system, we are quite excited about projects that explore the nature, role, and implications of schooling in their lives and work. To our knowledge, most, if not all of the research with undocumented students focuses on the role that lacking a legal status plays in their educational trajectories. Yet we believe it is also important to note the role that the educational system plays in further marginalizing communities as well as shaping the way students make sense of their lives. Similarly, there are many gaps in undocumented literature that would benefit from further research, such as the lived experiences of older immigrants and a further exploration of the intersectionality between citizenship and sexuality (see Abrego & Negrón-Gonzales [2020] for work on this topic by undocumented or formerly undocumented scholars). Ultimately, as we continue to highlight the heterogeneity of lived experiences of undocumented immigrants, it is also relevant to explore and stress that their epistemologies are neither homogenous, static, nor always undocumented.

Summary

In this chapter, we have discussed the intellectual tradition of UndocuCrit, the goals of the creation of UndocuCrit, and the research applications of this theory. UndocuCrit focuses on centering the lived experiences of those who are undocumented and marginalized, and with this piece it is our hope to continue building on a tradition that combats oppressive political and social systems to ultimately acknowledge and respect different ways of being.

FOR FURTHER THOUGHT AND REFLECTION

1. In what ways did UndocuCrit change your perspective on how you perceive, understand, and/or research undocumented communities?

2. How do you see this piece as impacting your relational lives, especially in the context of race, racial identity, and racism?

3. How might the ideas of the chapter relate to your own research or projects? For instance, do you think that the four tenets of UndocuCrit would apply to all undocumented immigrants in U.S. history—across time, political climate, region, culture, language, and the like?

STORIED REFLECTION
Does It Really Work Like That?

Britney N. Gilmore
Texas Christian University

Much of my relationship with theory revolves around the question "Does it really work like that?" By training, I am an educator. In 2014, interested in understanding the K–12 education system, I started teaching elementary aged children. The experience was rewarding and eye-opening. Even then, I knew I wanted to pursue a doctoral degree; thus, I analyzed many events during that experience through theoretical and research perspectives acquired in my master's degree coursework. That is where my interest in organizations, conflict, and identity began. More specifically, my relationship with theory started with training and working in community with others to understand problems plaguing organizations and groups—the districts, schools, teachers, and students in my life.

We never talked about theory, but it was always there. Theory was implicitly within the assessment practices, curriculum choices, and behavioral intervention programs we chose to follow. I remember sitting in yet another professional development seminar (we had a lot of those) with a handful of other teachers. As we listened to discussions about how to manage behavior in our classrooms and schools, I recognized that something did not align with my experiences. "Who are these practices for?" and "What are the implications of this program?" were questions that danced through my mind as I sat there and tried not to tune out. The program being sold was sound. It was researched. There were interesting findings. It also was not applicable to or wanted by myself or my fellow teachers. This prescriptive program did not represent the experiences of teachers in our schools or of the students we served. The reality of my school context, which included factors such as demographics of students, size of school, and amount of community support, made the program less likely to thrive in our school. What was less evident to me during this part of my career—but became illuminated when I started my doctoral program in 2016—was the frequent disconnect between what I saw and what I read.

Early in my graduate studies, I learned theories were meant to describe, explain, and/or predict. Attending my first graduate class, probably an introduction to communication studies, the topics and theories that interested me most were those where I saw potential impact related to challenges experienced by people I knew in organizations. Framed as a compliment, I've been told I like the "less popular theories," such as symbolic convergence theory and positioning theory. Based on my search history, I do not disagree. What I like are theories with practical utility and value and that are not too complicated for people to understand. Picturing myself back in that professional development session, two things are apparent to me: (1) Again, I did not see my students' experiences in these moments, and (2) I also saw the harm that could be done through well-packaged findings, if we do not consider other factors, voices, and experiences. The biggest validators of my perspective toward scholarship and theory during graduate school were the variety of divisions in the National Communication Association that support the type of research I want to do and learning about the use of qualitative methods. Making room to understand the lived experiences of individuals, groups, events, people, and organizations—that is what I wanted. Therefore, familiarizing myself with the theories that ontologically and epistemologically encouraged that perspective consumed my studies in the doctoral program and continues now into the start of my career.

Rather than a particular theory, my experience highlights the inability of some theories to capture and appreciate the lived experiences of the groups I serve as an educator and scholar. Theory has shown me that individual narratives and experiences do matter. From ideation through to production, my scholarly aim is to keep communities and their needs at the forefront of my mind. This small act keeps me invested in this work and helps me continue to elevate the voices of others in ways that provide value and resonate with them. So, I ask, "Does it really work like that?" I know now that the true answer to this question requires more research, more inclusivity in our theorizing, and more challenging of current theories to push their utility.

CHAPTER 2

Black Feminist Thought

Marnel Niles Goins

Marymount University

Jasmine T. Austin

Texas State University

B lack women are in a pivotal moment in history. Previously relegated to private spheres, the voice and advocacy of Black women are making waves in the United States and throughout the world in political, business, and creative realms. Black feminist thought (Collins, 2000), a framework that brings attention to the experiences of Black women, as well the knowledge that is produced by these experiences, argues that Black women are poised for these times and prepared to lead social and political movements. Black feminist thought serves as a theoretical foundation for much scholarship and theorizing of our discipline, as it provides a lens to view communication phenomena in a way that highlights and reflects the variety and beauty in Black women pertaining to our race, class, and gendered experiences.

This chapter begins with a discussion of the history of Black feminist thought, first detailing the origins of the framework that are crucial to understanding its assumptions. Following this is a discussion of the six tenets of Black feminist thought, including its basis in the knowledge of Black women and its goal of social advocacy for traditionally underrepresented and marginalized groups. Next, practical applications of Black feminist thought are examined, including notable Black women who have embodied Black feminist thought in their advocacy. Finally, recommendations for the future of Black feminist thought are discussed.

Intellectual Tradition of Black Feminist Thought

Black feminist thought was created to be uncomfortable. Pulling from the intersectionality of multiple group memberships, Black feminist thought engages race, gender, and social class in a manner that rejects labels and comparisons to white feminism and Black masculinity and instead differentiates itself as an approach founded on Black women's intersectional knowledge. Black feminist thought, created by sociology scholar Patricia Hill Collins (2000), highlights the *intellectual oppression* of Black women as its foundation. Collins states, "The assumptions on which full group membership are based—whiteness for feminist thought, maleness for Black social and political thought, and the combination for mainstream scholarship—all negate Black women's realties" (p. 12). These assumptions are embedded in U.S. society and, thus, the origins of Black feminist thought are quite significant and provide the framework from which its tenets are formed.

The racist, sexist, and classist domination of Black women is rooted in slavery and extends itself to present time (Collins, 2000). "To be a Black woman in nineteenth-century America was to live the jeopardy of belonging to the 'inferior' sex of an 'inferior' race" (Sterling, 1984, p. 1). Black women, relegated to the private sphere, were controlled by slave owners; their bodies were viewed and used as property to be sold as reproductive vessels and their intellect was violently muted.

The emancipation of slavery and the migration to cities in the north led to a decrease in Black women working in the fields on plantations and an increase in them working in domestic services in white environments (Collins, 2000). Black women tended to work jobs similar to those they had done while enslaved—jobs involving cooking, cleaning, and washing. Black women were not only relegated to the private/domestic sphere, but they were also dehumanized in the process. Collins (2000, p. 52) points out, "African Americans paradoxically were well integrated within, yet excluded from, the economic and political benefits of the market economy." Although employed and contributing to the economy, Black women were not recognized in the public sphere. Concomitantly, they were sociopolitically labeled as "domestics" and not afforded even the meager domestic power granted to white women, who at least were acknowledged as homemakers and mothers in the private sphere. Thus, Black women shared a commonality with each other that existed in what Collins (2000, p. 58) terms "frequently hostile environments," and through this they found a source of empowerment in each other. For Black women, their own shared private sphere became a place of power.

Racial oppression led to the primacy of race before gender for Black women; that is, many Black women identified with being Black but not directly with being a woman. Even still, though many Black women chose to "be Black," the Black liberation struggle has often been equated with men, just as the feminist liberation struggle has often been equated with white women (Collins, 2000; hooks, 1990). "It is not surprising ... that many Black women continue to fear that they will be betraying men if they support the feminist movement" (hooks, 1990, p. 59).

However, historical documentation of the 1830–1920 women's movement provides evidence that a number of Black women fought for gender equality in addition to racial equality, including Sojourner Truth, Harriet Tubman, Ida B. Wells, Victoria Earle Matthews, and Frances Ellen Watkins Harper. Yet the women's movement was still one that discriminated against Black women. Terborg-Penn (1978) criticizes the notion that in the 18th and 19th centuries, Black women were accepted by their white counterparts and highlights examples like women's clubs, the 1830–1860 temperance movement, and the suffrage movement of the early 20th century as groups and causes dominated by white women and which excluded Black women. This is not surprising, according to Cole and Guy-Sheftall (2003, p. 77), who reveal, "Given the acceptance by white society of the inherent inferiority of the Black race ... whites advance[d] the thesis that Black women were morally defective."

Within the Black community, the prevalence of gender inequality began to be magnified during the 1960s (Cole & Guy-Sheftall, 2003). Underlying messages in the Black Nationalist Movement, for example, have disregarded the Black women's desire for liberation—the Black feminist struggle was viewed as a threat to the Black struggle. hooks (1990, p. 58) declares that the "discourse of Black resistance has always equated freedom with manhood" (p. 58). She notes that the reluctance of Black men to take sexism seriously is as damaging as racism.

Black feminist thought recognizes that Black women are still oppressed in varying forms—sexism still exists within the Black community, racism still exists within white feminist environments, and classism exists within both communities (Collins, 2000; hooks, 1990). Black feminist thought represents a site of resistance from racial, sexual, and classist oppression and a safe space, particularly for Black women. "Only African-American women can ... 'feel the iron' that enters Black women's souls, because while U.S. Black women's experiences resemble others, such experiences remain unique" (Collins, 2000, p. 35). In essence, Black women have become their own supporters and listeners.

Main Goals and Features of Black Feminist Thought

Black feminist thought is based on six tenets that ultimately argue for the intellectual brilliance and variety of Black women that will lead to a better lived experience for us. A common misunderstanding of Black feminist thought is that it is about Black women's gendered experiences, negating the intersectional foundations of the framework. Instead, Black feminist thought is intersectional in its very nature, with all six tenets being grounded in an understanding and celebration of the various lived experiences of Black women.

First, Black women share common experiences of racism, sexism, and classism that have resulted in a "distinctive consciousness concerning our experiences and society overall" (Collins, 2000, p. 24). The oppressive experiences are not limited to certain contexts or arenas but are prevalent in everyday life. As such, Black women have found their homeplace with other Black women, using this as a method of survival in areas such as the workplace and even at home.

Second, Black feminist thought is grounded in the idea that, while Black women have shared experiences, they are different from each other and have the right to respond to intersectional oppressions in varied ways. These responses extend beyond the African American community in the United States to Black women throughout the world. There is no unified interpretation or response of Black women to their experiences, nor should there be an expectation of one voice or one perspective. Instead, the understanding is that there is beauty in these differences, though they all stem from the intersecting oppressions faced by Black women.

The third tenet of Black feminist thought highlights the lived experiences of Black women, with the goal to make those experiences better. Collins (2000, p. 32) states, "Black feminist thought can stimulate a new consciousness that utilizes Black women's every day, taken-for-granted knowledge. Rather than raising consciousness, Black feminist thought affirms, articulates, and provides a vehicle for expression in public consciousness that already exists." Collins argues that the relationship Black women have between activism and oppression is not dialectical but rather dialogical, in that activism informs oppression and vice versa. In other words, the knowledge of Black women demands activism, and the activism of Black women demands knowledge.

Fourth, Black feminist thought understands that the Black women's knowledge is special and important to social justice movements. This knowledge is not exclusive to Black intellectuals and, instead, is based on the very foundation of the lived experiences of Black women. As such, the intersectionality of Black feminist thought is again signified, in that the varied contributions of Black women are important, both "inside and outside of the academy" (Collins, 2000, p. 32). Black women's intellect and activism result in unique theoretical frameworks that have the power to change academies, communities, policies, and beyond.

It is important to note that Black feminist thought is not static; instead, it ebbs and flows just as the consciousness of Black women does. This is the fifth tenet of Black feminist thought, where Collins (2000) recognizes that while Black women have a shared consciousness, there are varied standpoints within that change. These changes include working conditions, political climates, as well as other contextual factors. The ebb and flow of Black feminist thought is not a negative feature but one that instead allows it to be adaptable and flexible to the needs of Black women.

The final tenet of Black feminist thought relates to "its relationship to other projects for social justice" (Collins, 2000, p. 41), differentiating itself from many other theories and frameworks. Black feminist thought is solution-oriented and framed around advocacy for the freedom of human society. It argues that one group cannot be free until all groups are empowered and free. The next section highlights Black feminists, theories, and frameworks that are grounded in the six tenets of Black feminist thought.

Research and Practical Applications of Black Feminist Thought

Black feminist thought plays a massive role in shaping culture and history. Over the years, several influential Black authors, educators, activists, and political figures have challenged and clarified what it means to be a Black feminist, advocate, and forerunner. What these women all have in common is living in and being change agents of "frequently hostile environments" (Collins, 2000, p. 58) and have been driving forces as Black women have moved (and are moving) from the private sphere into the public sphere. Through the lens of Black feminist thought, we will highlight some of those who were and are driving forces for social justice.

Black feminists have used their intellectual brilliance to dominate education sectors as authors and professors (tenets 1 and 3). Angela Davis and her notable works, including *Woman, Race, and Class* (Davis, 2011), focuses on social class barriers and racism and their impact on feminism and gender equity. bell hooks (2014) authored the staple book *Ain't I A Woman?*, which examines the history of Black womanhood, slavery, and the impact of sexism on Black women. Audre Lorde wrote about feminism, sexual identity, homophobia, race, sexism, and social class along with Nobel Prize- and Pulitzer Prize-winning novelist Toni Morrison, whose work explored Black identity and the Black experience. As Black feminist thought ebbs and flows, Black feminist authors have also challenged preconceived ideals and notions (tenets 2 and 5). For example, Roxane Gay challenges what it means to be a 'bad feminist' while Chimamanda Ngozi Adichie challenges the definition of feminism (De Fulviis, 2020).

In addition to these scholar-activists, we have Black feminists to thank for leading the charge on major social justice movements (tenet 4). Activists Patrisse Cullors, Alicia Garza, and Opal Tometi are the founders of the Black Lives Matter Global Network Foundation, an intersectional movement that affirms the lives of "Black queer and trans folks, disabled folks, undocumented folks, folks with records, women, and all Black lives along the gender spectrum" in addition to those victimized by police brutality (blacklivesmatter, 2021). In solidarity with sexual assault survivors, Tarana Burke began using the phrase "Me Too," in 2006 to raise awareness of women and children who have been abused (Wellington, 2017). Her use of the phrase launched a national #MeToo movement that raises awareness of the prevalence of sexual harassment.

Further, the political realm is drenched in #BlackGirlMagic (tenet 6), from Shirley Chisholm, the first Black woman to be elected to U.S. Congress, to the 40 years of public service by Representative Maxine Waters, to Kamala Harris, the first female, first Black, and first Asian American vice president of the United States. Another exemplar of Black feminist thought in the political realm is 2018 Georgia gubernatorial Democratic candidate Stacey Abrams, a politician, lawyer, *New York Times* best-selling author, and voting rights activist who served in the Georgia House of Representatives from 2007 to 2017, serving as minority leader from 2011 to 2017 (Epstein & Herndon, 2021). As Collins (2000) notes, Black women were integrated within, yet excluded from political benefits, but Abrams surpassed this oppression and created her own platform and politically focused organizations. Abrams founded Fair Fight Action and the New Georgia Project—organizations to address voter suppression in Georgia (Epstein & Herndon, 2021). Her efforts have been widely credited with boosting voter turnout in the 2020 presidential and 2021 special senatorial run-off elections, which led to Democrats taking control of the U.S. Senate for the first time since 1992.

As exemplified, Black women have helmed Black feminist thought, making willful strides into the collective consciousness surrounding equity and equality. Not only is Black feminist theory embodied in brilliant and powerful women, but it has also expanded by inspiring other scholarship in our communication discipline. Melbourne S. Cummings is a trailblazer in rhetorical, nonverbal, and intercultural communication, with her service and scholarship focusing on giving voice to differing Black and African perspectives. Brenda J. Allen is a forerunner in communication, infusing Black feminist thought into how we contextualize experiences of marginalized and underrepresented organizational members. Robin R. Means Coleman has influenced media communication scholarship with her line of research on horror noire—how Black people are portrayed in horror films. Black feminist thought can be seen as a foundation of theorizing within the communication discipline. For example, we can cite Amber Johnson's work on intersectional queer Hyper/in/visibility, which focuses on the performance and investigations of intersectional identities of BIPOC LGBTQQAIPPS folk (in this volume, Shardé Davis provides another example in her Strong Black Woman Collective Theory, which centers the strength of Black women's supportive friendship groups and how their solidarity can be used to confront external hostilities. These scholars were not only influential in their scholarship but also their mentoring, service, and scholar-activism.

Continuing the Conversation

Black feminist thought is an intersectional framework based on the resiliency, creativity, and knowledge of Black women. As seen in the previous section, Black women politicians, activists, and scholars have used the framework of Black feminist thought to advance social advocacy in the United States. Beyond the political and academic realms, however, Black women continue to take hold of the public sphere as artists, entrepreneurs, administrators, and visionaries. As such, those who seek to use Black feminist thought must continue to highlight Black women in the public sphere as advocates for liberation.

This chapter provides two recommendations for the future of Black feminist thought. The first is to use the framework in a manner that frees Black women from comparisons to other groups. Instead, we must continue to examine what the future will look like if Black women continue to move into the public sphere and advocate fully for historically marginalized groups. Black feminist thought is significant because it is based on the lived experiences of Black women, who, because of these unique experiences, have the ability to be change agents.

Collins (2000) intentionally includes the importance of social class, in addition to race and gender, as primary to the foundation and understanding of Black feminist thought. Much of the scholarship and many of the people who have been attributed to this framework, however, focus on race and gender, ignoring or diluting the significance of social class. Thus, the second recommendation is to create ways to bring the voices of all social classes of Black women into the public sphere and continue to join scholarship with community activism, ultimately recognizing that Black intellectuals come from "all walks of life" (Collins, 2000, p. 36).

Summary

This chapter offers an introduction to Black feminist thought, an intersectional framework that engages oppression and domination based on race, gender, and social class to carve a safe space for the intellectual freedom and varied experiences of Black feminists. The origins are rooted in slavery, exclusion, and present-day oppression, yet it is a framework of resistance, liberation, and intellectual brilliance. Six tenets of the framework were presented, along with examples of authors, educators, activists, and political figures who elevate the cultural and historical influence of Black feminist thought. Finally, we recommended that the future of Black feminist thought must free Black women from comparison to other groups, and we must continue to foster an intersectional approach that includes race, gender, and social class. Understanding the full intersectional foundation of Black feminist thought allows us to celebrate Black women fully. Black feminist thought, as it ebbs and flows, has deconstructed an oppressive past and continues to construct our present and future on fairer terms. Giving voice to the unheard and creating space for the uninvited, this Black feminist framework imbues society in possibilities.

FOR FURTHER THOUGHT AND REFLECTION

1. What are some of the advantages and disadvantages of Black women's ongoing journey from the private sphere to the public sphere? How does the notion of "Black Girl Magic" influence how Black women are viewed in both private and public spheres?

2. In addition to the examples of Black feminists provided in this chapter, who are other examples of influential Black women who embody Black feminist thought throughout their advocacy? In what ways did these examples elevate society? How might society look different without these examples?

3. As Black feminist thought engages the intersections of race, gender, and social class, we can see its influence on activism generated by and with other communities. In addition to Black Lives Matter and the Me Too movements, what are examples of activism that may have taken an intersectional Black feminist approach? How do these examples embody Black feminist thought?

STORIED REFLECTION
Black Masculinities Theory

Mark C. Hopson
Chapman University

The Autobiography of Malcolm X was my introduction to theorizing Black masculinities. I remember how the book was passed among my high school friends. I recall that we discussed Malcolm Little's transformation to Detroit Red, to Harlem Red, to Malcolm X, and ultimately to El-Hajj Malik El-Shabazz. Malcolm's transformation represented a change in image for young Black men coming of age at the dawn of the hip-hop era. In fact, Malcolm's story reflected our collective consciousness. He informed our Black intellectual thought. Malcolm's influence came full circle when I had the privilege to shake his mother's hand. I thanked Louise Little for her family's contribution to the world. Later, I also had the privilege to thank Malcolm's daughters Attallah Shabazz and Ilyasah Shabazz.

As an undergraduate student, my interests were cultivated further by Frederick Douglass's abolitionism and suffragism; W. E. B. Du Bois's intellectual activism; Richard Wright's focus on race, gender, and age in *Black Boy*; and Ralph Ellison's exploration of representation in *Invisible Man*. I was drawn to their articulations of voice, gaze, and space. I connected to the critical memories of Black men.

My research interests led me to a graduate program in communication. My master's thesis became a journal article titled "Playing the Game: Recalling Dialectical Tensions for Black Men in Oppressive Organizational Structures." This article was partially inspired by the work of Robert Staples. Known as a founder of U.S. Black masculinity studies, Dr. Staples authored *The Black Family: Essays and Studies* (1971); *Black Masculinity: The Black Male's Role in American Society* (1982); and *Exploring Black Sexuality* (2006). In 2011, Dr. Staples contributed a chapter to *Masculinity in the Black Imagination*, a book I coedited with Ron Jackson. The chapter came as the result of numerous emails and phone calls. I still have a hardcopy of the original essay printed and mailed from his home in Australia. Dr. Staples died on February 7, 2020.

Prior to my graduate studies, I worked for an alternative high school, which served largely Black and Brown student populations. During my graduate studies, I worked as director of an afterschool program that served low-income families. I also worked as a violence prevention facilitator in suburban and rural areas consisting of largely white student populations. These jobs helped me realize the complexities of relating to diverse populations, including communication tensions and strategies for Black male educators. For example, I came to know the value of Black/African American Vernacular English within Black communities. Conversely, I witnessed the institutional oppression of culture and communication at micro and macro levels.

Black feminist theory informs my respect and appreciation for theorizing lived experiences. As a graduate student, I was required to replicate Brenda J. Allen's ground-breaking essay "Black Womanhood and Feminist Standpoints." Dr. Allen's essay explores intersections of race, gender, and the labor of communication—locally and structurally. The essay spoke to my familiarity with feeling like a racialized and gendered body across my aforementioned organizational roles. Dr. Allen's work also led me to the works of Marsha Houston, Olga Davis, Geneva Smitherman, Patricia Hill Collins and others. Today I call Dr. Allen a mentor and friend.

I use Black masculinities theory to explicate overlapping dilemmas in social interaction and social identity. Black/African American men have historically felt the need to function with a double consciousness or a negotiated cultural identity that is constantly in flux. Black masculinities theory is based in pluralistic ontological and epistemological explorations of race, gender, and power; it focuses largely on four areas: (1) knowledge of the oppressed or outsider; (2) aspects of the social order that previously have not been exposed; (3) narratives, poetry, literature, art, and other discursive sites for identity exploration and development; and (4) nonmonolithic communicative experiences within education, law, economy, health, recreation, and other sectors of society.

Currently I am using Black masculinities theory to interrogate the U.S. phenomenon of killing Black bodies. These tragedies reflect disrespectful, irresponsible, and predictable behavior at local and national levels. Race-based murder—lynching—is an epidemic within a pandemic, subjected against Black people of all ages. Black children are particularly displaced within white institutional spaces. Historically they seen not as children but rather as adultified. Race, gender, and age can be used against them. For example, masculine dispensation in the United States constitutes white boys as being naturally naughty. Yet, Black boys are discerned as willfully bad. The consequences can be dire. There is a need to look more closely at this displacement. There is a need to foreground discourse pertaining to Black boys and Black men killed by U.S. law enforcement. Communication theory that centers Black masculinities in empowering ways has the potential to make great contributions to this social ill.

CHAPTER 3

Cultural Contracts Theory

Ronald L. Jackson II

University of Cincinnati

Gina Castle Bell

St. John's University

The murder of George Floyd demonstrates the preverbal nature of communication and helps demonstrate cultural contracts theory (CCT) in action. Officer Derek Chauvin travels to a particular area of town. The value judgments placed on this location (is it safe or unsafe?), as well as the cultural groups residing there (are they good or bad? law-abiding citizens or criminals?), are part of the identity ascription process. Chauvin's beliefs about Floyd and this location likely influenced his communicative behavior. Chauvin's discourse is hostile in tone and verbiage from the start of their interaction. Chauvin's refusal to take his knee off of Floyd's neck, even after it killed him, demonstrates that his mind was made up before arriving. In his mind, it seems Floyd was deemed a dangerous criminal who was violent and would resist arrest and would need to be apprehended forcibly.

The key to understanding how preverbal communication impacts dialogue lies in unpacking the definition of preverbal communication. Jackson (2006) maintains that all communication is preverbal: what we think about people, places, and things is influenced by our previous experiences; stories told to us by friends, family, acquaintances; and their reflections on television and in the news. Even in the absence of direct personal experience, we are inundated with stereotypes that influence our thoughts. We therefore form opinions and (un)consciously cultivate cultural contracts in this preverbal communicative state (think about the Chauvin example). This is problematic. Beliefs are rarely questioned and are accepted as facts; such preconceptions saturate and hinder communication. Chauvin did not reevaluate his assumptions of Floyd or seek alternative descriptors—his mind was made up in this preverbal state. This chapter describes a valuable theoretical framework—CCT—which helps to understand how individuals from different cultural backgrounds communicate with one another. We begin by describing the intellectual traditions that informed the development of the theory.

Intellectual Tradition of Cultural Contracts Theory

CCT is situated within an interpretive paradigm and situates communication as the central part of the identity negotiation process. Rooted in the premise that identities are fluid, the theoretical framework explores how identities shift over time. Interpretivism emerged in juxtaposition to positivism (Crotty, 1998). Positivism focuses on causal relationships and seeks to explain (*erklären*), predict, and control through objective inquiry using the scientific method (Crotty, 1998, p. 67). Interpretivism considers understanding (*verstehen*) as the goal of inquiry and positions subjective experiences as valid accounts of social scientific research. Interpretivism, in valuing subjectivity, documents the communicator's point of view where meaning is "culturally derived and historically situated" (p. 68). Interpretivism examines emic interpretations to which participants avow (Carbaugh, 2007), as well as the etic meanings observed from researchers.

CCT is rooted in the sociocultural tradition that explores how identities develop from communication with groups, communities, and cultures. CCT was significantly influenced by cultural identity theory, uncertainty reduction theory, social identity theory, and coordinated management of meaning. The CCT framework reflects the identity negotiation process in practice and notes the ontological, complex dialectical tensions at play as identities are ascribed (by others) and avowed (by one's self). Identities then are formed, shifted, avowed, and ascribed consciously and unconsciously before, during, and after interactions. Finally, CCT also shares values with the critical tradition. It aids in identifying, naming, deconstructing, and revealing prejudice to dismantle power, producing research to achieve social change. There are several features of CCT that reflect the critical theoretic tradition.

Main Goals and Features of Cultural Contracts Theory

Key Concepts in Cultural Contracts Theory

Communication is preverbal. Each of us is a cultural being who rhetorically transports our past-and-present values, beliefs, norms, and practices into our daily communication encounters (Hopson, 2011). We formulate our opinions about people, places, and things based on the following: (1) what we have "learned" through television, movies, and the news media; (2) the stories shared with us (whether factual or not) by family, friends, peers, and/or acquaintances; and/or, (3) our past and present experiences. This preverbal state is present within any social condition confronted by humans (racism, sexism, heterosexism, ageism, bullying, etc.) through which they understand themselves to be superior to others. Our prejudices remain with us, and impact our daily communication, unless we undergo radical self-examination.

Philosophical Premises of Cultural Contracts Theory

CCT is grounded in three original philosophical premises (Jackson et al., 2020). First, identity develops through validation from communication partners. Identity can also be challenged, when people see you differently than you see yourself. Second, "identities are constantly being exchanged, reflecting a dynamic process of activity" (p. 425). Third, "identities are contractual," scripted, and messy—resulting in the possibility of signing contracts that do not match from one person to another. Identity negotiation is a process where individuals seek to sustain, manage, and protect their identities, especially when confronted by an individual or institution that appears to pose a threat to one's identity.

Three Types of Cultural Contracts

People bring their perspectives into every communication encounter. Jackson (2002) presents three specific types of cultural contracts: *ready-to-sign, quasicompleted, and cocreated,* each of which reflects assimilation, accommodation, and acculturation, respectively. In other words, ready-to-sign contracts presume acquiescence with one's own perspective; therefore, this type reflects the greatest commitment to preserving self-interests. Quasicompleted contracts suggest a willingness to changing one's perspective within limits to facilitate relational harmony. Finally, a cocreated contract is one where the interactants place the relationship above self-interests; therefore, they are willing to be flexible enough to shift their orientation.

We reveal the specific cultural contract we sign during interactions through our communicative behaviors, which expose our cognitive biases. Below, we explain and provide examples of each of the three cultural contracts.

READY-TO-SIGN

A ready-to-sign contract is illustrated when an individual chooses to adhere to particular beliefs without a willingness to learn from an alternate perspective and/or alter opinions when presented with new information. Ready-to-sign contracts are fiercely maintained. Consider a family conversation about Brooklyn Center, Minnesota, police officer Kim Potter who killed Daunte Wright. This discussion takes place during a holiday dinner. Each person at the table has their mind made up, and nothing they discuss will change their opinions. On the one hand, the public learned from Police Chief Tim Gannon that Officer Potter mistook her firearm as a taser and unintentionally killed Wright. On the other hand, the history of anti-Black police brutality in the United States provides ample evidence that perhaps this was quite intentional. This example illustrates that multiple perspectives, personal histories, and orientations are simultaneously at work. Therefore, the complexity of ready-to-sign contracts is ever present. Ultimately, ready-to-sign contracts demonstrate how we hold onto and defend our ideas about people, places, and things since they constitute our values and belief systems (Castle Bell, 2019).

QUASICOMPLETED

Perhaps in another circumstance, you are partially open to acquiring new information about a particular topic. Let's consider members of the same family who are now in dialogue with friends. The individuals who thought that Officer Potter intentionally discharged the firearm that killed Daunte Wright explain their perspective to friends and surprisingly find that their friends have a more nuanced perspective that includes multiple contextual concerns about police training. Although the conversation becomes heated and at times a bit counterproductive, when the conversation is over, none of these friends hold the exact same perspective, because they are open to shifting their thinking a bit. They essentially agree to a quasicompleted contract. By definition, this type of cultural contract attempts to balance between maintaining the status quo and asserting one's identity.

COCREATED

In a third instance, the dinner table conversation occurs as multiple views are shared, differences are discussed, and space is provided to learn why and how differences matter. The hallmark of cocreated cultural contracts is the notion that perspectives and beliefs are *not* cemented; therefore, they are more fully open for negotiation. Here, individuals can share their opinions and respectfully come to understand each other's rationale. They don't have to agree entirely with one another's perspectives, and they do not force their views on the other person. Instead, they welcome sharing of one another's views while creating a safe space for the other person to hold a different view.

Research and Practical Applications of Cultural Contracts Theory

CCT has been utilized in a variety of research studies. Scholars have explored African American rural identities, white students' confessions about their Black male professors, "argumentative interactions," cinematic representations of Black rhetoric, interracial parenting decisions, cross-cultural perceptions of South African student teachers, face negotiation theory, American Indian identity negotiation in academe, biracial women's identities, cross-cultural adaptation in a European Union student exchange program, racialized masculinities in the context of a brotherhood kindled in a professional association, and white student positionalities (see Castle Bell, 2019; Jackson & Crawley, 2003; Jackson et al., 2020). In each case, the study is principally concerned with how identities are being negotiated. This section focuses primarily on Castle Bell's (2019) research to offer specific examples of cultural contracts theory in action.

Castle Bell (2019) interviewed 31 participants about their perspectives regarding the cultural contracts they ascribe to Black people. The results were powerfully important. This article suggested that those individuals who were interviewed had particularly strong perspectives about Black people being their own source of sociopolitical hindrance. Castle Bell concludes that these interviewees held ready-to-sign cultural contracts with no room for renegotiation. Their xenophobia of Black people was quite evident.

What is perhaps the most enlightening about the 2019 article is the sociopolitical context in which the article emerged. Even prior to 2018, President Donald Trump was campaigning for his second term. He pulled out all the stops related to his own privilege. When discussing border patrol, he tweeted on December 29, 2018, "Any deaths of children or others at the border are strictly the fault of the Democrats and their pathetic immigration policies." He tweeted over 100 times his position on immigration reform, border patrol, and the concrete wall. He reasserted that he was protecting our country and "making America great again." The media were replete with reports of President Trump blowing the neoliberal dog whistle to the white community, imploring them to resist the democratic political gymnastics that would try to convince the American people that his agenda was counterproductive. Each of these instances demonstrated President Trump's issuing of a ready-to-sign contract to American citizens. President Trump asserted his viewpoints via social media, especially Twitter, and tweeted every day about the "crazy liberals." His audience of mainly loyalists watched and reacted accordingly. Every time he mentioned that there was an unfair assault on American democracy due to unfair, "fraudulent," and "fake voter tabulation" voting practices, his audience reacted. When he implied that immigration was destroying our country and that the Democrats' "insane immigration plan completely eliminates US borders by implementing nationwide catch and release," his audience reacted. Ready-to-sign contracts are cemented over time through communities functioning as echo chambers that principally affirm likeminded perspectives and behaviors.

In Castle Bell's (2019) article, she interviews individuals who she regards as dominant group members (DGMs). Although dominance may imply privilege, it is only sinister when it is used to oppress others (Razzante, 2018). Many of us in a capitalist society have some measure of privilege and, consequently, some dominance. That dominance is not always intentional or direct. It does, however, afford certain kinds of opportunities, access, and privilege that marginalized others do not enjoy.

Castle Bell's article is an exemplar of CCT in action. CCT explores how people seek to hold onto their core identity through interactions with others. They may sustain their own worldview and create adaptive and protective behaviors to secure their identities against perceived attack. This becomes a reflex as identities shift in conversation. The identity negotiation comes in when they feel like they must shift their sense of self by changing what they believe, think, or do in order to accommodate other individuals' perceptions of them.

We all have our core identities. These are those things that we are willing to protect at all costs. If you are a devout Christian, then your religious identity is at the core of who you are. If you are a staunch Republican, then your political partisanship is an essential part of how you define yourself. These things represent the core. These are also the things that are least likely to be freely conceded or easily negotiated through everyday interaction with others. On the other hand, there are more flexible aspects of who we say we are, which we are open to change. Although it is possible to work within a conversation or a relationship to manage or negotiate things that we do not care as much about, we often seek to negotiate our identities and develop cultural contracts related to things that impinge upon our core sense of self.

Returning to Castle Bell's (2019) article, the white respondents describe feelings that suggested their core was being negotiated when interacting with the Black community. They tended to define Blackness vis-à-vis whiteness. According to the author, there were four ready-to-sign cultural contracts being presented across interviewees: "(1) fear of being the only white person in the room; (2) fear of predominantly Black locations; (3) "I avoid particular types of Black folks"; and (4) Black people are to blame. They hinder themselves" (p. 243).

The first ready-to-sign contract was related to an ingrown fear about being around Black people in low-income neighborhoods. This xenophobia has been cultivated and socially constructed over time. One of the interesting principles within CCT is related to preverbal communication. One of the respondents explains she already cognitively decided that she needs to prepare for the worst, because her cultivated perception of Black people is that they are violent. So when she talks about being the only white person on a public bus, she remembers it disturbed her and she felt very self-conscious. She admits she rarely interacted with Black people and relied upon stereotypes presented to her by family and the media to form her opinions.

The second ready-to-sign contract was fear of predominantly Black locations. This is an extension of the previous contract. The first contract centers on being afraid of being *the only* person in the room. This contract highlights fear associated with being in places primarily preoccupied by Black people; here, the person was concerned about being at a gas station that was either in a Black part of town or a place where Black people frequented. Keep in mind, it was a ready-to-sign contract, because it was based upon a fear that prevented the individual from having or coordinating a relationship with someone who was perceived as a cultural other. The only way that you can develop one of the other two contracts is through direct interaction. She basically held onto a belief that implicitly suggested that her fears made her hesitant to engage them.

The third contract is related to avoiding certain types of Black people. This is principally rooted in a myth of Black exceptionalism. The presumption is that anyone who is successful, well mannered, kind, intelligent, or the like is operating outside the norm. Obviously, the stereotype here is based upon a range of social scripts. Jackson (2006) talks about scripting the Black masculine body and indicates that there are several social prescriptions assigned to Black males, such as that they are dangerous, unintelligent, violent, and sexually aggressive. Perhaps this kind of script has motivated the third contract of avoiding people that might cause you harm. This individual convinces herself that her irrational fear is self-protective.

The final ready-to-sign contract identifies white interviewees' beliefs that Black people hinder their own success. For example, one respondent explains that Black people tend to have their pants halfway down their back sides, which provokes DGMs to see them as foreign. The problem with this assertion is that it does not describe the majority of Black people; it is based on an outgroup interpretation of this behavior. The ready-to-sign contract is enforced as a way of revealing the individual's stereotypical thinking about all Black people, which is false.

Ultimately, these research and practical applications reveal the significance of the theory. They help us understand why people do not get along or why people choose to behave one way around one set of individuals and another way around others.

Continuing the Conversation

CCT seeks to unpack a very common set of phenomena; it stems from sociocultural and critical traditions. That means that it tries to interpret and understand a set of social constructions that are tied to issues of power and dominance. There are many theories that explore issues of dominance; this one looks at a broader systemic set of issues that operate at a relational level. There are various strengths and limitations to the theory. Strengths of CCT include:

- *Advancing intercultural understanding.* The CCT is designed to address gaps in our capacity to bridge intercultural relationships. When we notice that individuals are at an impasse or find themselves unable to fully appreciate or value one another's cultural differences, usually one of CCT's three contract types is at the core of the issue.

- *Openness.* All effective theories should be open and flexible enough for change. That means they should be able to be extended in different directions and have the capacity to be applied in unforeseen areas of inquiry. This theory was initially used to explain how people in different racialized contexts worked to hold onto their sense of self. As noted earlier, the theory has been applied in a range of different institutional, global, relational, racial, cultural, and gendered contexts.

- *Heurism.* For a theory to be heuristic, it must contribute to new knowledge rather than replicate preexisting ideas. As stated earlier, CCT has been used to explain relational dynamics, classroom interaction, racial relations, and the like. The heuristic value of the theory is that it goes beyond simply talking about how we initiate and build relationships to how we consider facets of one's cultural identity that impinge upon the possibility of relationship growth.

- *Parsimony.* CCT is comprised of only three different contract types. Those three types (ready-to-sign, quasicompleted, cocreated) correspond with behaviors that can be understood as accommodation, adaptation, and acculturation, respectively. Such a straightforward and easy-to-understand typology reflects a clear and concise theoretical framework.

Of course, there are also limitations to any theory. For CCT, limitations include:

- *Conceptual scope generalizability.* Much of the research that has been done using CCT has explored race and racism. Some additional studies examined cross-cultural adaptation and parenting. Although CCT can be used to describe everything from aging to gamer identity, its main utilization describes the problems encountered when a part of one's identity is being rejected or dismissed. Additional scholarship should extend and demonstrate the elasticity of the theory as it relates to cultural identity, broadly defined.

- *Inherent ambiguity.* Over the years, several questions have emerged from those who have studied the theory. Some individuals want to know who issues the cultural contract. There are other questions, such as: Whose contract is it? What if contracts do not match? Do we all have contracts that inform every interaction? Can there be a relationship without a contract? Regarding social media use: What contracts are formed if you are engaging in a virtual space using artificial intelligence or virtual reality tools? When the relationship is not technically real, does it still conform to the same processes and have some of the same effects?

Summary

People are negotiating their identities on a daily basis. We see people code switching the way they talk to their friends versus their parents. We see how a president or political candidate speaks differently to different audiences. We notice how we respond differently to people based upon the uniform they are wearing. There are so many ways that identity shifting takes place in our everyday lives. What makes CCT unique is the way it seeks to capture the relational dynamics and socially constructed perceptions of others at the speed of thought.

FOR FURTHER THOUGHT AND REFLECTION

1. Think about the last time you felt you had to defend some part of your identity. What did that feel like? What cultural contracts were you reflexively agreeing to enact? What contracts of your own were you asking other people to sign?

2. What are some other areas where you have seen individuals negotiate their identities? What sort of studies can you imagine being done using CCT?

3. How can CCT help you to understand your career aspirations? What about your buying habits? How about how you interact on social media?

4. Where do you see CCT at play in your communication encounters? After reflecting on a communication occurrence, which cultural contracts do you observe in the interaction?

5. The findings of Castle Bell (2019) focused on ready-to-sign contracts within interracial contexts. What examples can you generate that highlight how quasicompleted and cocreated cultural contracts might foster more meaningful and authentic interracial relationships, especially those with self-defined white allies?

STORIED REFLECTION
It Hasn't Been What I Imagined

Ashlee Lambert
Arizona State University

My first introduction to theory was in my undergraduate interpersonal communication class at Jackson State University. I was mesmerized by theory and how it helped me better understand my own life. Theory just made life make sense ... until it didn't. When we started learning about Genderlect Styles Theory and discussing the book *Men Are from Mars, Women Are from Venus*, I no longer fit. The author and the folks in the class kept reminding me that the content wasn't for everyone, just *most* scenarios. Even when I considered it through that lens, I just couldn't get over the fact that I knew so many people who didn't neatly fit or fit at all into the categories the theory assumes, and I felt like the theory was missing some critical components on the sociopolitical construction of gender.

Nonetheless, I still loved the idea of theory and couldn't wait to learn more. When I transferred to Western Michigan University I took a class on human communication theory, we had to write Theory into Practice (TiP) reports, and we could write them at any time. In order to stay on top of things, I wanted to make sure I got mine in before the first deadline. One of the first theories we covered was symbolic interactionism. I really understood it, but when it came time for me to apply it to a situation, it was too complicated. I sat in front of my computer way too long pulling apart this theory to create unrealistic hypothetical situations that made the concepts within the theory fit. I found this to be true for many theories. I could talk about them but trying to apply the main concepts and premises to a real-life situation was hard. At least for my life.

It wasn't until we started discussing identity and cultural theories that I started to appreciate theory again. Even though I struggled to use them for research, I loved muted group and standpoint theories. I also grew particularly fond of co-cultural theory and cultural contracts theory as I could apply them effortlessly to real-world situations. They captured the complexities and allowed room for the ambiguity of my own lived experiences. They situated my lived experiences at the center, rather than how others might interpret my experiences. I then moved to learning more about how to apply theory, writing autoethnography through intersectionality, and reading scholarship by Black, Indigenous, or People of Color (BIPOC) who intersect with other marginalized identities, such as being first-generation college students, low-income, LGBTQ+, different abled, women, and the like. This led to great excitement to learn more within my graduate program. I couldn't wait to get my master's degree, be introduced to even more works by scholars of color, and find more theories that worked.

Well ... things didn't exactly happen how I'd imagined it. During my graduate program, I was introduced to hyper/in/visibility theory, and it has become one of my favorite theories! I also am better at understanding and applying theory, but even now some theories are just not useful in practice or they need critical updates. The more theory I learn, the less mesmerized I have become. I have been searching for theories to apply to the research that *I* want to do, but I haven't been introduced to many theories during my graduate program. In my foundational readings course, we centered white canonical theorists, such as Plato, Aristotle, Burke, which did very little for helping me with my research. Most of the time, I find theory constraining the work that I want to do.

I got what I wanted from my mentors (all people of color) and the classes they have taught (both undergrad and grad). Their work and classes made me so excited to attend my first National Communication Association conference in 2019. I anticipated trying not to fangirl in front of the scholars of color I read and loved. I imagined being overwhelmed by brilliance of all the other scholars of color who I had not met and relieved from the white scholarship I had been enduring. An unexpected reality hit entering the conference; it was overwhelmingly white. While I did meet some new scholars of color, I thought there would be so many more.

Overall, I am looking forward to having a book that centers scholars of color and that theorizes and reconceptualizes overcomplicated and uncritical theories. This book will contribute to the lives of so many scholars, from centering our experiences and providing representation to simply saving time searching for theories that apply to our research. I am excited to rebuild a connection to theory. While things haven't been what I have imagined, I imagine this book being what I have been looking for.

PART II

Interpersonal Messages

As summarized in the introduction to Part I, we communicate our identities to others through interpersonal messages that are enacted both verbally and/or nonverbally. While all messages may not carry direct references to one's identity, they do represent enacted frames of identity that can serve multiple functions. From conversations among friends and colleagues to discussions with family and romantic partners, we are unable to avoid crafting messages and message processing—they accompany our every interaction. Whether the messages are casual or formal and shared in person or digitally, each communicative effort is accompanied by decisions related to language and meaning-making that are made in concert with others.

As a process, interpersonal communication transactional models typically incorporate a variety of elements, including participants, frames of reference, encoding, decoding, messages, channels, feedback, context, and noise. This process typically focuses on the relationship between words and ideas as well as their use among conversational participants who fail or succeed in sharing meaning while occupying dual roles as senders and receivers. The emphasis on communicating meaningful messages links the efficacy of communicative encounters to conversational participants' goals (Canary et al., 2008). The use of language (e.g., abstract or concrete) in accomplishing effectiveness is paramount. Additional variables, along with the elements in a typical transactional model, become at play—gender, power, intimacy, knowledge, race, ethnicity, and culture are among them.

When theorizing about interpersonal messages, we have a fertile playground from which to center the experiences of marginalized groups. This requires probing the elements and variables of the communication process and use of language within the backdrop of *their* lived experiences to reveal *their* meanings and to understand *their* goals in interpersonal interactions. In Part II, we highlight the unique contribution of the theories offered in the chapters related to interpersonal messages after sharing the existing canonized theories.

Existing Canonized Theories

The landscape of theorizing about interpersonal messages involves a variety of existing theoretical frameworks related to meaning making, nonverbals, conversations, and communication behavior (including deceptive communication). We begin with three examples that acknowledge the mutual roles of conversational participants. First, is Pearce and Cronen's (1980) coordinated management of meaning (CMM), which views communication as a process in which participants cocreate social realities through stories; CMM provides an understanding of how stories lived and stories told are different, and it accounts for the complexities involved in the coordination of interactions. Another theory is Burgoon's (1978) expectancy violations theory (EVT), which incorporates proxemics. According to EVT, communicators hold a set of predictions (e.g., expectancies) about the use of personal space and normative behavior in conversations. When unexpected behavior occurs, participants evaluate these violations either positively or negatively (e.g., violation valence) and weigh the potential rewards and penalties (e.g., communicator reward valence) associated with the violation. EVT seeks to capture adjustments in communicator behavior and has been examined in cross-cultural interpersonal interactions. A third view of conversations in interpersonal interactions is Grice's (1989, p. 26) cooperative principle, which says to "make your conversational contribution such as is required at the stage at which it occurs, by the accepted purpose or direction of the talk exchange in which you are engaged." Grice's four maxims (quantity, quality, relation, and manner) assist individuals to fulfill the cooperative principle in interpersonal interactions. This view is prevalent as many theories import the degree of cooperation adhered to by conversational participants and incorporate the assumption of certain conversational moves as suitable or unsuitable. All of these frameworks are influential in illuminating factors that can shape or infringe upon interpersonal interactions.

To understand communication behavior, particularly among cultural group members, Giles and colleagues (1991) offer communication accommodation theory (CAT). Focusing on both verbal (e.g., specific word choice) and nonverbal (e.g., accent, eye contact, dress, proxemics) elements, this theory emphasizes how conversational participants interact while adjusting their communication behavior in ways that are more similar (convergence) or dissimilar (divergence) to their conversational partner. For example, when cultural group members seek approval or efficiency in their interactions, CAT predicts convergence is more likely to occur, whereas divergence is more likely when conversational participants seek to personally dissociate or portray a different self-image. CAT is a theory capable of acknowledging "how two people from different cultures interact in ways that reflect their personal goals and cultural identities" (Canary et al., 2008, p. 42).

Two additional theoretical frameworks are worth noting in acknowledgement that truth telling is not always a communication goal; theorizing also needs to account for the process of deceptive interpersonal interactions. One example is McCornack's (1992) informational manipulation theory, which relies on Grice's (1989) work to arrive at an explanatory model of the types of messages that create deception. McCornack argues that information can be manipulated in four ways that violate conversational maxims and thus create deception. His principal claim is "messages that are commonly thought of as deceptive derive from covert violations of the conversational maxims" (McCornack, 1992, p. 5). Another theory explaining the nature of deceptive communication is interpersonal deception theory (IDT). Burgoon and colleagues (1996) contend conversational participants make strategic choices when engaging in deceptive communication with information management (or managing message content and design) as one of those choices. From their perspective, IDT distinguishes "between how senders construct truthful and deceptive messages, receivers discriminate between them, and scholars theorize about them" (Buller & Burgoon, 1996, p. 95). While the central premise of these theories is not to center the lived experiences of racially and ethnically diverse conversational participants, the frameworks do account for the range of conversational exchanges that often involve cooperative and competing interpersonal messages.

Overview of Chapters

Within Part II, we remind readers of five fundamental principles in interpersonal communication that are germane to the theories in this area. As Orbe and Bruess (2005) offer, interpersonal communication is: (1) complex, (2) irreversible and inevitable, (3) rule-based, (4) always related to culture and power, and (5) changing with technology. These principles are relevant, and these theories contribute key aspects to inform our understanding of one or more principles. The principles are at play in the theoretical frameworks shared in Part II. Each theory can illuminate the deliberate and strategic creation and deployment of messages in interpersonal interactions involving those who are racially and ethnically diverse. The three chapters in this part position the lived experiences of the marginalized as central to our understanding of daily interpersonal interactions. Each theory yields research capable of informing communicative behaviors from the perspectives of those with salient cultural and ethnic identities. Each uniquely accounts for the positionality and desired aims of marginalized group members in communication interactions. And each holds promise for prompting even greater heuristic value in understanding the lived experiences of racially and ethnically diverse communicators.

Chapter 4, in Part II, focuses on conflict face negotiation theory (FNT). The theory's originator, Stella Ting-Toomey, introduces FNT, which illuminates the conscious and unconscious choices of communicators in managing face in everyday interactions, particularly in culture-sensitive conflict situations. Stemming from a post-positivist theoretical framework, FNT offers a window for explaining or predicting how communication functions as individuals seek to save, defend, threaten, attack, improve, elevate, or position the image of self or others through facework. Ting-Toomey walks the reader through FNT's maturation across three decades offering an overview of FNT's refined assumptions and propositions. As a cross-cultural communication theory, FNT orients us to differences and similarities in face concerns across cultures. Ting-Toomey incorporates three mini-cases that illustrate face concerns in what can be viewed as common communicative encounters. Dubbed by Ting-Toomey as a "work-in-progress," FNT holds great promise for understanding the series of strategic moves and countermoves associated with facework across a variety of intercultural and interpersonal contexts, including situations with greater complexity and with varying levels of perceived privilege and power.

In Chapter 5, co-cultural theory is examined by Mark P. Orbe, who is the theory's originator, and Fatima Albrehi. Given the commitment of this book to foreground racially diverse and inclusive perspectives, co-cultural theory offers powerful contributions. First, it situates our understanding of interpersonal communication within the lived experiences of marginalized groups. Second, it accounts for the power imbalances that exist in communicative encounters but that are often omitted in communication theory. Drawing from muted group and feminist standpoint theories, Orbe and Albrehi share co-cultural theory's five core assumptions and the key research that aided in the development of co-cultural practices. With great lucidity, the co-cultural framework offers insight on the six factors that shape the strategic communicative choices of co-cultural group members and the nine co-cultural orientations that emanate from selections of preferred outcomes and communication approaches. Their chapter includes a co-cultural case study of an Afro-Arab Muslim that elegantly demonstrates the theory's utility. Co-cultural theory remains a unique vehicle for understanding the real-time communicative practices of marginalized group members.

Ethnic communication theory (ECT) is the topical focus for Chapter 6 and is written by theory originator Uchenna Onuzulike. ECT probes the communication of Igbo immigrants from Nigeria and emphasizes how second-generation individuals sustain ethnic identity within two main cultures—their ethnic culture and the United States' main culture. Through ECT, Onuzulike's work provides a theoretical window that makes it possible to see the traditions, customs, and values of Igbo culture in the communication style and interactions of Igbo immigrants. The work of ECT informs transnational identity and hints at the role that transnational media, social media, ethnic functions, ethnic literature, ethnic artwork, and ancestral homeland visits play in informing communicative behavior when ethnic identity is salient. ECT is insightful for understanding interpersonal interactions when communicators are attached to their ancestral origin.

Overview of Storied Reflections

In addition to the main theoretical contributions in each chapter, Part II includes three storied reflections from Dalaki Livingston, Dorthy Pennington, and Pavitra Kavya.

Livingston, a doctoral candidate at the University of Oklahoma, shares an *upward journey and sunwise path* through the lens of dawn, day, and dusk that led to a presence in and out of academia. Using the three distinct moments of twilight, he reflects on his grievances with communication theory and research to arrive in a space where Native scholarship and community intertwine. Pennington, an associate professor at the University of Kansas, recounts her *behavior in search of theory*. She recalls her roots studying English literature at a historically Black college and university (HBCU) and shares the impetus for her investigation of power in communication inquiry. Through her mispronunciation of "paradigm" coupled with a focus on Black rhetors, she reminds us of the importance of humility. Kavya, an assistant professor at California State Polytechnic University, Pomona, elaborates from her practitioner-informed view on the importance of *using theories for skill building in the frontlines of organizations*. She offers communication theories as a readily accessible toolkit capable of shaping or shifting the mindsets of business leaders and helping them to cultivate skills for tackling complex organizational challenges and issues.

CHAPTER 4

Conflict Face-Negotiation Theory in Intercultural-Interpersonal Contexts

Stella Ting-Toomey

California State University, Fullerton

Intercultural conflict refers to the perceived or actual incompatibility of cultural beliefs, values, situational norms, goals, face orientations, emotions, scarce resources, styles/processes, and/or outcomes in a face-to-face (or mediated) context within a sociohistorical embedded system. The study of intercultural conflict communication involves, at least in part, cultural group membership differences and face-identity dissonances. Competent facework communication involves the integration of culture-sensitive knowledge, mindfulness, and adaptive facework skillsets in managing the vulnerable, face-sensitive situation skillfully and adaptively.

This chapter is organized into three sections. First, the historical backdrop and the intellectual tradition of the conflict face-negotiation theory are mapped out. Second, boundary conditions, building-block constructs, and application illustrations are discussed. Third, strengths, limitations, and directions for future research are identified.

Intellectual Traditions of Conflict Face-Negotiation Theory

The root of the conflict face-negotiation theory (FNT) was influenced by Hsien Chin Hu's (1944) anthropological essay entitled "The Chinese Concepts of 'Face',"

Erving Goffman's (1955) sociological article entitled "On Face-Work: An Analysis of Ritual Elements in Social Interaction," and Penelope Brown and Stephen Levinson's (1987) linguistics monograph entitled *Politeness: Some Universals in Language Usage*. The originally developed FNT explains the culture-based, individual-based, and situational-based factors that shape communicators' tendencies in approaching problematic face-sensitive situations. FNT is cast as a cross-cultural conflict theory due to its focus on a comparative analysis on how members of individualistic and collectivistic cultures approach and manage diverse interpersonal conflicts (see Ting-Toomey, 2017).

The meaning of *face* is generally conceptualized in the FNT as how we want others to see us and treat us and how we actually treat others in association with their social self-conception expectations. *Face* is a relational meaning phenomenon—what you want to claim for your own *face* ("avowed face") may not be how others treat your *face persona* ("ascribed face"). In everyday interactions, individuals are constantly making conscious or unconscious choices concerning face-saving, face-recouping, and face-honoring issues across a wide range of problematic interpersonal encounters. On the surface, *face* is about the "claimed sense" of socially approved self-image and other-image consideration issues; on the deep level, it involves the emotional streams of shame and honor, guilt and pride, and identity disrespect and respect phenomena. *Facework* is about the verbal and nonverbal interactional behaviors or strategies that we use to defend or save self-face, to threaten/attack the other person's face, or even to elevate the *face image* of self, others, and community. While the conflict FNT has been primarily used in the context of explaining and predicting culture-sensitive conflict styles and facework tactics, other researchers have used the FNT to generate insights on other cross-cultural discourse or interactional strategies (e.g., request, apology, compliance gaining).

While the seed of the FNT first appeared in a chapter Ting-Toomey wrote in 1985, the first rendition of the formal theory was presented in Ting-Toomey's (1988) theoretic essay in Kim and Gudykunst's *Theories in Intercultural Communication*. This first version of the FNT included five assumptions and 12 theoretical propositions. A second rendition of the FNT (Ting-Toomey & Kurogi, 1998) contained seven assumptions and 32 propositions stating the relationship among an individualism-collectivism value spectrum, face concerns, and conflict styles, and it was extended to include optimal facework competence issues.

Based on the results of several large-scale cross-cultural data sets (e.g., Oetzel & Ting-Toomey, 2003), a third rendition of the FNT appeared in a handbook chapter (Ting-Toomey, 2005). This third version of the FNT contained seven assumptions and a fine-tuned 24 propositions. More recently, a fourth rendition of the FNT appeared in a conflict chapter in Ting-Toomey and Dorjee's (2019) advanced text, with a dual emphasis on studying intercultural and intergroup facework competence via the particular practice of mindfulness.

The author considers conflict FNT as a postpositivist theory. *Epistemologically*, the FNT emphasizes the cultural, individual, and situational standpoints of how *face* is being constructed and known. The "knowledge world" of where the FNT resides is a multiplex mini-cultural world in which both outsiders and insiders can walk away with distinctive interpretational facets of what had occurred in the *face* collusion encounter. *Face* is in fact an identity-communication resource (e.g., reputation, prestige) that is being constantly renegotiated and bargained over, with strategic interdependent moves and countermoves. Methodologically, under the FNT canopy, the initial study of cross-cultural face concerns and conflict styles started with an interpretive paradigm methodology—from narrative interview method, to open-ended response method, to Q-sort method. The follow-up research studies then followed the functional paradigm methodology—painstakingly constructing cross-cultural face concerns and conflict styles' surveys to capture the conceptual and functional equivalence of various facework constructs (e.g., data collection in Germany, China, Japan, South Korea, Mexico, and the United States; and including U.S. domestic ethnic identity salience issues). Additionally, personality traits and situational parameters (e.g., ingroup-outgroup) were added into the conflict FNT research design. Thus, while the structure of the face-negotiation theory sounds positivistic and operated under the functional paradigm framework, the methodologies that have been employed are pluralistic in emphasis. Hence, the theory itself is viewed by the researcher-creator here as a post-positivist theory.

Ontologically, the FNT theorist, in looking out to the "world of reality" concerning the mirage and meaning of *face*, relies heavily on probabilistic theoretical statements (e.g., independent self tends to be more self-face concern, and interdependent self tends to be more other-face concern) versus deterministic claims in the construction of the FNT. Based on their sociocultural lived experiences, different cultural members would decode the different face-sensitive situations at times similarly and at times differently.

Axiologically, no theory construction process is ever value-free. Even three-year-old children learned from their family socialization process of the normative standards of how to behave compliantly or rebelliously depending on who is watching. At such a young age, toddlers can already formulate complex self-conscious emotions such as embarrassment, shame, beaming pride, or frowning guilt. To be completely transparent here, the theorist did not set out in the 1980s to construct intentionally an Asian or Chinese theory of face-negotiation. However, it is without doubt that her traditional Chinese Confucius upbringing shaped her theorizing process.

Main Goals and Features of Conflict Face-Negotiation Theory

It appears that when an individual's face image is being threatened in a conflict situation, she or he would likely experience identity-based frustrations, emotional vulnerability, anger, defensiveness, hurt, or even vengeance. The threats to face can be on a group membership level or an individual level. In the FNT third version, the following conditions were posited concerning the valence direction of an *intercultural face-threatening process (FTP)*: First, the more the culturally appropriate facework rule is violated, the more severe the perceived FTP. Second, the larger the cultural distance between the conflict parties, the more mistrust or misunderstanding cumulate in the FTP. Third, the more important the perceived conflict topic or imposition of the conflict demand, as interpreted from distinctive cultural angles, the more severe the perceived FTP. Fourth, the more perceived power the conflict initiator has over the conflict recipient, the more severe the perceived FTP by the recipient. Fifth, the more harm or hurtful the FTP produces, the more time and effort are needed to repair the FTP. Self-face concern becomes incrementally more salient if several of these conditions are present in a face-threatening process.

For example, individuals are likely to move toward self-face-saving and ingroup communal face-saving emphasis as they perceive the escalation of the various face-threatening conditions directed at them or their salient ingroups. Cultural worldview perspectives, individual personality tendencies, relational parameters, and situational pressures frame the underlying interpretations of what count as a severe "face-threatening" interaction episode.

The struggles for face respect or face deference in an identity-sensitive episode consists of three core facets: (a) locus of face—concern for self-face orientation, other-face orientation, mutual-face orientation, plus communal-face orientation; (b) face valence—whether face is being defended, saved, maintained, honored, or even elevated; and (c) temporality—whether face is being restored/recouped or proactively protected. Locus of face is the primary dimension of face that has been tested extensively, and this face orientation facet shapes the direction of the subsequent conflict responses and facework tactics. *Self-face* is the protective concern for one's own image when one's own face is threatened in the conflict situation. *Other-face*, on the other hand, is the concern for accommodating the other conflict party's image in the conflict situation. *Mutual-face* is the concern for both parties' images or the expectancy relational identity image of the interpersonal pairing. *Communal-face* is the concern of upholding ingroup membership face in comparative assessment of ingroup/outgroup face expectancies, estimated net worth, and anticipated future interactions. *Facework* is the communication strategies used to defend, challenge, support, or even upgrade self-face and other-face identity issues in an emotionally vulnerable, identity off-balance encounter.

The overall findings in testing the conflict FNT revealed that individualistic cultural members and independent types have more self-face concern and less other-face and mutual-face concerns than collectivists and interdependent types. In comparison, collectivistic cultural members and interdependent types have more other-face emphasis in managing conflicts with others than individualists and independent types. In testing the FNT within the pluralistic U.S. culture, multiethnic conflict research has uncovered distinctive conflict interaction styles in relationship to particular cultural/ethnic identity salience issues.

Research and Practical Applications of Conflict Face-Negotiation Theory

The following two mini-dialogue scenarios reinforce learning about *self-face* and *other-face* concern constructs across cultural-ethnic or personality lines. The first scenario reflects an interaction between two individualistic-independent personality types; the second scenario reflects a conversation between two collectivistic-interdependent personality types in an acquaintanceship setting (Ting-Toomey & Chung, 2022).

FNT: A FIRST-INTERACTION MINI-DIALOGUE

KALENE (knocks on her neighbor's screen door): Excuse me, it's past 11 o'clock already, and your loud music and dancing around are really disturbing my sleep. Please stop your jumping and banging around right away! I have an important job interview tomorrow morning, and I want to get a good night's sleep. Some of us *do* need to pay rent!

KELSEY (resentfully): Well, this is the only time I can rehearse! I have an important audition coming up tomorrow. You're not the only one who's starving, you know. I also need to pay my rent. Stop being *so* petty!

KALENE (frustrated): I really think *you're* being *very annoying* and *intrusive*! There is an apartment noise ordinance, you know. And if you don't stop banging around immediately, I'm going to file a complaint with the apartment manager and he could evict you.

KELSEY (sarcastically and turning up the music louder): Whatever! Do what you want. I'm going to practice as loud as I want. Don't bother to ask for my autograph when I become a Hollywood star!

FNT: A SECOND-INTERACTION MINI-DIALOGUE

MRS. NGUYEN: Hello, Mrs. Trang. I heard your son Minh-Ha is entering his high school karaoke contest, isn't he? I envy you, because you must be so proud of his talent. You must be looking forward to his future as a pop singer. I'm really impressed by his enthusiasm—every day, he practices so hard, for hours and hours, until late at night.

MRS. TRANG: Oh, I'm so sorry. Minh-Ha is just a beginner in karaoke singing. We don't know his future yet. He is such a silly boy singing so late. We didn't realize you can hear all the noise next door. I'll tell him to stop right away. I'm so sorry about all your trouble. It won't happen again.

In the first-interaction scenario, both Kalene and Kelsey emphasized self-face concern needs and used "I-centered" discourse messages to protect and defend self-interest and personal-interest conflict goals. The use of direct evaluative language, personal attack and blaming statements, and sarcastic and defensive tone further escalated the runaway conflict spirals.

On the content conflict goal analysis level, it seems Kalene and Kelsey were arguing about the "loud music and dancing around and banging" noise level; however, on the deeper identity level of analysis, they were arguing over their rights and freedom to do what they want between apartment units and also defending their spatial boundary domains. In utilizing the FNT vocabulary for analysis, Kelsey then used a direct face-threatening attack message that undercuts Kalene's social self-image persona: "Stop being *so* petty!" In reciprocation, Kalene used a counter-face-threatening message that she was ready to "file a complaint with the apartment manager." At that point, the rubber-band polarization between the two neighbors was ready to snap. If both Kalene and Kelsey had some training on facework competence issues, they may have realized that beyond self-face protection and defensiveness, they could work on more mutual-face saving and mutual-face giving and respect. Through mindful listening and collaborative dialogue, they can also uncover some common ground.

In analyzing the second-interaction scenario between Mrs. Nguyen and Mrs. Trang, Mrs. Nguyen approached the neighborly conversation with an initial strong positive face-giving message, complimenting the hard work of Mrs. Trang's son Minh-Ha. She then followed up with a bonus face-honoring verbal message of "you must be so proud of his talent," thereby uplifting Mrs. Trang's social image and motherly pride. Mrs. Nguyen's skillful use of a facework-honoring message reached the culture-sensitive ears of Mrs. Trang. She expressed her facework embarrassment by sharing that she did not realize her good neighbor could hear the nonstop singing of her "silly boy son," and closed the dialogue with expression of regret.

However, if you use your imagination for the next three minutes, what do you think would happen if Mrs. Nguyen was the neighbor of Kelsey? If Mrs. Nguyen used the same facework request message with Kelsey, would Kelsey stop singing into the night, or would she sing louder and dance louder thinking that she is now offering a free concert to entertain her neighbor, Mrs. Nguyen?

Extending the above interpretive dialogue analysis lens, let us check out one more real-life case study and use the key constructs from the FNT to analyze the disruptive event sequences (Ting-Toomey & Chung, 2022).

> ### A CASE STUDY: "DOING LUNCH—MISTAKEN IDENTITY OR RACISM EPISODE?"
>
> My work colleagues and I met for lunch at the university restaurant. As we were being seated, I could not help but notice another table nearby. The table was beautifully decorated with rose petals, fancy packages, and wine glasses. The women at the table were immaculately dressed in designer couture—Chanel, Gucci, and Dior. I was curious and walked over to their table. "Excuse me, your table is absolutely stunning! I hope you don't mind me asking what the special occasion is." One woman, Ms. XX, smiled and replied, "We are celebrating friendship day. We do this every year. Since you are here, may I have a glass of ice tea with no ice cubes?" I was shocked and stunned, and said, "I am so sorry I did not introduce myself properly. I am an assistant dean in the College of Arts and Sciences." Ms. XX apologized and then ended with this statement: "Oh, I thought you were the maître d'—I mean, the *head* maître d'."
>
> As an African American woman who has worked on this campus for over a decade, I am still disappointed and somewhat dismayed that after all these years, color matters. It is a daily reminder that I am different. For those who are ignorant (and/or racist), this is a teaching moment. For me, these moments keep me grounded and motivate me to keep being an outspoken, positive change agent in my community—with my students and others who I may encounter daily.
>
> — PBP, Assistant Dean

Well, what do you think? Can you reach into the FNT toolkit and use some of the FNT core constructs to analyze this case study? To start you off, let's briefly apply the constructs of self-face and other-face and perceived face-threatening messages that manifested in this story.

The story took place at a formal university restaurant, and Dean PBP noticed a table nearby and that was beautifully decorated. Out of her curiosity and trying to *give face* to the next-door table guests, Dean PBP approached the table graciously and inquired about the festive occasion. While Ms. XX did answer with politeness, the quick follow-up, matter-of-fact request triggered shock waves and face-threat emotions to Dean PBP's identity being. As Ms. XX cavalierly requested: "Since you are here, may I have a glass of ice tea with no ice cubes?"

It is no doubt (from this researcher FNT's analytical lens) that Dean PBP at that moment experienced strong emotional flooding of instantaneous surprise, frustrations, outrage, and a mix of flabbergasted emotions. As her own *avowed face* as a dean did not match the implicit *ascribed face* (being mistaken or stereotyped as a "waitress") imputed by the well-coiffed Ms. XX, Dean PBP, however, maintained her poise and used an assertive-clarification line: "I am so sorry, I did not introduce myself properly. I am an assistant dean in the College of Arts and Sciences." Thus, Dean PBP reclaimed and elevated her own face prestige via the formal self-introduction line. Instead, the final zinger came flying back sharp and furious and creating more face-insult "ouch!" when Ms. XX actually amended her earlier *facework-embarrassment message* with a quick *facework-repair* message: "Oh, I thought you were the maître d'—I mean, the *head* maître d'."

As a minority member, if you've experienced racism episodes directed at you historically, it is hard to scrub away the racism stain that you have absorbed constantly, even if it was only for a nanosecond. From perceived self-face being invalidated and insulted, Dean PDP, understandably, tied the face-insulting episode to her larger reflection of being an African American dean on this elite campus. Despite all her lifetime campus hard work, it appears that inclusive face-respect communication training sessions need to be continually promoted, advocated, and practiced by all. The FNT lens helps to flush out some complex emotions underlying unintended to intended microaggression messages.

Continuing the Conversation

Conflict FNT is an original theory in the field of intercultural communication and has been tested, expanded, and refined through three decades of research studies from both functional and interpretive methodologies. The following evaluative criteria will be used to assess the strengths and limitations of the conflict FNT: cross-cultural scope, communication-centered focus, explanatory power, parsimony, and testability/predictive power.

First and foremost, conflict FNT is a cross-cultural communication theory with its onset goal of comparing differences and similarities of various face-concern orientations with particular conflict styles. Second, conflict FNT has a strong communication-centered focus due to its emphasis on how different value patterns shape different face-concern priorities and, subsequently, connected to the different use of particular conflict communication styles. Third, on the explanatory criterion level, the five boundary conditions, seven assumptions, and 24 propositions appear to be logically consistent with one another and in persuasive alignment within and between structural elements. Fourth, conflict FNT is a parsimonious theory, especially the essential assumptions of the FNT that provide broad coverage for researchers from different disciplines to extrapolate selective assumptions to explore face-sensitive situations. Finally, the 24 theoretical propositions have testable predictive power, and other conflict researchers have used selective propositions as a springboard to construct specific hypotheses among predictor factors, face concerns, and diverse facework strategies.

Three possible limitations (and more) of the conflict FNT potentially exist. First, on the cross-cultural scope criterion, conflict FNT has been tested primarily in Western cultures such as the larger U.S. society and Germany, with additional research findings reflecting primarily of Chinese, Japanese, Korean, and Mexican face-concern issues. Thus, data-collection scope sites can be widened and expanded. Second, in terms of the communication-focused criterion, the FNT remains a cross-comparative theory, and more studies can be designed to capture the intercultural or intergroup face-negotiation, back-and-forth discourse exchange process level. Lastly, on the heuristic value level, the next rendition of the conflict FNT must consider the role of digital media usage between members of different cultural/ethnic members in face-violation settings as a sorely neglected area of study.

In addition to the above points on the strengths and limitations of assessing conflict FNT, here are three directions for future research: First, the advancement of the FNT can only be made by instilling a strong sense of situational complexity and sociocultural identity complexity in its further theorizing development. Second, the progress of the FNT is dependent highly on rigorous and creative comparative methodological testing—from postpositivist research design to the use of multimethods or mixed methods. Third, where do the twin concepts of privilege and power fit in the FNT theoretical schema? *Face* is both an affective-embodied identity construct and a cognitive appraisal resource. In a problematic intergroup facework situation, we gauge each other's sense of worthiness filtered through our mindless stereotypes and biased perceptual lens. How we calculate our own sense of rights and privilege in a face-sensitive situation may be in total misalignment with how others assess our social net worth. Thus, facework can be misfired, misinterpreted, and misconstrued. More attention can be given to facework-repair competence work and mutual power-honoring facework. Particular power-related conditions and propositions can be more fully developed if scholars would like to play with conflict FNT from a critical/cultural studies lens.

Summary

The conflict face-negotiation theory is a work-in-progress kaleidoscope. Although the structure of the theory skews towards the functional postpositivist paradigm, the testing of the FNT can be drawn from any of the paradigms or even a mixed-method toolkit. More importantly, the ultimate decision of using a particular method should be in general alignment with the conceptual spirit of the FNT core conditions, assumptions, and theoretical propositions. More collaborative research effort among international and domestic diversity theorists and researchers can help to understand the underlying metaphors, communication repertoires, and situational complexity of the net meaning of *face* and the creative facework strategies that are needed to promote genuine intergroup facework respect, understanding, and inclusion.

FOR FURTHER THOUGHT AND REFLECTION

1. Think of a past conflict at work with your coworker or a team project conflict with a classmate. What was your overall conflict approach with your coworker or your class-mate? Using FNT core constructs, analyze how you negotiated *face* with your conflict partner. How did your partner negotiate *face* with you? How did the conflict end?

2. Have you ever encountered a similar story like that of Dean PDP? Share your story with a classmate. How did that face-threatening episode make you feel? What facework repair communication strategies would you wish you had used in that episode?

3. If you want to work on the conflict FNT for the next 10 years, what do you think are the two most fruitful directions for future research? Can you frame these two research directions into two "answerable" research questions? What methodological approach would you pick? Why?

STORIED REFLECTION
An Upward Journey and Sunwise Path

Dalaki Livingston
University of Oklahoma

Black-Night

When I was younger, I would wake up early on weekends to watch cartoons. *Justice League*, a show of superheroes, had Green Lantern. He was my favorite; he was brown like me! Time passed, and I found out that Green Lantern was a different brown than me. I continued my search for that Native American superhero. I was a child search-ing for myself in the dark. I just wanted to see myself doing those amazing things. Thankfully, among my family of six sisters, two brothers, and a mother and father, I had role models aplenty. Yet I would keep watching the screen, hoping to see myself represented.

Dawn

Before theory was introduced, I saw communication work like magic in my high school career. I wanted to know how people can use their words to inspire, motivate, and influence their audi-ence. Being from a small town with a graduating class of 33, I saw firsthand how a network of people can be forged through communication. Friendships spawned across county and state borders in dazzling arrays. Communication became the connecting factor.

Day

Time continued to tick, and I found myself in my Ph.D. program. The words still ring in my ear: "If you don't do better work, you'll end up as a diversity hire." An advisor uttered these words to me. In academia, I needed to be like a certain type of scholar, or the consequence was to be irrelevant. I yearned to fit. The reality of being a diversity hire was like a scorching noon-day, and I burned. I retreated into my insecurities and tried to shelter myself from the reality I thought to be true.

The doubt crept in; maybe getting into the Ph.D. program truly was a diversity pick, and what I had done up until then did not matter since I was selected because of pity or charity. Once again, I could not find myself in where I was looking; I traded the screen for my career. Scholarship did not have a place for me. Four years into my Ph.D. program and I kept grab-bing for theories that resonated with my experience. Though I sought to find my voice, it hid.

My mother, of European decent, was just as much a part of me as my father's Navajo lin-eage. My skin darker than my mother's side but lighter than my father's, I had a leg in two cultures but a home in neither. I felt the same way with academia. Colonial constructs devel-oped through the Western view of academia sometimes rejected Native ways of knowing. Native scholarship criticized and sometimes rejected Western practices, for good reason. I was either a diversity hire or a researcher who forsake half of who he was.

Dusk

I left academia for a time and season. Between my own personal decisions and various compounding factors, I spiraled. Twilight has three distinct moments; so did my return to communication research. I was a graduate research assistant with the Center for the Ethics of Indigenous Genomic Research (CEIGR) and a member of the Genomics and Ethics Program for Native Students (GEN) before my departure from my graduate program. Though my con-flict between research and my identity remained, my colleagues, CEIGR, and several members in the Communication Department did not give up on me. Emails and text messages would find their way through my solitude and offered a different path. The civil twilight, just before the sun meets the horizon, was those messages that reached me and encouraged me. The messages offered a return to academia and it was not only possible but could be different.

The nautical twilight—when the sun's center is just below the horizon—of my path back was the conversations with my new advisor. Deliberation (Gastil, 2008) was the answer to several of my concerns. The CEIGR uses community-engaged research with Indigenous communi-ties to utilize ethical means of meaning making and research. We see a meshing of my two worlds in research. We can have Native ways of knowledge creation and Western practices intertwined into what communities need and want.

Astronomical twilight—when the sun is below the horizon—is the dusk of my previous grievances with theory and research. I am currently working towards my dissertation, which champions the voices of Black, Indigenous, or People of Color (BIPOC) and ethical research with Indigenous communities. The days of seeing myself as a diversity hire are ending, and something new is beginning to form. Communication theory and community-engaged research are beginning to do something miraculous in my eyes: I am starting to see myself in it.

CHAPTER 5

Co-cultural Theory

Mark P. Orbe

Western Michigan University

Fatima Albrehi

Wayne State University

How do people without equal access to societal power communicate? That is the core question that co-cultural theory, the focus of this chapter, is designed to address. While there isn't a simple "correct" answer to that question, co-cultural theory provides a productive framework to understand the power dynamics that exist in every society. Within the United States, for example, certain groups—European Americans, men, heterosexuals, the able-bodied, Christians, and the middle and upper-class—have been in power as dominant group members. Other groups have not had equal access to power, including people of color, women, LGBTQ persons, persons with disabilities, those from nonmainstream religions, and/or the lower/ working class. The theory applies the term *co-cultural* to describe individuals from these groups. This term is embraced to avoid negative connotations of other terms such as *minority, subordinate, subcultural,* or *nondominant.* Co-cultural group members and dominant group members simultaneously exist in a society where the latter have greater access to macro-level power structures that impact communication at the micro-level.

This chapter offers an introduction to co-cultural theory and the insight that it provides into understanding the diverse ways that individuals communicate. We begin by describing the key components of the theory. Then we present a case study of how the theory can be utilized to understand experiences nonwhite Muslims face in America. The chapter concludes with a summary and discussion of the future of the theory.

Intellectual Tradition
of Co-cultural Theory

In its most general form, co-cultural communication refers to interactions among traditionally marginalized and dominant group members. While other interpersonal and intercultural communication theories offer general approches to studying human interactions, co-cultural theory is one of only a few that is grounded in the lived experiences of the individuals it seeks to describe. In this regard, difference—from the perspective of underrepresented group members—is acknowledged as central to communication. Accordingly, the theory focuses specifically on situations when co-cultural group members perceive cultural difference as salient. Within this section, we track the developmental process through which the theory emerged from the experiences of people who have been traditionally marginalized in society.

Co-cultural theory is a humanistic, interpretive theory designed to provide understanding into the complex, nuanced ways that people communicate with others. Grounded in the idea that individuals make communication choices based on free will and what makes the most sense at the time, the theory also highlights how oppressive societal structures (i.e., racism, sexism, classism, heterosexism, and the like) function in similar ways. Because co-cultural theory is based on power imbalances that traditionally have gone unaddressed, it also has been described as a critical theory. Accordingly, it draws upon intellectual traditions rooted in feminist theorizing.

Two theories serve as foundational building blocks for co-cultural theory: muted group theory and feminist standpoint theory. As described in the book *Constructing Co-cultural Theory* (Orbe, 1998), both theories insightfully focus on unequal power dynamics and the impact they have on individual experiences, perceptions, and communication. Muted group theory (Kramarae, 1981), for instance, posits that women perceive the world differently than men, and because men's system of perception is dominant, they must adapt to men's system of communication to participate. Over time, women—as a co-cultural group—have creatively and effectively communicated in ways to overcome attempts to mute them. Feminist standpoint theories (Harding, 2004) are rooted in the idea that the world is understood from particular social locations that inform one's sense of reality. As opposed to general knowledge that purports to offer a neutral account of reality, this family of theories highlights the importance of localized knowledge that is situated within a particular time, place, experience, and relative power. The vast majority of research generated by muted group and standpoint theories has focused on the experiences of women in the context of male-dominated societies, yet both theories have highlighted their relevance to other power-laden societal relationships like those based on race and class (Orbe, 1998).

Drawing directly from these intellectual traditions, co-cultural theory is based in five core assumptions (Orbe, 1998). First, each society has hierarchies that provide privileges to certain groups of people and not others. Second, dominant group members, based on varying levels of privilege, occupy positions of power that are used to create and maintain communication systems that reflect, reinforce, and promote their

5 core assumptions

life experiences. Third, these dominant communication structures, directly and indirectly, impede the progress of group members whose lived experiences are not valued in such systems. Fourth, co-cultural group members' experiences will vary; however, they will also share a similar societal position that renders them marginalized and underrepresented within dominant societal structures. Fifth, co-cultural group members strategically adopt certain communication behaviors to negotiate their standing in oppressive societal structures.

Main Goals and Features of Co-cultural Theory

The main goals and features of co-cultural theory can be traced to a series of research projects in the early 1990s that focused on the communication practices of different marginalized groups (Orbe, 1998). These studies created a foundation for the core concepts of the theory, namely the identification and conceptualization of co-cultural practices, factors, and communication orientations.

Orbe (1996) was the first to identify and describe a typology of different co-cultural communicative practices. Through the inductive, discovery-oriented process of phenomenological inquiry, 26 different strategies demonstrated a wide variety of responses to communicating within a society that marginalizes one's experiences. These responses ranged from those seeming obvious and straightforward (censoring self, overcompensating, increasing visibility, intragroup networking, confronting, and avoiding) to those that appeared more covert and nuanced (gaining advantage, reappropriating/embracing stereotypes). Table 5.1 defines each of the 26 different co-cultural practices revealed in the initial research that created the foundation of the theory. The most striking finding of these initial research projects was the interesting ways in which co-cultural group members communicated in both similar and different ways. The conclusion was that no one co-cultural group, say African Americans, are a monolith. Instead, the diversity *within* any one co-cultural group was great—even greater than the diversity *between* different groups.

TABLE 5.1 Co-cultural Communication Practices (Orbe, 1998)

Examples of Practices	Brief Description
Emphasizing commonalities	Focusing on human similarities while downplaying or ignoring co-cultural differences

(continued)

TABLE 5.1   Co-cultural Communication Practices (Orbe, 1998)

Examples of Practices	Brief Description
Developing positive face	Assuming a gracious communicator stance in which one is more considerate, polite, and attentive to dominant group members
Censoring self	Remaining silent when comments from dominant group members are inappropriate, indirectly insulting, or highly offensive
Averting controversy	Averting communication away from controversial or potentially dangerous subject areas
Extensive preparation	Engaging in an extensive amount of detailed (mental/concrete) groundwork prior to interactions with dominant group members
Overcompensating	Conscious attempts—consistently enacted in response to a pervasive fear of discrimination—to become a superstar
Manipulating stereotypes	Conforming to commonly accepted beliefs about group members as a strategic means to exploit them for personal gain
Bargaining	Striking a covert or overt arrangement with dominant group members in which both parties agree to ignore co-cultural differences
Dissociating	Making a concerted effort to elude any connection with behaviors typically associated with one's co-cultural group
Mirroring	Adopting dominant group codes in attempt to make one's co-cultural identity more (or totally) invisible
Strategic distancing	Avoiding any association with other co-cultural group members in attempts to be perceived as a distinct individual
Ridiculing self	Invoking or participating in discourse, either passively or actively, which is demeaning to co-cultural group members
Increasing visibility	Covertly yet strategically maintaining a co-cultural presence within dominant structures

(continued)

TABLE 5.1   Co-cultural Communication Practices (Orbe, 1998)

Examples of Practices	Brief Description
Dispelling stereotypes	Myths of generalized group characteristics and behaviors are countered through the process of just being one's self
Communicating self	Interacting with dominant group members in an authentic, open, and genuine manner; used by those with strong self-concepts
Intragroup networking	Identifying and working with other co-cultural group members who share common philosophies, convictions, and goals
Utilizing liaisons	Identifying specific dominant group members who can be trusted for support, guidance, and assistance
Educating others	Taking the role of teacher in co-cultural interactions; enlightening dominant group members of co-cultural norms, values, and so forth
Confronting	Using the necessary aggressive methods, including ones that seemingly violate the rights of others, to assert one's voice
Gaining advantage	Inserting references to co-cultural oppression as a means to provoke dominant group reactions and gain advantage
Avoiding	Maintaining a distance from dominant group members; refraining from activities and/or locations where interaction is likely
Maintaining barriers	Imposing, through the use of verbal and nonverbal cues, a psychological distance form dominant group members
Exemplifying strength	Promoting the recognition of co-cultural group strengths, past accomplishments, and contributions to society
Embracing stereotypes	Applying a negotiated reading to dominant group perceptions and merging them into positive co-cultural self-concepts
Attacking	Inflicting psychological pain through personal attacks on dominant group members' self-concepts

(continued)

TABLE 5.1 Co-cultural Communication Practices (Orbe, 1998)

Examples of Practices	Brief Description
Sabotaging others	Undermining the ability of dominant group members to take full advantage of their privilege inherent in dominant structures

Subsequent analysis of existing and new data provided additional insight as to the process through which co-cultural group members strategically enacted different communication practices. Specifically, six different factors emerged as most salient:

1. *Field of experience:* The sum of one's life events that directly and indirectly influences perceptions, expectations, and understandings of the world. This broad concept includes one's upbringing and socialization, interactions with family and friends, educational experiences, and past interactions with co-cultural group and dominant group members.

2. *Abilities:* The capacities of individuals to access and perform different communicative practices. Abilities exist within a larger context of nature and nurture influences; it is important to recognize that all individuals do not have the same level of aptitude, skills, and mastery when communicating with others.

3. *Communication approach:* The attitudinal perspective of one's verbal and nonverbal expression, ranging from prioritizing others' needs and expectations over one's own (nonassertive approach) to regarding one's own needs and expectations as more important than others (aggressive approach). In the center of the communication approach continuum is assertiveness, which reflects a balance between attending to the needs and expectations of self and others.

4. *Preferred outcome:* The desired, ultimate consequence that co-cultural group members have for interactions with others. Three options emerged from co-cultural data: assimilation (deemphasizing cultural differences to fit in with dominant group members), accommodation (working within dominant group societal structures to make them more reflective of co-cultural experiences), and separation (creating societal spaces where co-cultural group members authentically interact with one another without dominant group members).

5. *Perceived costs and rewards:* The imagined and predicted consequences of one's communication choices. All communication behaviors have potential repercussions—those that are anticipated and unanticipated, desirable and undesirable, and so on. Depending on the individual, and their field of experience, the same predicted consequence can be perceived differently.

6. *Situational context*: The broadly conceptualized setting of a communication event. This includes the physical environment, geographical location, time of day, relational and organizational histories, and the presence or absence of other co-cultural and dominant group members.

These six factors help to explain, from the perspective of co-cultural group members, why individuals choose to enact certain practices over others. While described individually, the factors are inherently interdependent. For example, one's communication approach naturally is directly tied to a person's field of experience, which also affects their abilities to enact different approaches; a particular communication approach also can be impacted by perceived costs and rewards and the situational context.

As explained by Orbe (1998), phenomenological inquiry evokes ongoing interpretation of findings in order to discover the interrelatedness among the concepts that link the phenomenon under investigation with consciousness. Bringing to light conceptualizations that were not immediately apparent during earlier analyses is part of a process known as hyper-reflection (p. 45). This ongoing process led to the following articulation of co-cultural theory's main idea:

> Situated within a particular *field of experience* that governs their perceptions of the *costs and rewards* associated with, as well as their *ability* to engage in, various communicative practices, co-cultural group members will adopt certain communication orientations—based on their *preferred outcomes* and *communication approaches*—to fit the circumstances of a specific *situation*. (Orbe, 1998, p. 19)

This summary statement highlights the ways in which the six different factors work together to synergistically influence co-cultural group members' strategic communication choices. It also introduces a new concept, co-cultural communication orientation, which is central to the theoretical framework.

Co-cultural orientation refers to a specific communicative stance that co-cultural group members assume during interactions with others (Orbe & Roberts, 2012). This concept emerged out of data whereby individuals highlighted how a preferred outcome (assimilation, accommodation, separation) and communication approach (nonassertive, assertive, aggressive) aligned with one another to forumulate nine different co-cultural communication orientations. In addition, a reexamination of earlier co-cultural studies generated insight into the ways in which different communication practices, briefly described in Table 5.1, aligned with one or more orientation.

TABLE 5.2 Co-cultural Theoretical Framework

	Separation	Accommodation	Assimilation
Nonassertive	• Avoiding • Maintaining Interpersonal Barriers • Leaving the Situation • Isolating Self	• Increasing Visibility • Dispelling Stereotypes	• Emphasizing Commonalities • Developing Positive Face • Censoring Self • Averting Controversy • Remaining Silent • Interrogating Self
Assertive	• Prioritizing Self-Love, Pride, and Agency • Ingroup Cooperative Networking • Exemplifying Strengths • Embracing/ Reappropriating Stereotypes	• Communicating Self • Intragroup Networking • Utilizing Liaisons • Educating Others • Reporting Incident to Authorities	• Extensive Preparation • Overcompensation • Manipulating Stereotypes • Bargaining • Rationalization • Intellectualizing
Aggressive	• Attacking • Sabotaging Others • Intimidating Others • Micro-protests	• Confronting • Gaining Advantage	• Dissociating • Mirroring • Strategic Distancing • Ridiculing Self • Showing Appreciation • Deception

The framework illustrated in Table 5.2 captures the essence of co-cultural theory. It features nine different co-cultural communication orientations, starting with the upper-left hand corner and moving vertically: (1) nonassertive separation, (2) assertive separation, (3) aggressive separation, (4) nonassertive accommodation, (5) assertive accommodation, (6) aggressive accommodation, (7) nonassertive assimilation, (8) assertive assimilation, and (9) aggressive assimilation. Each of these boxes includes specific communicative practices that are consistent with the larger co-cultural communication orientation. Table 5.2 includes the original 26 practices, as well as additional strategies described by various research studies (see, for example, Castle Bell et al., 2015). This promotes deeper understanding on the relationship between specific practices and orientations.

For example, a co-cultural group member who works assertively with a goal to fit in a dominant organization would adopt an assertive assimilation communication orientation and engage in practices such as extensive preparation, overcompensation, manipulating stereotypes, bargaining, rationalization, and intellectualizing. If the person decides over time to work toward accommodation, they would utilize different communication practices associated with other orientations. According to Orbe and Roberts (2012), co-cultural group members typically adopt one or two primary communication orientations. However, it is also common for individuals to embrace multiple orientations over time and for different situational contexts. This helps to reinforce the idea that while preferred outcome and communication orientation emerged as most salient, they exist within the context of the four other factors. An extended, focused case study helps to demonstrate how co-cultural communication functions.

Research and Practical Applications of Co-cultural Theory

Co-cultural groups exist in different capacities, whether as people of color, women, LGBTQ persons, persons with disabilities, those from nonmainstream religions, and/or the lower/working class. Given Islam's presence as a nonmainstream religion in the United States, Muslims construct a co-cultural group. While Muslims are not a monolith, there are common experiences that inform the communication strategies employed when interacting with dominant, non-Muslim populations.

Bilal, an Afro-Arab Muslim in the United States, is a part of three co-cultural groups: Muslims, Black persons, and Arabs. His presence as a Muslim man of Arab and African descent makes him hyperaware of his communication behaviors. Bilal's hometown is known for its large Muslim and Arab population, therefore providing him with relief of not having to downplay his religiosity or cultural background in fear of being misunderstood and/or harassed. For instance, his Arabic prayer app goes off three times a day to remind him of his religious duty. While he feels comfortable with the app going off in his hometown where co-cultural separation is the norm, being in a public space outside of his hometown is a different story. When traveling to areas unfamiliar with Muslim populations, Bilal silences his prayer app to avoid strangers' eyes widening in fear and/or narrowing in disgust or confusion. This approach aligns with the preferred outcome of disassociating from his co-cultural group, highlighting Bilal's aggressive approach to assimilating into the dominant group. He also refuses to pray in a public space such as parks outside of his hometown or ask business owners to use a secluded room, despite knowing that prayer is a main pillar of Islam. Bilal chooses to delay prayers rather than show others his religious affiliation for fear of being misunderstood and judged. In the unfortunate event that Bilal forgets to silence his prayer app, he immediately scans his surroundings to identify other co-cultural group members for support should he be harassed. This intragroup networking is based on his ability to empathize with the struggles and fears other co-cultural groups may have when interacting with dominant groups. After all, there is strength in numbers.

Interestingly, while Bilal's religious beliefs place him as a dominant group member within his hometown, his racial background attests to his continued co-cultural status.

While it is easier for Bilal to engage in disassociation and censorship as a member of a nonmainstream religion outside of his hometown, a first glance at Bilal reveals that he comes from a lineage of Black predecessors. His African lineage makes him hyper-aware of negative stereotypes he may face, as it is more physically noticeable than his Arab background. For instance, a non-Black gas station attendant suspiciously eyeing and following Bilal as he browses the snack aisles serves as motivation for him to be very kind towards the attendant. This involves a greeting, asking "How are you?" and inquiring about the attendant's snack recommendations. This communication attests to his desire to achieve assimilation as a preferred outcome through nonassertive behaviors such as developing a positive face through polite small talk. Given the surveillance he experiences in public spaces as a Black man, if he notices that a business owner or worker is visibly Arab, he makes sure to greet them in Arabic to emphasize his similarities to them and their identification within that co-cultural group.

Continuing the Conversation

Over the past two decades, co-cultural theory has been embraced as a productive lens for scholars interested in understanding how macro-level oppressive structures inform everyday interpersonal interactions. Multiple research projects have continued to study people of color, women, LGBTQ persons, and people with disabilities in local, national, and international contexts. In addition, other research studies have broadened the theory's research and applied it to the communicative lived experiences of others who exist on the margins of different social contexts: The Roma people of Europe, people without homes, male nurses, punk culture, and high school academically talented students (for summary, see Orbe & Roberts, 2012). The quantity and quality of co-cultural studies demonstrates the productive ways in which the theory has offered fresh insight into understanding how culture and power affect one's communication. In doing so, the theory has cultivated increased awareness of individual and societal values regarding difference, something that has been embraced by scholars who advocate for engaged scholarship that makes a difference by increasing awareness, offering new perspectives, cultivating a sense of agency, and generating change. As demonstrated in Figure 6.2, the theoretical framework is easy to understand; descriptive data featuring the voices of diverse co-cultural group members provides powerfully meaningful evidence supporting the framework.

While the foundations of co-cultural theory have been laid, the theory continues to grow and develop as different scholars engage the theory (Castle Bell et al., 2015). For instance, some international scholars have noted that the theory and its focus on personal strategic choices are embedded within a Western, individualistic orientation (Matsunaga & Torigoe, 2008). This limitation provides an excellent source to extend the theory's relevance across the world. Other scholars have insightfully criticized how the theory oversimplifies co-cultural group and dominant group membership as uni-dimensional, distinct, and binary. Who is the co-cultural group member and who is the dominant group member in an interaction between a white woman and an African American man (Orbe & Roberts, 2012)? While the latter may see his racial identity as most salient, the former may perceive her gender identity as the most central to their interactions. The future of co-cultural theory, then, must embrace the challenge of multiple identities enacted simultaneously within each interpersonal interaction and explore how this dynamic functions within the existing framework. Toward that direction, a dominant group theory (Razzante & Orbe, 2018) has emerged that promotes advanced understanding of the diverse ways in which those in the majority communicate in their everyday lives. As an outgrowth of co-cultural theory—and by extension muted group and standpoint theories—this new theoretical framework demonstrates the value of embracing communication theory as dynamic, ongoing, and vigorous in its attempt to provide insight into the complexities of human interaction.

Summary

This chapter offers an introduction to co-cultural theory, a valuable interpretive theory for understanding the diverse ways that underrepresented group members communicate. We have presented the key concepts of the theory and used a case study of an Afro-Arab Muslim man to demonstrate some of the complexities of co-cultural communication. Over the past 30 years, co-cultural theory has emerged as a framework that centers the experiences of those who have traditionally been marginalized in most interpersonal communication theories. Given the increased saliency of cultural identities in today's world, the theory's relevance will only continue to grow.

FOR FURTHER THOUGHT AND REFLECTION

1. In what ways, do you identify as a co-cultural group member? How has this theory helped you to understand your own communication choices? If you primarily identify as a dominant group member, how does the theory help you understanding others?

2. In addition to the examples provided, what other examples of co-cultural groups exist? How might co-cultural/dominant group dynamics shift in different micro- and macro-level contexts given the changing demographics of different societies?

3. In what ways did the chapter increase your understanding of how individuals identifying with multiple co-cultural groups negotiate their communication practices when interacting with dominant groups? How might the saliency of different identities shift in different contexts and, consequently, impact one's communication?

STORIED REFLECTION
Communication Modalities:
Behavior in Search of Theory

Dorthy L. Pennington
University of Kansas

As an undergraduate student at a historically black college/university (HBCU), it had not dawned on me that years later I would be welcomed as a graduate student at a predominantly white university for advanced degrees; this realization came later in undergraduate studies, as those were the years of institutionalized racial and social segregation in my native South.

During my undergraduate years as an English major, it never fazed me that the English curriculum was comprised of American and English literature classes, with the one exception being a class in Black literature, in those days called "Negro Literature." This was prior to Black consciousness and diversity politics. Upon reflection, I think, how ironic, for mine, like most HBCUs in those days, were purveyors of a Eurocentric education, but those were the times.

More irony awaited me in graduate school where the first course I took in Black rhetoric was developed and offered by a white male professor, Dr. Wilmer Linkugel, someone who was endowed with diversity sensibilities and power as social capital used in a positive way. It was in that class that I gleaned how Black orators eloquently encapsulated the plight of our people, a plight undergirded by the social hierarchy of racism, discrimination, and violence, fortified by power machinations. I later explained to a graduate adviser that I was intrigued by studying power as a variable in communication and that I wanted to begin my initial investigation by engaging the classic John French and Bertram Raven power paradigm. Before then, the term *paradigm* had not been a part of my vocabulary, and my vivid recollection of that conversation was that I mispronounced the word, emphasizing the syllable *dig*. This neophyte graduate student had much to learn. Semideterred by my later discovery of my verbal faux pas in that conversation, I was humbled, an attitude that marked me for life, while also charting my course for the systematic investigation of power as a significant variable in communication. Later, I would write about power in interracial and interpersonal communication.

I was fortunate to study under the late Dr. Nobleza Asuncion-Lande at the University of Kansas. She was a leader in pioneering the field of intercultural communication, and I became hooked for life because intercultural communication and its off-shoot, interracial communication, spoke to my identity and positionality. While my gravitational leanings were materializing, I was not oblivious to the value of required courses in communication such as those on Ernst Cassirer, Susanne Langer, and Kenneth Burke. I appreciated Cassirer and Langer for their discussions of symbolic, nondiscursive, nontraditional forms of communication and of myth, discussions that would serve me well later as I taught courses in Black rhetoric and in religion. Growing up with clear religious values enabled me to find an intriguing resonance with Burke's discussion of consubstantiality. Also, I found resonance between Burke's discussion of darkness and light and Martin Luther King's discussion of the same oppositional images and metaphors and how these two authorities narrated humans' struggle with the two dialectical pulls. King, like other Black rhetors I studied in graduate school, would go on to share another concept with Burke—that of guilt, which I later described in a Black rhetoric article on guilt-provocation as a strategy employed by King and other Black rhetors such as Frederick Douglass, Henry Highland Garnet, and Malcolm X. Guilt results when covenants are broken. These rhetors reminded America of its broken covenant with Black people, in hopes of creating what King called the "beloved community" among all races, imbued with a great sense of equality.

In his 1968 speech "The Drum Major Instinct," King provides an imaginary response to the dominant view expressed by rhetor Albert Beveridge in his 1898 classic speech, "March of the Flag," in which he claimed whites as God's chosen people and as superior to other races. King metaphorically alludes to the drum-major instinct as some whites having the need to be superior and to be first, to march in front of the marching band, as in real-life performance. However, King strategically and theologically changes the valence of "being first" from negative to positive, by advising there is nothing wrong with wanting to be first—but be first in love and in kindness and in helping one's fellow humans. Therein lies hope beyond view, embodying the reason I am sentimental toward my first course in Black rhetoric, taught by a white male professor who embodied King's dream and mentored me throughout graduate studies. If I were to have the drum-major instinct, it would be toward King's prescription, in my goal of remaining humble. I remember how I first pronounced the word *paradigm*—and that, among other things, keeps me humble.

CHAPTER 6

Ethnic Communication Theory

Uchenna Onuzulike

Bowie State University

Ethnic communication theory (ECT) was developed by communication scholar Uchenna Onuzulike to explore the communication style of second-generation Igbo young adults. The Igbo are one of the three largest ethnic groups in Nigeria; the others are the Yoruba and the Hausa. The Igbo people can be found in every state in Nigeria, although their ancestral homeland is concentrated in the southeastern region of Nigeria. The Igbo language is their language. and it has a variety of dialects. There are two major phases of Igbo migration to the United States, which include the Atlantic slave trade and the waves of immigration, which span decades. This chapter refers to the latter phase.

The second generation referred to in this study is those who were born to Igbo immigrants, mainly in the 1980s and 1990s. For context, the second generation refers to individuals born in the United States or those who migrated to the United States before five years of age (Padilla, 2006). ECT draws attention to the ways in which people, especially the second generation, maintain their ethnic identity while residing in the diaspora with two main cultures. First is the ethnic culture received from their parents, siblings, co-ethnic memberships, and various media outlets. Second is the culture of their new host nation.

The aim of ECT is to decenter communication theory, which has been dominated by Western perspectives. Theorizing communication through the perspective of the Igbo has attempted to decenter Western communication theory by centering African Igbo perspectives to the discussion. In this way, Igbo traditional communication continues to evolve.

ECT was conceptualized to give a voice and offer a platform for individuals to be able to partake in two or more cultural identities. The empirical study of the Igbo second-generation young adults residing in the Washington, D.C., area was used as the initial application. Practically, the theory uses second-generation Igbo to articulate their ancestral style of communication. Generally, it can be applied to people in the diaspora who care about their ethnic cultural identity.

This chapter begins with consideration of ethnic communication theory, focusing on the theory's purpose, intellectual tradition, main goals, and features. Foundational assumptions and premises/propositions, key concepts, and research and practical applications are provided. Finally, the chapter concludes with a discussion of the future of the theory.

Intellectual Tradition of Ethnic Communication Theory

I stated elsewhere that "ethnic communication theory posits that second-generation individuals gain competence of their ethnic communication style through their parents, family members, and co-ethnic members. The Igbo communication style is learned within the primary socialization process of the Igbo ethnic group" (Onuzulike, 2014, p. 42). I further argue that the second-generation Igbo young adults' articulation of their Igbo ancestral communication style empowers them to gain more insight into their "imaginary" ancestral homeland as they face challenges in their new host or homeland. They utilize "their communication styles for code switching, engaging in conversations with their co-ethnic membership, as well as interacting with family members in their ancestral home" (p. 42).

ECT emerged out of research, in part, as empowering second-generation Igbo who are experiencing cultural adjustment as well as responding to such Western theories, which do not center African perspectives. Specifically, the idea and influence of conceptualization of ECT was developed from a study that explored second-generation young Igbo adults who were residing in the Washington, D.C., area as they dealt with their ethnic and transnational identities (Onuzulike, 2014). That work demonstrated the need for a theory that would frame second-generation individuals in the diaspora. Then the empirical research about the phenomenological study of second-generation young Igbo adults on how they articulate their ethnic and transnational identities was used for the practical application.

The study revealed that participants struggled with their ethnic and transnational identities. Therefore, there was a need to build a theory from an African perspective that illuminates the competency of current second-generation individuals in the diaspora in relation to their ethnic communication styles. De-centering Western communication theory helps give a voice to second-generation Igbo or any other individuals facing ethnic or transnational struggles.

The discipline of communication is overdue in acknowledging and showcasing communication theories based in the continent of Africa. Some of the concepts that influenced ECT include the second-generation ethnic identity, transnational identity, and emotional transnationalism. These key concepts are discussed in the ethnic communication theory section. To theorize beyond the West, Onuzulike (2021) advanced critical intercultural communication concepts of ECT and co-culturation by analyzing ethnicity and belonging among young Igbo in the United States.

Main Goals and Features of Ethnic Communication Theory

Assumptions of Ethnic Communication Theory

The initial theorization of ECT through the analysis of the second-generation Igbo young adults produced five underlying themes: (1) figurative language: proverbs, metaphors, and idioms; (2) oratory and storytelling; (3) respect for elders; (4) directness in communication; and (5) ambassadorship and diplomacy (Onuzulike 2014, 2018). Even though these themes are core and specific to the Igbo, they may not apply to all Igbo. This is because cultures are not static; rather, cultures evolve and people adapt to the circumstances that serve their interest. Other influences, such as those found in host countries and media, may determine whether each person adheres to and applies the themes. Along the same lines, five assumptions were formulated in conceptualization of ECT (Onuzulike, 2018):

ASSUMPTION 1

Assumption 1 states: "*Figurative language: proverbs, metaphors, and idioms* involve developing a holistic view of meaning and critical thinking, belief, values, and behavior" (Onuzulike, 2018, p. 45). The first assumption infers communication styles of second-generation Igbo young adults in the United States make them think critically about every situation. Igbo people are known for using figurative words. One popular Igbo proverb says, "*ilu bụ mmanụ ndị Igbo ji eri okwu.*" Literally, it means the (cooking) oil that the Igbo use to eat words. The Igbo bury wisdom and knowledge in their figurative language and conversations. Also, the essence of using figurative language is beyond just the incident or issue at stake. The Igbo use figurative language not just about the current conversation but beyond, so individuals can apply it in other areas of their life. This phenomenon is not limited to the Igbo people; it also applies to other African nations.

ASSUMPTION 2

Assumption 2 indicates: "*Oratory and storytelling* entail assertiveness and competence in communication. The second assumption asserts that communication styles of the second-generation Igbo young adults enable them to excel in speech" (Onuzulike, 2018, p. 46). It is not unusual for a traditional Igbo person to use a story to answer a question. Also, a story may be used to formulate the background to enable the individual to answer the question. In terms of oratory, the Igbo are known to have a command of public speaking and an appeal to emotions. In the traditional Igbo society, when the community is gathered in the public square, people take turns speaking concerning the subject matter. This type of performance is ingrained in their culture.

ASSUMPTION 3

Assumption 3 states: "*Respect for elders* encompasses facework management: saving face, giving face, and face honoring, as well as acknowledging wisdom" (Onuzulike, 2018, p. 47). Ting-Toomey (2005) referred to facework as "the specific verbal and nonverbal behaviors that we engage in to maintain or restore face loss and to uphold and honor face again" (p. 73). In Igbo culture, facework management skills can be used to validate elders during conflicts as they maintain their "social self-esteem and social worth" (Ting-Toomey & Oetzel, 2001, p. 186). Essentially, facework management skills in the Igbo context involves respecting and honoring your elders both at home and particularly in the public. Moemeka (1997, p. 181) observed that in traditional African societies, "the elderly are seen as the true repositories of wisdom and knowledge and, therefore, as assets of great value to the community."

ASSUMPTION 4

Assumption 4 claims: "*Directness in communication* involves a dialectic process. The fourth assumption suggests the Igbo communication style of second-generation Igbo (SGI) may take forms or approaches of assertiveness, straightforwardness and confrontational and dialectical patterns" (Onuzulike, 2018, p. 48). Although the Igbo traditionally apply figurative speech in their communication, they also employ direct communication, which, among Igbo, is situational and can be explicit or implicit. It is situational and explicit when the speaker communicates his or her message or instructions without any ambiguity and in a clear and forceful manner to make the receiver somewhat uncomfortable. Igbo people can also engage in direct communication in ways that are not so direct, but subtle and implicit. In this case, the receiver may have to read in between the lines, listen attentively, and make certain inferences to get the full message, as when the message is direct, but the speaker's intention may be hidden. Someone can tell a person something serious in a very polite and courteous manner; in this case, the speaker will be direct and not explicit, as with some use of proverbs. Thus, it is common for age grades (age mates) to be direct in their communication among themselves. But it is traditionally frowned upon to be (too) direct with elders.

ASSUMPTION 5

Assumption 5 states: "*Ambassadorship and diplomacy* comprise flexibility, adaptability, and mutual face giving. The fifth assumption posits that the Igbo communication style enables them to flourish in foreign lands" (Onuzulike, 2018, p. 48). For example, the Igbos' ambassadorial and diplomatic skills can be displayed through adaptability and cordiality, and they are well traveled. An Igbo "proverb that says, '*e be onye bi ka ọ na-awachi*,' or where one lives, the person thrives. It means that wherever an individual lives, that is the place the person calls home and thrives. '*Ojemba enwe ilo/iro*' means a traveler has no enemy" (Onuzulike, 2014, p. 97). The literal translation of "*Oje mba enwe ilo*" is that the sojourner or traveler does not have enmity. Contextually, it means that he or she lives an honorable lifestyle, follows the conventions of the host culture, and respects the people and the host culture. This concept is a propositional one about the Igbo migrants' enculturation. The concept implies that the Igbo coexist with the host culture as their entrepreneurship and economic growth thrive in the diaspora.

Key Concepts in Ethnic Communication Theory

The key concepts in ethnic communication theory are ethnic identity, transnational identity, emotional transnationalism, the second generation, and communication style:

ETHNIC IDENTITY

The concept of ethnic identity is central to this theory. Ethnic identity or group membership links generations together with shared ancestry, history, origins, and ethnic characteristics and cultures; this includes traditions, customs, values, behaviors, belief systems, language, dance, and music. It is a group's membership in a social system that is bonded with common ancestral heritage. Ting-Toomey (2005, pp. 8–9) reminds us that "before we understand the significance of an individual's ethnicity, the salience of the individual's ethnic identity has to be understood."

TRANSNATIONAL IDENTITY

Transnational identity involves "having two geographical experiences by the virtue of traveling and experiencing two communities or countries. It is an identity involving both a host nation and a nation of origin—usually the ancestral home" (Onuzulike, 2014, p. 16). Second-generation young Igbo utilize social media to negotiate and articulate their ethnic and transnational identities in the United States. Vertovec (2001, p. 575) attests that "transnational connections affect migrants as never before with regard to practices of constructing, maintaining and negotiating collective identities. This has a significant bearing on the culture and identity of the so-called second generation, or children born to immigrants."

EMOTIONAL TRANSNATIONALISM

Emotional transnationalism can be experienced when second-generation individuals are embodied and situated "between different generational and locational points of reference, both the real and the imagined—their parents', sometimes also their grandparents' and other relatives', and their own" (Wolf, 2002, p. 258). These individuals' appreciation of their ancestral cultural experiences is explained or embodied through their parents. One does not need to travel to the ancestral lands to experience emotional transnationalism; it can be triggered or experienced through social media. Yearning for the ancestral culture triggers imagined emotional transnationalism. The study on SGI young adults indicated that engaging "social media serves as segue in connecting and emotionally experiencing the ancestral or 'imagined' homeland" (Onuzulike, 2014, p. 177).

THE SECOND GENERATION

The second-generation Igbo (SGI) young adults were used as a case study in the application of ECT. Second generation is characterized as those individuals born in the United States or who moved to the United States at a very early age or before they turned six years old (Padilla, 2006). The notions of second generation and first generation can be applied to other countries, groups, and similar situations, such as first- or second-generation students. Second generations across the globe operate within transnational social fields linked by familial, cultural, social, economic, religious, and political networks. Among second-generation individuals, transnational practices vary across country of origin. Some may prefer to visit their homeland, while others may prefer to send remittances.

COMMUNICATION STYLE

Communication style is "the way one verbally, nonverbally, and paraverbally interacts to signal how literal meaning should be taken, interpreted, filtered, or understood" (Norton, 1983, p. 11). Besides the above definition, communication style can be learned and solidified through social media. For example, an Igbo born in the diaspora can watch Nollywood films about the Igbo, then emulate and internalize Igbo characteristics and behaviors.

Claims of Ethnic Communication Theory

Ethnic communication theory offers six empirically testable propositions to explain and predict how ethnic communication styles play out within the context of "ethnic identity competence in relationship to the second-generation and their parents, family members, and co-ethnic members" (Onuzulike, 2014, p. 49). The following propositions are formulated based on the phenomenological research of second-generation Igbo (Onuzulike, 2014, 2018).

PROPOSITION 1

Proposition 1 states: *The more the second-generation individuals communicate with their parents, family members, and coethnics, particularly in relation to their ethnic culture, the more the children become competent in their ethnic communication styles.* Proposition 1 is concerned with how second-generation people comprehend and practice their ethnic speech styles from those who are already proficient or at least familiar with their ethnic patterns of communication. Research has demonstrated that children learn their ethnic identity firsthand from their parents. This shows that parents are the prime source for their children in learning and gaining competence in their ethnic identity.

PROPOSITION 2

Proposition 2 proclaims: *The more the second-generation individuals visit their ancestral homeland, the more they become competent in the Igbo communication style.* Proposition 2 suggests that visiting the ancestral homeland of Igboland or sending children to attend part of their schooling in their ancestral homeland enhances Igbo communication style competency. The study of the SGI indicates that those who visited the ancestral homeland or who had been sent there to partly attend school (e.g., high school) had a higher probability of increasing competency in the Igbo communication style (Onuzulike, 2014).

PROPOSITION 3

Proposition 3 indicates: *The more second-generation individuals attend to and participate in their ethnic functions, the more they become competent in their ethnic communication styles and cultural traits and the deeper their appreciation of the culture.* Proposition 3 deals with the question of attending and partaking in ethnic cultural functions in the diaspora. This proposition is consistent with the young SGI partaking in ethnic cultural functions in the Igbo community in the United States, for example, during their youth. Some of the participants indicated that they attended some Igbo functions to keep them informed and connected to Igbo culture and identity. Likewise, coethnics through social networks and other coethnic young Igbo organizations, associations, and social groups play a major role in how they form their ethnic and transnational selves. Some of the young Igbo organizations such as the Nwannedinamba Youth Branch, Umu Igbo Unite, and the Umu Igbo Alliance create the platform for the SGI to sustain their ethnic identity. These organizations and associations serve as a place of cultural reproduction, socialization, and competency.

PROPOSITION 4

Proposition 4 asserts: *The more second-generation individuals consume transnational media and ethnic media, the more they appreciate and improve their ethnic communication styles.* Proposition 4 addresses how transnational media and ethnic media such as Nollywood films and Igbo music proliferate second-generation individuals' proficiency of Igbo communication style.

PROPOSITION 5

Proposition 5 attests: *The more second-generation individuals access ethnic culture online and through social media, the more they gain additional knowledge and competence about their culture.* Proposition 5 is concerned with how the second-generation individuals utilize social media and the Internet to assert their ethnic identity in relation to the ethnic communication style. Empirical study of SGI indicated that they recognized the dominant force of social media, and they make use of social media to widen their knowledge in relation to Igbo history, language, culture, identity, and more.

PROPOSITION 6

Proposition 6 indicates: *The more second-generation individuals read ethnic-related litera-ture and engage in ethnic artwork or aesthetics, the more they increase their knowledge about their ethnic culture and communication styles.* Proposition 6 answers the question about how literature and art impact ethnic communication styles of second-generation indi-viduals. The answer is that second-generation individuals use literature and artwork to enact, articulate, and learn their ethnic culture and communication styles. The empir-ical evidence comes from study of SGI in the Washington, D.C., area.

Research and Practical Applications of Ethnic Communication Theory

Ethnic communication theory suggests that second-generation individuals accumulate competence in their ethnic communication style through the parents, family members, and coethnic members. In addition, they can increase their ethnic competency through social and transnational media. One of the practical applications of the ECT includes communication between second-generation young Igbo adults with their parents in the diaspora. One example is the research of the second-generation Igbo young adults in the Washington, D.C., area. Onuzulike (2014) used a qualitative approach of thematic analysis of in-depth interviews and open-ended questions. The analysis involved 12 par-ticipants (M = 6 and F = 6) who were aged between 19 and 34. There was a focus group of some participants (M = 3 and F = 2) that provided supplemental information so the researcher could further probe and explore recurring patterns found in the interview sessions. An observational method was used as well. During the focus group, it was observed how participants interacted among themselves and how they code-switched sometimes. Their verbal and nonverbal communication exuded Igbo communication traits. For example, some of them snapped their fingers when they were talking about Nollywood movies.

Practical applications of ECT evoke the notion of multicultural leaning due to chal-lenges manifest in many areas, including ethnicity, race, language, religion, and other forms of identity markers. Research on SGI indicates that some of them faced identity and cultural challenges while going through primary and secondary schooling in the United States. Some of them indicate that they experienced mockery and bullying in school. Some were concerned about it, some said it is kids just being kids and picking on each other, and some said that it is typical for students to undergo that experience. Furthermore, the research on SGI shows that learning about African culture was very pertinent to them despite the mockery they faced about Africa and the way their par-ents dressed or talked with an accent. One can feel insecure or ashamed of his or her culture based on derogatory remarks and negative treatment. One of the participants, Agbonma, indicated that she rejected her Africanness and Igboness when she was younger because of the way the media depicted Africa. She said that she has learned that things have improved by talking to her young niece, who is in elementary school, which is facilitated by increasing ethnic, cultural, and religious diversity in schools, colleges, and universities in the United States. For the SGI, the results show that learning about African culture is very pertinent to them.

Igbo is the heritage language of the SGI. It is not uncommon for the parents and other family members to speak Igbo to them in the household. Therefore, children who are exposed to multiple languages may code-switch and mix up languages during their conversations. Some of the SGI blend English and Igbo, which is referred to as "Engligbo." This phenomenon was experienced by some of the participants who learned Igbo in the United States.

In terms of reconnecting ethnic identity via social media, all participants acknowledged the dominant force of social media, and they utilize social media to learn and to connect to Igbo history, culture, identity, and more. Obiageli stated that she uses Facebook mainly to keep abreast of Igbo cultural events. She says that she goes to the site to promote and support Igbo events and the Igbo people as much as she can. Agbonma said that even though she has used social media to articulate Igbo culture, she has no intention to do so in the near future.

All participants expressed their love for Nollywood and cited it as a primary source for connection to the ancestral homeland. For transnational Nollywood flows to occur, the SGI need to watch Nollywood movies.

Continuing the Conversation

ECT has advantages, including that it provides a platform for individuals besides the second generation to partake in their ethnic cultural heritage. That is, the theory can be used to relate to someone from another ethnic group besides the second generation. People from different generations and ethnic backgrounds are welcome to apply the theory in terms of relating to others. Even though this theory was conceptualized based on the experiences of second generation, it can be applied to any individuals of different generations who are attached to their ancestral origin.

Summary

In this chapter, I have discussed ethnic communication theory, which emerged from research on second-generation Igbo young adults who resided in the Washington, D.C., area. Ethnic communication theory predicts that second-generation folks increase the competence of their ethnic communication style via their parents, family members, and coethnic members. They also use media to gain entrance to and to reconstruct their ethnic, cultural, and transnational identities. This theory, which can be applied to multigenerational groups, has contributed to generating a platform to decenter communication theories, which are dominated by Western perspectives.

FOR FURTHER THOUGHT AND REFLECTION

1. In what ways did the chapter increase your understanding of second-generation young Igbo or other ethnic groups?

2. What research projects might be a good fit for ethnic communication theory?

3. How might the ideas in the chapter relate to you, your upbringing, and your ethnic or cultural identity?

4. How might any assumptions in the chapter relate to you?

5. How might this chapter impact you in terms of maintaining and dealing with transnational ties, struggles, or identities?

STORIED REFLECTION

A Practitioner's Journey With Theory:
Using Theories for Skill Building on the Frontlines of Organizations

Pavitra Kavya
California State Polytechnic University, Pomona

8:01 AM. It was an early autumn day in 2013. The city of gardens was in *mostly* full bloom. On a hot and uncharacteristically sticky morning, about 30 senior sales and marketing leaders gather for a two-day workshop. They are excited to engage in learning and take back some communication tools to enhance the work life of self, peers, subordinates, supervisors, and clients. We kick-start the day by writing down our operational goals. The training focused on learning communication skills for high stakes moments. The training is attentive to helping participants enhance their repertoire of dialogic skills. The goal of the present module is to help participants stay focused on the goals they ultimately desire. The objective of this module was to help participants align their work outcomes with their heartful values. The ultimate purpose is to help participants, 'restart their brain' by asking the following questions:

1. "What do I really want—
    *   for myself?"
    *   for others?"
    *   for my relationships?"
    *   for the organization?"

2. "Is my behavior going to get me what I want?"

1:11 PM. Thirty high-performing, talented leaders enter the room after enjoying a scrumptious lunch. We begin reviewing the content and discussing operational challenges, when voices pipe up:

Participant 1: "I am struggling; I don't know if I can get this deal."

Participant 2: "I will do *what* it takes, if *that* helps me secure a deal."

Facilitator: "What concerns you? Which stakeholders have been impacted?"

Participant 3: "My situation is complex. I cannot be too authentic. These communication skills may not be helpful in *my situation!*"

Facilitator: "Let's go back to the core questions. What do we really desire? Why are we learning these skills today?"

The back-and-forth interaction piqued the interest of the entire class. Progress halted around this single concern: the various difficulties in their work situations made it difficult for participants to connect with the value of the new communication skills they were learning. It became important to help participants restart or shift their mindsets about communication skills by asking themselves: What do I really want?

This training workshop was inspired by communication theories developed over many decades with care and concern by social science scholars. I can envision these experts at their desks, talking to students as they wove their wisdom into concepts, assumptions, and propositions accompanying their theory. I hope these scholars know that their work made its way into a training classroom where it became a lantern in the dark by illuminating a way forward for business leaders.

Some examples of how theory came in handy during that transformative training session are as follows: First, framing tools (metaphors, stories) allowed the *facilitator* to shift the focus and provide inspiration and hope to the participants. It was evident that anxiety and stress from stiff competition were plaguing the minds of individuals. Second, influence appeals (e.g., stating the company value of integrity and transparency that required all members to be ethical and sincere in every transaction) alongside advice-seeking (e.g., how would you encourage your subordinates to accomplish the operational goal alongside maintaining the highest moral ground?) provided easy communicative nuggets that helped the group push past the critical challenge.

In a stroke of luck, six years after this incident, I had the opportunity to use advice-seeking theories in my dissertation. This story is focused on exploring the utility and efficacy of theory. Does learning theory transform the post-college work lives of our students? Is it necessary? How does teaching theory make a dent in the lives of our students? My takeaway from time as a consultant seeking practical answers and as a graduate student exploring theories is, "Yes! We need theories." I envision our theories as a toolkit that we can dive into while navigating the complex challenges and problems facing our organizations, teams, families, and personal lives. Theories have played an important role in my work life, and my current story is a testimony to the value of teaching theory to undergraduate students. It illustrates how theories can open the minds of our students to creative possibilities in artistic and inspired ways while engaging in problem solving and decision making at work.

I have hope that theories will enable, equip, and empower our students to create inroads across other organizations and other areas of their life. The communication discipline can be a trailblazer in bridging the gap between theory and practice. After all, a great practitioner can be a fine theorist. These are not separate.

PART III

Relating and Relationships

Communication in everyday conversations and otherwise trivial interactions form the fabric of our relationships. Communication in relationships, at its core, is about the dyad—how two committed people perceive one another and navigate their relationship. Therefore, relating and relationships are about the viability of connecting, building healthy ties, and improving communicative interactions. These relationships can vary from family members and intimate partners to mentor-mentee and close friend connections.

A traditional view of how dyads relate is through Knapp's relational development model (1978) in which relationships were conceptualized as moving in a linear fashion. Knapp's model suggests the five stages of coming together (i.e., relational development) and five stages of coming apart (i.e., relational dissolution) should be accomplished one at a time, in sequence, to make sure they are effective. Later, communication scholars realized relationships do not always proceed or dissolve in a staircase progression. Instead, relationships ebb and flow in closeness and separation and Knapp's model accounts for neither the fluidity of relationships nor the navigation of tensions—particularly those brought upon by racial, cultural, and ethnic factors. The scholarly contributions of this part of the book do, in fact, center the tensions and fluidity of relationships, while centering race, culture, and ethnicity.

Before we delve into those chapters, we will situate ourselves in a foundational view of relational theories that are built with less regard to racial and cultural differences of members entering and maintaining relationships. In this introduction, first, we elaborate on five foundational theories of relational communication, provide an overview of the four theoretical contributions, and describe the three storied reflections embedded in this section.

Existing Canonized Theories

An often-cited relational theory is social exchange theory (SET), which explains human behavior as it pertains to relational development and decision making (Homans, 1958). SET pertains to scholarship that focuses on how individuals weigh the costs and benefits of their decision to select, enter, maintain, and end social relationships. Simply put, the more benefits an option has, the more likely a person is to choose that option.

Uncertainty reduction theory (URT; Berger & Calabrese, 1975) is a relational development theory that can focus on ways strangers reduce uncertainty about each other. The theory identifies two types of uncertainty (i.e., cognitive and behavioral) that are prominent in initial interactions and social situations. Cognitive uncertainty may arise when individuals are unsure about their own beliefs or the beliefs of others. Behavioral uncertainty commonly occurs when people are unsure about their own actions or the actions of others (Berger & Calabrese, 1975). Like SET, if there are evident benefits to engaging with someone, then uncertainty reduction is necessary. According to URT, uncertainty can be reduced in multiple ways, including interactive communication and observational strategies, while maladaptive ways of reducing uncertainty can include stereotyping or avoiding the interaction. Gudykunst (1995) extended URT with a culture-centric approach by developing anxiety/uncertainty management (AUM), in which the outcome of the initial interaction is to manage uncertainty, instead of reducing it. Based on AUM, the interaction is driven by a motivation to understand and adapt to other cultures. In this way, AUM is a necessary extension of URT as it is applied to sociocultural interpersonal interactions.

As URT and AUM focus more on the initial relational development stage, relational dialectics theory (RDT) focuses on the relationship maintenance stage and the varying contradictions that arise (Baxter, 2004). These contradictions, known as dialectical tensions, arise whenever two interdependent, yet mutually exclusive, forces, tendencies, or behaviors come into play. The three most common dialectical tensions are labeled in a variety of ways, but at their core, they are (a) openness and closeness (i.e., wanting consistent communication, yet wanting privacy), (b) certainty and uncertainty (i.e., wanting dependability, yet not wanting predictability), and (c) connectedness and separateness (i.e., wanting a physical and mental bond, yet wanting individuality). Relational dialectics gets at the tensions within relationships but does not focus on racial, cultural, or ethnic factors. Cultural dialectics (Martin & Nakayama, 1999) is a framework nestled in navigating the push-pull tension and contradictory nature of intercultural interactions; however, it still does not center racial and ethnic factors that influence relationships. In this part of the book, our contributors do a masterful job of centering the complexities of the dyadic relationship, while centering race, culture, and ethnicity in their theorizing.

Overview of Chapters

In Part III, *Relating and Relationships*, we continue with Gudykunst's culture-centric extension of theory and highlight four theoretical contributions that center racial, ethnic, and cultural experiences and one's agency in developing and maintaining fruitful relationships. The themes of this section are unity and community developed and maintained amid racial and ethnic turbulence. These four theoretical contributions are authored from a communal standpoint in which one's "village" is essential in operating in relationships. In addition to our four theoretical contributions, we spotlight three storied reflections from new and tenured communication scholars. These vivid and engaging stories suggest that Black, Indigenous, or People of Color (BIPOC) individuals are nested in cultural and racial values, tensions, and experiences, so much so that even when engaged in relationships, much of their identity and many of their decisions remain an extension of the collective.

Chapter 7 focuses on the topic of social networks. Though social network theory is credited to Lazarsfeld, Berelson, and Gaudet (1944), we are fortunate that Wenlin Liu authored this chapter, as her research applies and extends the traditional social network theory into one that benefits from a diverse lens from which to view networks. Liu takes a novel and invigorating approach to social network theory by adopting and recognizing the importance of a diversity perspective. First, Liu discusses the basic assumptions of social network theory, including ego-network, whole network, degree centrality, betweenness centrality, closeness centrality, and structural equivalence, among other concepts. Then, she takes on a different approach in the practical applications section by focusing on how immigration status influences membership of social networks and how networks can be a source of upward mobility in organizational contexts. Liu provides the perfect chapter to start this section on, as the following two chapters on ethnic-racial socialization mapping and strong Black woman collective theory both have roots in social network theory.

Mackensie Minniear authored Chapter 8 on the topic of family communication about ethnicity and race. Minniear's ethnic-racial socialization (ERS) mapping, is a tool for understanding an individual's social support network regarding their identities and experiences surrounding ethnicity and race. Reaching out beyond their nuclear family, ERS tends to include messaging from extended family and fictive kin. In particular, after experiencing a critical incident in which one's ethnic or racial identity is made salient, individuals tend to reach out to their social network to express vulnerability and mental health matters, gain strength and empowerment, or receive guidance on how to respond to bias and discrimination. Minniear supports these claims with evidence gathered from BIPOC individuals who completed a creative arts-based activity that allowed them to draw their ERS map and identify who they receive ethnic and racial socialization messages from. In sum, ERS mapping is a tool that helps socializers (e.g., parents) understand and see the importance of raising a child within a community. Minniear concludes the chapter with recommendations for future research to extend ERS mapping to encompass additional marginalized identities.

Chapter 9 is authored by Shardé M. Davis and Martinque K. Jones on the strong Black woman collective (SBWC) theory. This chapter authors a powerhouse duo as Davis is the creator of the SBWC theory and Jones has utilized the theory in much of her work, along with expertise in topics pertaining to women and gendered communication. The SBWC theory stems from the gendered and racialized archetype of the strong Black woman (SBW) characterized by independence, self-sacrifice, resilience, caregiving, strength, and emotional (lack of) control. Despite the negative *inter*personal consequences of being expected to serve others without support in return and negative *intra*personal outcomes of psychological stress, according to the SBWC theory, the SBW image is reappropriated and personified in communication practices of Black women. When Black women gather as a collective, members jointly participate in reinforcing virtues of strength within themselves and other group members and thereby are capable of confronting oppressive external forces. Following this argument, Davis and Jones engage the readers in the complexities of how this strength regulation within the collective can also serve to impede the expression of vulnerability. The authors conclude the chapter by applying the SBWC theory to sistah friendships and blood-linked kinship among other relational and communication contexts.

Similar to Liu's focus on the immigrant experience, paired with Minniear, Davis, and Jones's discussions of how marginalized group members seek support from members of their networks, Antonia De La Garza joins the conversation by adding a framework that acknowledges the agentic efforts of immigrants to navigate societal and identity-related pressures about their migrant experiences. De La Garza distinguishes the differential adaptation theory (DAT) from previous interculture research on assimilation as an adaptation process in which newcomers relinquish their cultural traits in place of adopting that of the host's. Instead, DAT is a process in which the individual retains one's agency and the migrant and host culture relate to one another through a series of negotiations that may lead to mutual accommodations. This is a huge theoretical contribution as DAT parts ways from previous assimilation literature and provides an alternative to the previously misconceived notion that immigrants will assimilate into a homogeneous society and that would be the test of "successful" adjustment. De La Garza's alternative notion involves three prevailing assumptions that guide DAT— immigrant agency, barriers faced by immigration, and contextual factors. In sum, De La Garza provides a framework for the divergent, which accounts for the complex social and political realities that shape an immigrant's adaptation experience.

Overview of Storied Reflections

In addition to the main theoretical contributions, this section offers three storied reflections from Ajia Meux, Kristina Ruiz-Mesa, and Nickesia Gordon. Meux, a doctoral candidate at the University of Oklahoma, reflects on the ways in which her mom instilled in her an unapologetic confidence in her being *blackity Black*. Reluctantly participating in a daily call and response about loving their blackness held more significance as community engagers, relationship builders, and proud members of their collective than Meux was able to comprehend until adulthood. Thanks to her mother's influence and her engagement with social identity theory, Meux can be a source of empowerment in academia and within her Black collective. Ruiz-Mesa, an associate professor at California State University, Los Angeles, describes her experience with *the magic of mentors and theory*. Ruiz-Mesa provides a fitting reflection for this section of this book as she discusses the important professional relationship she built with her mentor, whose lessons influenced her ability to cultivate healthy and lasting relationships with others. Engaging with expectancy violations theory, Ruiz-Mesa manages to take us along her journey of building relationships over a 20-year period. Nickesia S. Gordon, an associate professor at Rochester Institute of Technology, reflects on *making ourselves visible* within a colonized ethnocentric monoculturalistic environment. Focusing her interests in critical/postcolonial studies, Gordon can empower others by resisting academic colonization. Closely related to De La Garza's DAT, Gordon can infuse her postcolonial pedagogy into the classroom to foster trusting relationships and a dialogic environment.

CHAPTER 7

Social Network Theory

Wenlin Liu

University of Houston

F ocused on social relationships and their implications for human interaction, social network theory has a long tradition on diversity and inclusion. Although many networks are formed around shared identity, network theory recognizes the importance of diversity—the extent to which a network is made up of heterogeneous actors—in shaping various outcomes such as the diffusion of information, accumulation of social capital, and many more. At the individual level, as social networks significantly influence an individual's attitudes, behaviors, and the opportunities that one has access to, the lack of diversity within these networks may create inequitable systems and reinforce echo chambers of perspectives. At the organizational level, diversity of a social network is linked to critical organizational outcomes such as organizational innovation and survival. Recognizing the intricate connection between social networks and diversity, this chapter provides an overview of social network theory, with a particular emphasis on the application of the theory in communication research that advances equity, diversity, and inclusion.

Intellectual Tradition of Social Network Theory

Stemming from multiple disciplines including psychology, sociology, anthropology, and mathematics, social network theory seeks to understand the formation, structure, and consequences of social relations among individuals, organizations, and other social actors. According to Scott (1991), three lines of early research have collectively shaped the current state of social network theory: the sociometric analysis tradition, which was pioneered by psychologists in the 1930s to study group dynamics; the interpersonal relations tradition, which focused on social clusters, or *cliques* that form among a group of individuals; and an anthropology tradition, which studied the family and community structure in tribal communities. Two central tenets characterize the early work on social network theory. First, the network approach shifts the focus from examining actor attributes to the web of relationships in which actors are embedded. Second, this approach posits that the web of relationships can cast powerful influences on actors. For example, an actor's position in a network may afford or constrain the actor's opportunity to acquire novel information; the immediate network environment also determines the number of resources that an actor has access to.

Social network theory was first applied in the field of media and communication in the 1950s, when Lazarsfeld, Berelson, and Gaudet (1944) conducted the classic study to investigate how personal influence transmitted through individuals' social networks may impact voting decisions. Ever since then, the field has seen continued waves of scholarship applying the network approach in various communication research contexts. For example, a keyword search of "social network" in the Communication & Mass Media Complete database returns over 6,000 published scholarly pieces. The growing adoption of this theoretical approach is further fueled by the ubiquitous use of social networking sites, the platforms that thrive on connectivity and social relations.

Tracing the intellectual trajectory of communication scholarship on social network theory identifies the following research traditions: first, there is a media and communication effects tradition that stems from Lazarsfeld and colleagues' research on the "two-step flow of communication" and opinion leaders. The fundamental question from this tradition asks how various network properties, ranging from the density of a network to a particular network position of an actor, may influence various outcomes such as civic participation, immigrant acculturation, organizational resilience, and so forth. The second communication research tradition revolves around the understanding of social network structure, as well as the formation and dissolution of ties among a certain social network. This tradition thus focuses more on the antecedents rather than the consequences of social networks, such as how different communication dynamics may drive the presence or absence of network ties.

Main Goals and Features of Social Network Theory

Different from other social scientific approaches that view actor attributes as basic units of analysis, a social network approach is concerned with relations among actors. Depending on whether a single actor or multiple actors are the focal points of analysis, there are two types of social networks: ego network and whole network. An ego network is a local network with one central node or *ego*. Egos can be individuals, organizations, communities, or other social entities. In an ego network, the focal actor is connected to multiple alters, and their relationships constitute a micro network environment where the ego actor is embedded. An example of an ego network is an individual's discussion network. Research has found that different individuals' discussion networks vary in dimensions such as size and heterogeneity (or the level of diversity), and both characteristics can influence individual attributes such as political knowledge or their attitudes towards social issues.

Meanwhile, whole networks, also referred to as complete networks, consist of multiple actors and all the social relations among these actors. For a whole network, the focal unit of analysis is not just a single actor but all actors in the network and their interrelationships. An example of a whole network is the friendship network of an elementary school class, where all students from the class are nodes in the network, and the ties among them indicate the friendship relations. Compared to ego network analysis, which typically just examines the dyadic interaction between an ego and alters, whole network analysis provides a macro-level view of the entire network.

Two levels of concepts are central to social network theory: the actor-level concepts that identify important actors and positions in a network, and the network-level concepts that characterize the structural pattern of an entire network. Below, we will use a specific communication network to illustrate actor-level concepts. Figure 7.1 shows a communication network based on a group of team members' collaboration relations. The team consists of ten members who regularly work together on job-related tasks. In the network, each node represents one of the ten team members, and a network connection (indicated by the arrow in Figure 7.1) represents that members A and B have collaborated at least once. A network approach is helpful to understand the collaboration dynamics, such as who are commonly regarded as popular collaborator partners, who tend to be isolated from the rest of the group, and who may play an instrumental role in connecting otherwise unconnected social circles.

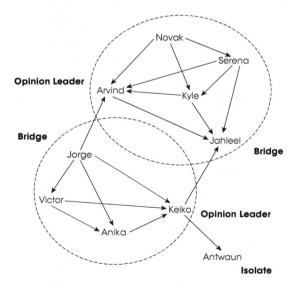

FIGURE 7.1 A Collaboration Network Among Ten Team Members

The concept *degree centrality*, also called Freeman centrality, measures the number of connections to and from an individual in the network. Actors that are high in degree centrality are often regarded as leaders, and they occupy important structural locations in a sense that (1) they have more channels (i.e., network ties) to send and receive information, and (2) they may have a greater capacity to influence others as more connections indicate likability or respect. In the collaboration network shown, Arvind and Keiko enjoy the highest levels of degree centrality among all. Meanwhile, it is important to identify actors who have few to no connections. These actors are often called *isolates* (Antwaun in the network). Isolates are actors at peripheral positions in a network, due to various reasons. For example, race and class have been found to explain individuals' peripheral positions in a network. A study of individuals' expertise network suggested that racial minorities and members of the lower and working classes tended to have fewer ties to experts within their personal networks (Cornwell & Cornwell, 2008). Meanwhile, as isolates are distant from the rest of the network, these actors are therefore less likely to be influenced by other network actors. They also tend to possess different traits in terms of demographic background, socioeconomic status, or ideology.

Other than degree centrality, *betweenness centrality* and *closeness centrality* are two related concepts that help identify structurally important actors. Betweenness centrality measures the frequency at which an individual actor sits on the shortest path connecting all other nodes in the network, whereas closeness centrality measures the average distance between an individual actor and all other actors in the network. In the network shown, Jorge and Jahleel have the highest betweenness centrality, and their positions are important because they both serve as the bridge connecting two otherwise unconnected clusters. Without Jorge and Jahleel, the two clusters will have no other way to connect, and this means information or resources are not able to travel from cluster A to cluster B.

Another critical concept in network theory is the notion of *structural equivalence*, which describes two network positions that are equivalent in terms of having the same social environment, or in other words, connecting to the same others. Sociologist Ron Burt (1987) develops the concept of structural equivalence, suggesting that actors who occupy structurally equivalent positions tend to have similar characteristics, or they may adopt similar attitudes and behaviors due to the similar network environment around them. For example, Burt's study finds that doctors who occupy structurally equivalent positions are more likely to adopt new medications around the same time, suggesting an equally, if not more, important role of structural equivalence in facilitating the diffusion of innovations as network cohesion (i.e., influence through direct connections).

While actor-level concepts are useful in identifying the structural locations of individual actors, network-level concepts provide a bird's-eye view of the entire network. Network-level concepts thus allow one to compare one network with another with important structural characteristics. The first network-level concept is *density*, which indicates the extent to which a network is densely or sparsely structured. Density is calculated as the number of existing network ties divided by the maximum number of ties that are possible in the network. To use disease spread as an example, a disease is more likely to spread in a densely connected community than in a sparsely connected counterpart. This explains why social distancing may be an effective prevention measure during a pandemic like COVID-19, as social distancing helps reduce the density of a community network, therefore decreasing the chance that a disease is actively transmitted in the network.

In addition, a network can be characterized by concepts like *reciprocity* and *transitivity*. Reciprocity is measured by the percentage of reciprocal ties in a network. Certain networks may have higher levels of reciprocity than others. For example, a friendship network among a group of college students is more likely to demonstrate greater reciprocity than a celebrity follower network on Twitter, due to the different nature of social relationships in these contexts. Along with reciprocity, another concept that characterizes a network's local structure is transitivity, which describes the tendency of one actor connecting to its third-party, indirect ties. The phrase "my friend's friend is also my friend" reveals the prevalence of transitive ties in various social networks, such as friendship networks or organizations' alliance networks. Research has found that organizations are particularly likely to collaborate with transitive actors both because the search cost is usually lower and the third party's trustworthiness has already been verified by its partner. For a network, a high level of transitivity thus indicates the presence of tightly connected sub-communities. Finally, a network may be characterized by the level of *centralization*, that is, the extent to which network ties are clustered around a few actors rather than evenly distributed in the network. Centralization indicates the level of hierarchy in a network. If we compare a communication network in the military versus that in a tennis club, it is likely that the former is more centralized than the latter.

Research and Practical Applications of Social Network Theory

Over the past two decades, a growing body of research has taken a social network approach to understand human communication dynamics. In mass communication, for example, social network theory has been applied to understand how new media platforms, particularly social media, interact with individuals' social behaviors ranging from information seeking to social movement participation. In organizational communication, network theory is widely applied to explain how organizations build interorganizational alliances during regular times as well as emerging disasters. In health communication, network theory is a powerful tool to guide public health campaigns such as mapping disease spread networks and offering network-based interventions.

The following section will focus on one example that uses social network theory at the individual level. In this example, the researcher examines the nature of immigrants' social networks and assesses the relationship between network characteristics and individuals' cultural attitudes and beliefs.

Communication Networks of Immigrants

Communication networks have been a central subject of interest for communication scholars. For one thing, the way a communication network is structured often represents an individual's interpersonal communication preferences as well as their social position. For another, the configuration of one's communication network can be predictive of outcomes such as civic participation level and, in this example, cultural attitudes and beliefs.

Lee (2014) studies the structural composition of the communication networks of Korean immigrants from an ethnic church community, with immigrant groups rapidly growing in population but often less examined in relevant literature. Lee argues that immigrants' social networks are not only important in generating social capital, providing immigrants with physical resources and social support, but they are also heavily influenced by a cross-cultural adaptation process. Specifically, Lee (2014) distinguishes between a monocultural orientation and an intercultural orientation. Individuals with monocultural orientation tend to identify only with one's own cultural worldviews, thus being less receptive to values from alternative cultures. Meanwhile, individuals' intercultural orientation is an important indicator of acculturation, that is, the extent to which individuals adjust to or even get integrated into a new culture.

In the study, Lee (2014) examines several aspects of Korean immigrants' communication networks, including the network size, diversity, and an immigrant's centrality in an ethnic community network. Lee posits that an immigrant's communication network size may be positively associated with network diversity. The more diverse one's communication network is, the higher the level of intercultural orientation, and the lower the level of monocultural orientation. Finally, the researcher investigates the relationship between one's centrality within an ethnic community and their intercultural, monocultural orientations.

Through a network survey, Lee finds that even after controlling for immigrants' English proficiency, an important indicator of one's intercultural acculturation level, the communication network size is indeed positively associated with network diversity. Furthermore, as predicted, the diversity of immigrants' communication networks has a positive influence on intercultural orientation, whereas network centrality has a positive influence on monocultural orientation. These findings thus suggest that to facilitate immigrants' cross-cultural adaptation, diversifying one's social and communication networks may play an instrumental role, whereas the overembeddedness in one's ethnic communication networks tends to slow down the process.

Continuing the Conversation

Several decades have passed since the network concept was first introduced in communication research, and the research guided by social network theory is still booming. The advancement in social network research has particularly benefited from the recent development in network modeling techniques, a family of network statistical methods that enable researchers to model the complex network tie formation and evolution dynamics. The current research can not only *describe* how a social network configures or how network ties are associated with various outcomes; researchers can now uncover the underlying factors that shape the existing network configuration and *predict* how the network may evolve over time.

To sum up, there are several strengths of social network theory. First and foremost, compared to other social scientific approaches that only focus on actor attributes, the network approach provides a relational view of social phenomena, which is much needed considering our entire social life is connected in one way or another. This means that social and communication processes are always examined in their relational environment, not isolated from relevant actors and their behaviors. For example, a network view of disease and risk prevention would not only consider an individual's predispositions and current behaviors but also the network embeddedness of the individual. Second, a social network approach offers a structural view that often goes beyond individual observations. This higher level of analysis thus can provide a more holistic answer to a research question. For example, semantic network analysis, a sub-category of social network analysis examining the associations among words and semantic concepts, can be used to detect latent frames emerging from a large body of communication text (Liu et al., 2018). The ability to produce a "bird's-eye view" of the entire communication text could well supplement traditional methods such as content analysis or discourse analysis. Third, social network theory is uniquely equipped to examine dynamic communication processes. As the very concept of social network recognizes interdependence among actors, the theory posits that the change of one actor's behavior may easily scale up to the entire network and influence other actors. Cutting-edge network methodologies have further made it possible to conduct longitudinal analysis such as examining the evolution of a social network and its consequences.

Meanwhile, there are less-explored territories of social network theory that merit more future research and theorizing. First, the idea of disparity in social networks is a promising avenue for future theorizing. While a social network may be a neutral concept, the social processes that shape network configurations are not. Specifically, certain actors in a social network may be negatively predisposed or marginalized due to their initial network position, or the external forces keep making it difficult for these actors to grow network ties. For example, in terms of capitalizing informal social networks for career advancement, African American female managers were found to experience lower acceptance rates into informal social networks by both male and female White peers (Combs, 2003). Such network-based disparities are particularly manifested along the lines of race and ethnicity, class, and gender.

In addition, network disparities can be observed on social media, where prominent social media users, such as celebrities or influencers, can easily gain new followers and grow their social networks, whereas it is significantly harder for ordinary users, including both individuals and organizations, to gain influence or visibility. This phenomenon may be explained by a well-known network property called "power laws," that is, the tendency for already well-connected network actors to keep developing new connections, whereas the "resource-less" actors face disproportionally more challenge to gain new ties.

Second, social network theory can be better leveraged to devise interventions to alleviate structural inequality in various forms, such as existing gaps in civic engagement, health well-being, and other domains across different population groups. In health communication, there is already a growing use of network-based strategies to help improve health outcomes like promoting cancer-screening behaviors and HIV prevention among minority populations. However, more research and practical projects are needed to fully unleash the potential of network-based interventions. There are urgent needs for scholars and practitioners to first understand the unique social networks among minority communities, and then adopt strategies that are tailored to the respective network properties identified.

Last, but not least, there are more opportunities for researchers and practitioners to utilize social network theory and methodologies as a diagnostic tool for social problems. In a disaster coping and recovery context, for example, network theory can be used to understand residents' varying connections to resources, such as disaster aids or disaster-related information. The concept of "communication ecology" describes a communication resource network that individuals can rely on to obtain disaster-related information and coping strategies (Liu, 2020). Different racial and ethnic groups have long been observed to experience disparity when it comes to disaster coping and recovery. Guided by social network theory, future research may map diverse residents' communication resource networks to identify any discrepancies across different racial and ethnic groups.

Summary

This chapter has provided a brief history and overview of social network theory, reviewing key concepts and its recent applications in the field of communication. The theory is not only useful as a theoretical lens to understanding social and communication processes, but its practical potential can be further unleashed to informing policy making and catalyzing social change. As reviewed in the chapter, a network approach has increasingly been used to understand the communication dynamics among diverse communities, and it provides a unique social structural perspective that is otherwise unavailable. With ongoing theoretical and methodological advancement, social network theory will continue contributing to the building of a more diverse and inclusive research agenda in the communication field.

FOR FURTHER THOUGHT AND REFLECTION

1. Think about all the social contacts that you frequently interact with. Can you draw an ego network where network ties represent your social connections? What are some of the characteristics of this network, such as density or the extent to which network actors exhibit diverse traits (e.g., race/ethnicity, age, occupation, gender)? Who is the bridge, opinion leader, and isolate in the network?

2. Based on the overview provided in this chapter, what research projects may be a good fit for social network theory?

3. Researchers often integrate social network theory with other communication theories in formulating research questions. Can you think of a project that extends an existing communication theory with a social network angle?

4. Along with the practical applications provided, can you think of other practical projects that social network theory can help diagnose and offer interventions?

STORIED REFLECTION
"I'm Blackity Black, and I'm Black Ya'll!"

Ajia Meux
University of Oklahoma

"Say it loud!" she would yell.

"Moooommmm," instinctively, I whined. My disdain was almost a part of the call and response.

"C'mon. Say it! Say it loud!" she'd say again.

"I'm Black and I'm proud," I would respond, unenthusiastically.

"Say it louder!" Her pitch, slightly higher.

"I'm Black and I'm prouder," I would say, even less enthused.

"Say it loudest!" She'd be shouting by this point.

In almost a whisper, I'd respond, "I'm Black and I'm proudest."

"Ungawa!"

On cue, "Black Power." Our fist in the air in solidarity.

It took me well into adulthood to realize the role my mother's routine call and response moments would have in socializing me into being exceedingly comfortable with my Blackness. Outside of the embarrassment of the overall performance, I wasn't entirely aware of what it all meant so early in my life, nor did I fully comprehend the roots from which I had sprung, both literally and figuratively. It was true that, at a surface level, I knew that my hometown of San Francisco was the birthplace of the Black Panthers and the Ebonics movement, but I didn't know how my mother's rearing in the counterculture of the city's Haight-Ashbury neighborhood transferred into her radical perspectives. I was 15 when I learned that she'd received food from the Black Panthers' free lunch program when she was in junior high school. And though I knew she was spending her lunch breaks attending the murder trial of the man who killed Black Panthers cofounder Huey P. Newton, my 13-year-old self didn't fully grasp what that time spent meant to her—and, ultimately, what it would mean for my life's trajectory.

During a time when so many urban communities were marred by drugs and death—mine in particular—my mother lived in the beauty and struggle of Blackness—its lament in the past, its hold on the present, and its push toward the future. She, like so many other Black mamas balancing the beauty and the struggle, absorbed and emitted messages that focused on pride and love. Pride in our hair, our complexion, our music, and our love of our collective. She also fostered an understanding that oppressive systems exist and taught my brother and me to actively challenge what we believed were right and wrong.

Pragmatically, I've been intentional about my life's work since leaving my mother's home some 25 years ago. I joined a Black sorority in undergrad. I moved to Washington, D.C. (also known as Chocolate City), after completing my bachelor's degree and attended Howard University to study social work from within the Black paradigm.

My social identity as a mass communication scholar influences my work in different ways. Just as my mother gave me the gift of understanding the beauty and struggle, I believe I owe the world that same gift in scholarship. My social identity is rooted in radical decolonization and collective and community support, which fuels a desire to understand how we are represented in the messages we consume, how we consume those messages, and how the consumption can bring about change. Because I have been situated in Blackness, my position is from inside the collective, not on influencing others outside the collective.

My mother and I are doing our part to change the narrative to the collective about who Black people are to themselves in this life. Theoretically, this is precisely what Tajfel and Turner (1986) explicate in their theory of social identity when groups work to change the negative self-images assigned to the attributes of a group. The theory suggests that when groups want to change negative attributes, they will change or select the outgroup with which the ingroup is compared—in particular, ceasing or avoiding using the high-status outgroup as a comparative frame of reference. The "Black is Beautiful" campaign that's been going on since about the 1960s is a reflection of this assertion. The campaigns have taken on different elements of

Blackness—size and width of features, hair texture, and skin tone/complexion—with the goal of encouraging Black folk to be proud of the physicality of Blackness. By using the Black collective as a frame of reference only, we've removed the hegemonic structures by which we judge ourselves. My research employs similar tactics. I do not care what others think of us, I care what we think about us.

Now, when my mom launches into our call and response, I poke my sister and niece to join in and shout as loud as she did when I was a kid: "I'm Black and I'm proudest!"

CHAPTER 8

Ethnic-Racial Socialization and Communication
Mapping New Trajectories

Mackensie Minniear

University of Georgia

W hen I was a small child, my parents noticed a troubling theme among my picture books—all the characters were white. As one of the few interracial couples
in our neighborhood, my mom, a Black woman, and my dad, a white man, wanted to
make sure I saw myself in the books I read. With careful precision, my dad went to
the local art store and bought several shades of brown markers. My parents carefully
combed over each page of my books, coloring in the characters, transforming each
image from a sea of beige to a vibrant rainbow of brown hues. They even let me color
in a few pages as well, although my lines were not as clean as theirs. As I grew older,
they sought out books to represent a range of different cultures and traditions. They
found a book of traditional African American folklore filled with detailed illustrations. We poured over stories of Iktomi, a Lakota spirit known for causing mayhem.
As we read books on civil rights, Japanese internment, immigration, and slavery, my
parents sprinkled in their own stories and experiences. Little did I know that my
parents were engaged in the activity to which I would dedicate my scholarly career.
These were my earliest experiences of ethnic-racial socialization.

Ethnic-racial socialization (ERS) refers to the explicit and implicit messages that
individuals receive about ethnicity and race (Hughes et al., 2016). For me, sometimes
these were the direct conversations my mom and grandma had with me about growing up as Black women. Other times, it was the books my parents carefully curated
for me. ERS is a staple not only in Black families but also in all Black, Indigenous, or
People of Color (BIPOC) (Hughes et al., 2006). This chapter provides an overview
of ERS and introduces a new framework for studying, researching, and conceptualizing ethnic-racial socialization mapping. Before exploring mapping, I review how

scholars have conducted ERS studies and how communication scholars and psychology scholars have researched race and ethnicity in distinct but complementary ways. I then integrate this work to showcase ERS research's core assumptions, which are reflected in the ERS mapping process. I demonstrate how ERS mapping can provide a more nuanced understanding of how meanings of ethnicity and race change for individuals and end with future directions.

Intellectual Tradition of Ethnic-Racial Socialization

Before overviewing the research on ERS, I want to elaborate on my decision to use the term *ethnic-racial* rather than *ethnic or racial*. Traditionally, ethnicity refers to a "cultural" difference based on descent and cultural communities, while race refers to a physical or visible difference based on descent and cultural communities (Fenton, 2010). However, definitions of ethnicity and race are constantly changing, and steadfast definitions depend primarily on social context. For example, the U.S. Census classifies "Hispanic" as an ethnicity, although some people conceptualize being Latinx as being more akin to a racial group. Due to changing tides of immigration, changing demographics (particularly in North America), and moving definitions of ethnicity and race, combining the term *ethnic-racial* allows us to encapsulate a more holistic experience, particularly for BIPOC (Umaña-Taylor et al., 2014).

It is also imperative to note that while every person goes through ERS, this chapter focuses on the experience of ERS for BIPOC. While there are growing and robust literature on white racial socialization, this piece, instead, focuses on BIPOC for several reasons. First, ERS has shown positive well-being outcomes for BIPOC (Wang et al., 2020). Second, ERS is generally a much more explicit conversation in BIPOC families when compared to white families. Third, while each ethnic-racial group in North America has a unique and rich legacy, and no one group is a monolith, the racial classification system of North America does position all families of color as nonnormative. Therefore, all families do have to engage in ERS similarly. There are common messages and themes of ERS across all nonwhite groups in North America (Hughes et al., 2006).

ERS research began in the 1980s as Black scholars began investigating how parents instilled a positive racial identity in Black children while also preparing them for racism and discrimination. Daniel and Daniel's (1999) seminal piece likened this process to teaching the children about a hot stove. You must always tell them that a stove is hot and will burn them, but you must also understand that the children must touch the stove itself to understand the danger entirely. As research continued, communication and psychology scholars began to study the phenomenon of ERS in separate but complementary ways.

[handwritten margin note: everyone goes through E.R.S.]

Communication Approaches to Ethnic-Racial Socialization

Daniel and Daniels' (1999) chapter laid the groundwork for family and interpersonal communication scholars to investigate race and ethnicity's role in shaping family contexts. Despite calls from scholars as early as 2001, literature on ERS in communication studies remains scant. Those who study race and ethnicity have demonstrated three approaches: intergroup dynamics, sibling interactions, and critical incidents.

An intergroup approach to ERS examines how our ethnic-racial group membership is highlighted and shaped by our family interactions. One's ethnic-racial group membership is an example of one of many social identities a person has, and there are times when that social identity is salient and times when it is not. For instance, Soliz et al. (2009) examined how intergroup tensions can arise in multiethnic-racial families or families with multiple salient ethnic-racial group memberships. Multiracial families are unique in that numerous social identities are present. Parents have individual social identities compared to each other, and their children also have individual social identities. According to intergroup theorizing, strains between different social identities may occur when the disparities between ingroup and outgroup members are highlighted. Soliz et al. (2009) found that tensions in ethnic and racial identity can still arise in multiracial-ethnic families. However, how families support, discuss, and negotiate identity differences is a strong predictor of relational solidarity. In this way, family is not insular from the larger discourses of ethnicity and race—rather they are more likely to address and discuss these differences.

Another avenue in highlighting how family members socialize ethnicity and race is through siblings and extended family interactions. While most literature examines parental messages of ERS, Cardwell and Soliz (2020) highlighted siblings' role in establishing ethnic-racial identity. Cardwell and Soliz (2020) found that in multiethnic-racial families, siblings are often the only family members who feel they are in the same ethnic-racial group. Therefore, important messages about ethnicity and race stem from sibling interactions. Additionally, Minniear and Soliz (2019) also found that messages about Black racial identity came not only from parents but also grandparents, siblings, and extended family members. In this way, multiple family interactions shape ERS.

[handwritten margin note: critical incident is when "the hot stove" is touched.]

Lastly, critical incidents play a vital role in ERS. Critical incidents refer to significant events in an individual's life where they feel personally and directly involved. For example, social issues, geographic location changes, and direct prejudice experiences play a meaningful role in how Black young adults negotiate their racial identity (Minniear & Soliz, 2019). Multiracial-ethnic individuals also report that critical incidents serve as a vital part of their socialization (Cardwell et al., 2020). Even if parents or family members have warned individuals about discrimination and prejudice, the critical incident serves as a crystallizing moment. The critical incident is when the individual "touches the hot stove," so to say.

Overall, communication scholars have highlighted the role of intergroup tensions, sibling and extended family interaction, and critical incidents. Psychology approaches to ERS also provide a valuable lens for influences of ERS.

Psychology Approaches to Ethnic-Racial Socialization

Psychology scholars have played a significant role in establishing scholarship on ERS, particularly in youth development (Hughes et al., 2006). In general, psychology approaches have examined ERS through message types, sociopolitical influences, and socialization patterns.

Hughes et al. (2006) established four types of ERS practices—cultural socialization (messages regarding cultural values, history, and pride), preparation for bias (messages about how individuals should cope with discrimination), egalitarianism (messages emphasizing equality), and promotion of mistrust (messages that promote wariness of other ethnic-racial groups and do not prepare individuals for how to cope). These types of messages are common across all nonwhite ethnic-racial groups in North America, highlighting the need these families feel to have these conversations. These messages do more than simply provide individuals context for ethnicity and race. ERS messages also have powerful positive effects across ethnic-racial groups. Overall, these messages' presence is predictive of improved psychosocial outcomes and academic adjustment for BIPOC populations (see Wang et al., 2020 for meta-analysis).

Beyond the presence or absence of ERS messages, scholars have highlighted how contextual and dynamic ERS is. Messages about ethnicity and race will change based on social contexts, such as police brutality, immigration rhetoric, and xenophobia. For example, Thomas & Blackmon (2015) found that the murder of Trayvon Martin radically changed the way parents spoke to their children about navigating the world while Black. ERS messages do not occur in a vacuum. Instead, discourses, laws, social events, and politics impact BIPOC families in a way that white families do not experience. BIPOC families must adjust their messages about ethnicity and race out of necessity, to protect children and family members from danger.

Additionally, scholars have examined not simply the presence of messages but patterns of ERS as well. How these messages work together is an essential indicator of child adjustment and well-being. Parents may rely on particular messages more often based on geographic location or socioeconomic status. Neblett et al. (2008) showed that specific messages work together to promote different well-being outcomes for Black youth. ERS does not operate as a checklist, in which certain messages automatically indicate a positive relationship with one's ethnic-racial identity. Instead, messages and message frequency work in tandem to create a positive ERS experience.

Main Goals and Features of Ethnic-Racial Socialization

As I worked through the literature on ERS and began collecting data for my research on how Black families discuss race and ethnicity (Minniear & Soliz, 2019), I began trying to weave the scholarly work with participant experiences together visually. My conversations, academically and with my participants, started to showcase a set of assumptions about ERS. Throughout the literature reviewed above, we know that ERS varies largely and depends on social identity salience, sociopolitical context, patterns, and message types. This scholarship leads to the following three of five assumptions underlying work on ERS.

1. ERS messages are repeated implicitly and explicitly from numerous family members throughout one's life.

2. Sociopolitical context constantly changes conversations and meanings of race, such that BIPOC families are continually adjusting their ERS practices.

3. People often reach out beyond their nuclear family to extended family and fictive kin throughout their lives to understand their ethnic-racial identity.

With these assumptions in mind, I developed a tool for understanding ERS entitled ERS mapping. First, participants listed all of the people they consider to be family in a circle outside of a piece of paper and labeled "self" in the middle of the circle. Participants then drew different types of lines to the people they talk to about various topics. Participants drew lines to those who taught them to be proud of their culture (cultural socialization), who taught them how to respond to bias and discrimination (preparation for bias), who always emphasized the importance of equality (egalitarianism), and who told participants to be careful around certain other ethnic-racial groups (promotion of mistrust). As previous scholars have demonstrated, ERS is dynamic and transactional, so participants also drew lines to people they talk to when they experience discrimination, have trouble fitting in, and talk to about news coverage and social issues.

Additionally, in concordance with the Strong Black Woman Collective (see chapter 9 of this volume), some participants, particularly Black women, may seek strength from others and struggle with vulnerability. Participants also draw lines to those they talk to when they desire to be empowered and the people they talk to when they need to express vulnerability. Lastly, as many mental health disparities between ethnic-racial groups persist, participants also draw lines to the people they talk to when they have concerns about mental health.

Figures 8.1 and 8.2 provide example maps from participants. From these examples, we can see how different family messages are and how dramatically these maps can vary. These findings lead to the final two assumptions of ERS.

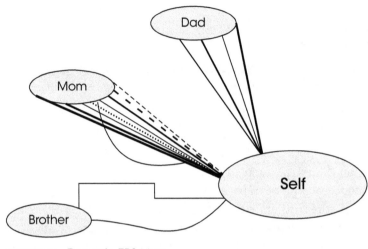

FIGURE 8.1   Example ERS Map

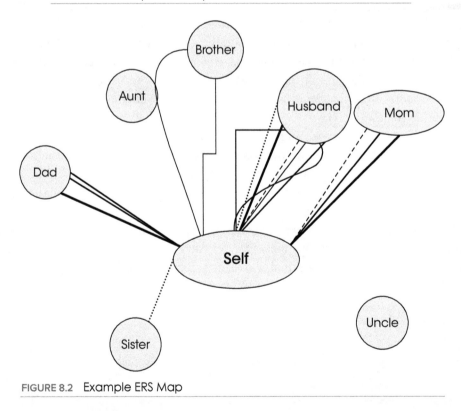

FIGURE 8.2   Example ERS Map

ERS messages will vary dramatically among families based on family communication climate, demographics, and location, creating specific familial conversation patterns.

4. ERS is transactional, such that messages one receives about ERS will be negotiated and processed between family members.

ERS mapping allows a way to integrate multiple strands of ERS literature to see patterns, the influence of sociopolitical contexts, and differing social identities and tensions among members. These maps allow us to integrate all five underlying assumptions of ERS and visually represent these nuances.

Research and Practical Applications of Ethnic-Racial Socialization

The inspiration for this mapping came from interactions with participants. At the beginning of my work with Black college students (Minniear & Soliz, 2019), I fell under the trap of previous ERS research. I assumed that most messages would come from parents in a very top-down manner. However, through initial focus groups, I realized how dynamic conversations were and how participants went to multiple family members. Additionally, they were not simply "recipients" of ERS. Instead, they were also conduits for ERS, sparking conversations with parents, siblings, nieces, and nephews. When reflecting on what I had heard, I struggled to visualize the stories and experiences participants shared with me.

These ERS maps provided a visual representation of participants' experiences. I was able to begin developing and understanding the assumptions of ERS more clearly. Expanding beyond only Black participants, participants filled out these maps across ethnic-racial groups (Minniear, 2020). These maps allowed me to connect with the participant and ask essential research questions. What do the maps show me that I might have missed previously? What assumptions of ERS do these maps reflect? Initial results demonstrate patterns in ERS conversations that were more indicative of family type than an ethnic-racial group.

Not only do the maps serve as an essential research tool, but they also allow individuals to process and reflect on their conversations. For example, a Black woman may be struggling with the difference in how family communication literature generally depicts "normative" (e.g., Eurocentric) families compared to her own, or perhaps she wants to discuss police brutality and protests at her predominantly white institution. Participating in ERS mapping may serve as a way to highlight the social support that exists outside of her immediate circle. If Figure 8.3 showcases her ERS map, she can see who she typically would talk to about these issues and how family members can speak to her about her struggles. In this way, ERS mapping serves several vital functions. First, it helps to create a reminder of the family as self-defined and in a way that may differ from a nuclear family. This map allows participants to define family on their terms, rather than feeling pressures to conform to one family type. Second, the maps highlight the social support she can receive from multiple family members, which we often forget as we go day to day through our lives. Third, she can see who the best person to call may be when struggling to fit in. In this example, even though she does not have as many lines to her cousin as she may to her mother, she can see that her cousin is someone she feels comfortable talking to, prompting her to reach out. Fourth, simply completing the map may result in increased well-being upon reflection. Initial results indicate that completing the map itself may result in increased self-compassion (Minniear, 2020).

Continuing the Conversation

As we reflect on the utility of ERS mapping, there are several chances to improve, refine, and enhance the study of ERS. First, this chapter presents assumptions of ERS, which are reflected in ERS mapping. However, there remain questions about paradigmatic approach to ERS paradigmatically. Many scholars have used post-positivist approaches to test the relationships between ERS messages and well-being outcomes (Neblett et al., 2008). However, the nature of ERS focuses on a critical question—what dominant discourses about race and ethnicity exist, and how do BIPOC families resist and create resilience in the face of these complicated structures? Understanding the influence of discourse is central to several ERS studies (e.g., Thomas & Blackmon, 2015). However, other critical studies have taken a genuinely interpretive approach, focusing on meaning-making from participants and exploring how they negotiate the world around them (Cardwell et al., 2020; Minniear & Soliz, 2019). Paradigms offer us valuable insight into the assumptions that theories and frameworks have about the world, but scholars have not fully explored paradigms in ERS. Perhaps this is due to the difficulty communication and psychology scholars had in having mainstream academia center questions of race and ethnicity for years.

As we question if ERS is a framework, a lens, or a theory, young scholars can utilize EFRS mapping in several ways. Currently, ERS mapping has not thoroughly examined how gender dynamics play into conversations about race and ethnicity, nor has it truly highlighted how intersectionality plays a significant role in ERS. We know that ERS messages will vary based on gender, sexual orientation, and social class, yet how can we use this to understand better how these differences manifest? Additionally, ERS mapping provides us the opportunity to understand resilience in BIPOC families. Native, Latinx, Asian, and Black families have all faced laws, acts, and policies that disenfranchise families based on their ethnicity and race. Despite these attempts, BIPOC families continue to thrive and counter these assumptions. Interested scholars can use ERS assumptions and the different map types to investigate resilience in BIPOC families when encountering problematic representations about race and ethnicity.

Summary

Overall, ERS mapping provides us a new lens to examine family communication about race and ethnicity. By integrating research on different ERS areas, we can see how other individuals process and understand ERS. Further, we can see the extended family's role and how ERS is a dynamic and transactional process. Communication scholars are unique in highlighting the role of family and interpersonal relationships in resisting the problematic narrative of BIPOC families. ERS mapping provides participants a unique way to understand their social support regarding ethnicity and race and allows scholars to reflect on their assumptions and become better scholars in the process.

FOR FURTHER THOUGHT AND REFLECTION

1. Reflecting on past interactions, what memorable messages do you remember receiving about race and ethnicity?

2. In what ways does ERS mapping help participants process ERS messages?

3. What benefits may participants receive by completing ERS mapping?

4. How can ERS mapping help researchers and scholars reflect on their paradigmatic assumptions?

5. In what ways can these maps be adapted to understand white racial socialization?

STORIED REFLECTION
The Magic of Mentors and Theory

Kristina Ruiz-Mesa
California State University, Los Angeles

My first connection to communication theory began on a warm Pennsylvania afternoon in April 2001 during "Accepted Multicultural Students Day" at my undergraduate university. This event was designed for prospective students of color and their families who were considering attending the university. As a 17-year old from a Caribbean family in southern New Jersey, I felt anxious as my parents, sister, and I sat in a large ballroom with hundreds of students and their families. As I nervously flipped through the campus brochures and pondered my future, I heard a voice that changed the trajectory of my life. Dr. Terry Nance, a communication professor, took the stage, and her powerful voice filled the room. During Dr. Nance's speech, I leaned over to my dad and told him that I wanted to learn to speak like her. Little did I know then that Dr. Nance would teach me more about life and communication than I ever hoped and that she would become my role model and mentor for the next 20 years.

Throughout my undergraduate studies, I, like many students, sought out classes taught by Dr. Nance. As a teacher, Dr. Nance used her experiences as an African American woman and as a scholar of Black rhetoric to design engaging courses and assignments, challenging us to learn communication theories by building on our lived experiences. As a Latina attending a predominately white, wealthy, private university, I sometimes felt that my communication norms and expectations for interactions were different from the communication expectations of some of my peers. For example, when meeting my residence hall roommate and her family on my first day of college, I immediately hugged all of them. This was a perfectly normal greeting for me as a Puerto Rican-Cuban Latina who was raised to greet people warmly and who was taught not to shake hands in personal interactions. For my conservative, white, New England roommate and her family, apparently, I was a little different from what they expected.

One afternoon in our Introduction to Human Communication course, Dr. Nance explained expectancy violation theory and my entire view of communication shifted. Dr. Nance spoke to us about social scripts, identities, cultural norms, and explained how our individual and group connections and socialization help us to figure out who we are in the world and condition us to have certain expectations in our communication with others. Dr. Nance went on to teach us that when these expectations for interaction are violated, it can lead to a host of feelings and reactions that can positively or negatively influence relationships. I realized that while I did not know all of the key terms, theorists, or theoretical underpinnings, I did know what it was like to feel like an outsider; now, through theory, I had a way of making sense of peer interactions. Understanding how culture and experiences help us to know what is expected in interactions prepared me to accept or to challenge norms (depending on the situation) and to strategically think about how I want to move in spaces and with whom I want to engage in a variety of places.

Since my time as an undergraduate student, I have found it productive to think of theories as guides that contribute to my understanding and processing of interactions with others and as resources that help to prepare me for speaking, writing, teaching, and engaging diverse audiences in my personal and professional life. During difficult times of insecurity and self-doubt, understanding critical race theory and imposter syndrome helped me to understand how social and legal structures and practices led to unequal access to resources and systems of oppression that, sadly, leave some feeling like they don't belong. As the first person in my large extended family to move thousands of miles away to attend graduate school, I felt awful guilt associated with leaving my family behind and accessing education that was inaccessible to others. When I later read about family achievement guilt, I immediately felt seen and understood and learned that I was not alone in having these feelings.

Reading theories can sometimes feel like getting a *CliffsNotes* version of what to expect in life's many bumps and challenges. Not all theories make considerations for diverse voices and experiences, and some oversimplify interactions and practices, but some theories are like a crystal ball that lets us know what is happening and what is likely to happen next. In those moments when theories are inclusive, precise, and clear, I see the magic of theory and the possibilities of improving our communication, our connections to one another, and of making our world a kinder and more just place for all of us.

CHAPTER 9

Strong Black Woman Collective Theory

Shardé M. Davis

University of Connecticut

Martinque K. Jones

University of North Texas

The strong Black woman (SBW) controlling image is a gendered racial archetype characterized by emotional control, independence, and self-sacrifice (Woods-Giscombé, 2010). The image is one of several archetypes (e.g., Mammy; Collins, 2000) that have been used to justify the subjugation of Black women. Because of its deleterious impact, the image has traditionally been considered a negative ideology by Black feminists (Collins, 2000), and this assertion has been corroborated by a long line of empirical research (e.g., Abrams et al., 2019; Watson & Hunter, 2015; Woods-Giscombé, 2010). According to such studies, the SBW image is lauded and widely accepted by members of U.S. society, including Black women, but its embodiment presents interpersonal and intrapersonal consequences. Interpersonally speaking, when Black women embody the SBW image, we are often perceived by outsiders as aggressive and expected to serve and care for others, oftentimes without any reciprocation of support or care (Jones et al., 2021). Challenging this negative perception and contending with the internal and external pressures to uphold the attributes of the SBW contribute to intrapersonal issues such as psychological distress and depression (Abrams et al., 2019). Despite the established link between the SBW image and negative outcomes, we (the coauthors, who self-identify as Black women) pressure ourselves and each other to be strong, indicating that the "functions" of strength may outweigh the consequences (Davis & Jones, 2020). Part of the reason that we cling to the SBW image is because we have resolved that it is a resource that plays critical functions in our lives.

Intellectual Tradition of Strong Black Woman Collective Theory

The Strong Black Woman Collective Theory (SBWC, Davis, 2015) reconciles both perspectives—the functionality and consequences of the SBW image—into one comprehensive framework that is rooted in the critical tradition. It posits that the SBW image is consciously reappropriated and embodied in the communication practices of Black women during relational encounters. One of the key elements of the SBWC is acknowledging the tension between the concurrent liabilities and benefits of *strength* (which we use to refer to as the adaptive and maladaptive manifestations of the SBW image). Prior research (specifically in the field of psychology) has illuminated this important point by noting that the SBW image is not entirely "good or bad; rather, it is functional" (Watson & Hunter, 2015, p. 25). That is, it suggests that the functionality of the SBW image is rooted in its ability to offer Black women a sense of psychological fortitude against oppression as well as greater levels of self-esteem and cultural pride (Jones et al., 2021; Watson & Hunter, 2015; Woods-Giscombé, 2010). Further, studies show that Black women have begun to reappropriate and redefine the SBW image in ways that maximize the benefits associated with the image and minimize negative consequences (Jones et al., 2021; Nelson et al., 2016). This line of research encapsulates the entry point and essence of the SBWC theory. The internalization and reappropriation of strength do important work that should not be overshadowed by their liabilities. At the foundation of the theory is the premise that strength is a resource that functions to facilitate Black women's resistance, survival, and even resilience in societal contexts where Black women are disenfranchised. With that said, there are key departures of the SBWC theory from prior research (e.g., field of psychology). Prior studies connect macro-level issues (e.g., the controlling image) with psychological processes (e.g., coping, Abrams et al., 2019) and mental and physical outcomes (e.g., depression, Abrams et al., 2019). The SBWC theory shifts the lens to connect the macro level with the meso level, thereby illuminating how Black women take up our agency to contend with the image within the domain of our interpersonal communication and relationships (see Figure 9.1).

Main Goals and Features of Strong Black Woman Collective Theory

The SBWC theory provides a lens to examine the lived realities of Black women in the United States and advances four propositions about the way we contend with strength communicatively within our sistah spaces. First, Black women communicate strength using distinct behaviors that cohere to characteristics of the SBW image (i.e., assertive and direct messages, code-switching, culturally nuanced speech codes). Second, a group of Black women communicating strength composes the strong Black woman collective (referred to as "the collective" henceforth). Third, members of the collective participate by reinforcing virtues of strength in oneself and others. And fourth, the regulation

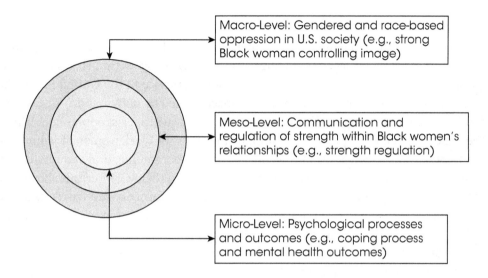

FIGURE 9.1 Connections drawn between micro-, meso- and macro- levels of society by the strong Black woman collective theory.

of strength enables the collective to confront oppressive external forces and develop a retreat space; but strength regulation also impedes the expression of vulnerability and emotionality within the collective (Davis, 2015).

Communicating Strength

At the heart of the first proposition is that strength is a critical feature of Black women's verbal and nonverbal communication, a point that extends prior research on the SBW image. To explain, strong Black women want to mask vulnerability and emotionality, persevere through challenges, resist oppressors, maintain power and control, and independently handle our own problems (even when the task is unbearable). These goals can be reached using the communication practices that are prevalent among—and empirically attached to—Black women. For instance, Black women often avoid sensitive or feeling-oriented topics during conversations, and when emotions are heightened, we might dampen emotional expression by palliating the encounter with humorous and playful messages. Additionally, Black women often communicate forthright messages, encourage honesty in others, share unsolicited advice about what others should do, and present oneself with authority and assuredness (for further discussion, see Davis, 2015). While many of these communication practices occur during interactions with cultural outsiders, the theory hones in on the way Black women encourage the use of strength-accordant communication (i.e., fortitude and stoicism) and discourage strength-deviant communication (i.e., emotionality and vulnerability) when Black women gather together (Davis, 2015).

Forming the Collective

The starting point of the SBWC phenomenon is when Black women come together and communicate messages that cohere to the SBW image within that space. The gathering of Black women is a common relational practice in the United States. In fact, the collective likens a homeplace—a space coined by hooks (1990)—in which Black women seek respite, heal, and strategize about ways to resist oppression. While the collective and homeplace share similar functions for Black women, it is important to note that a key feature of the collective is the communication *and* regulation of strength (further discussion of strength regulation is below). There are, however, instances when a gathering of Black women may shift to form a collective. To explain, individual Black women might encourage the SBWC phenomenon to emerge by signaling to a woman that she needs strength (e.g., a woman seeks out female elders in her family to help her cope with a divorce). Additionally, as Black women come together for sistahly connection, individuals may see a woman "be strong" and, in turn, model that behavior during the conversation. External forces can also encourage a normal gathering of Black women to shift to an SBWC. For instance, a cultural outsider can transgress against a member of the collective (e.g., a woman's romantic partner commits adultery) or an oppositional force can signal to Black women that their livelihood is in jeopardy (e.g., a police officer wrongfully murders a Black girl). Given the long and troubling history of misogynoir and anti-Blackness in the United States, it is likely that Black women will begin to communicate strength during ordinary gatherings as an exigent response to the systemic oppression that indisputably affects one, multiple, or all members of the collective.

Regulating Strength

Though the SBW image is most known as a controlling image with negative implications for Black women (e.g., Abrams et al., 2019; Collins, 2000; Woods-Giscombé, 2010), scholars note that Black women have reappropriated this image so that its adaptive functions can be optimized (Jones et al., 2021; Nelson, 2016). Accordingly, this theory is built upon the premise that *strength is functional* (Davis & Jones, 2020; Watson & Hunter, 2015), and it extends this idea to consider how Black women leverage the benefits of strength within the relational domain by encouraging each other to embody strength via our verbal and nonverbal communication. Accordingly, the theory advances the construct of *strength regulation*, which denotes an attempt to control the way characteristics associated with the SBW image are embodied by one's self and others in the collective (Davis, 2015). One empirical example of strength regulation is from a memoir by Danquah (1998) when she recounts a time she sought support for her depression from her group of Black women friends, and her friends associated her depression with weakness and supported her by affirming her identity as a strong Black woman. While strength regulation emerges in the context of Black women peer groups, prior research suggests that strength regulation can begin in childhood when socializing agents such as parents, relatives, and media

teach Black women the essential elements and outcomes of a "successful" strength performance (for discussion, see Davis, 2015). Over time, Black women habituate what we
observe in others by embodying strength in our personal lives and encouraging other
Black women to do the same (Davis 2015).

Research suggests that the nature of strength regulation may change to adapt to the
social norms and established knowledge claims of the modern era. For instance, studies
show that older generations of Black women perceive strength regulation as a necessary
mandate for Black women's survival and, thus, seek to reify the traditional components
of strength in oneself and others (e.g., emotional control; Bailey, 2018). Comparatively,
younger generations of Black women (who have greater access to knowledge about the
deleterious impacts of the SBW image) might challenge themselves and other Black
women to reimagine how we can repurpose aspects of the SBW image in a way that
poses *less* harm to their physical, mental, and emotional health (Jones et al., 2021).

Outcomes and Implications

Strength regulation among members of the collective has three distinct implications
according to the theory: (a) delineate a safe space for Black women who share racial
and gender identities; (b) confront hostile forces that exist beyond the collective; (c)
and discourage members of the collective to express vulnerability, thereby reifying
strength in members of the collective. To explain, the process of communicating and
regulating strength can foster solidarity among members. In fact, prior research suggests that Black women affiliate with each other through a unique communicative style
that is laden with sociocultural and historical properties. Culturally derived words,
phrases, and colloquialisms can be used as identity markers in Black women's everyday
conversations to invoke solidarity and identification with the social group (e.g., Davis,
2019). Because strength is considered a critical element of Black women's gendered
racial identity (see Davis, 2015), women can draw upon strength to reify Black womanhood. Some researchers have attempted to disentangle the SBW image and Black
women's gendered racial identity (Jones et al., 2021; Nelson et al., 2016) but admitted
that this goal is rather difficult to achieve; in fact, Nelson and colleagues (2016, p. 10)
note "maintaining a facade of strength may be difficult to abandon" for Black women.
Therefore, members of the collective may mark their shared identity by reinforcing
strength in self and others (e.g., "don't let those white folks see you cry"); such rein-
forcement fortifies the relational bonds within the collective and establishes a sense
of belonging within the group and a safe space for them to display a more authentic
and unapologetic Black womanhood.

Strength regulation within the collective also serves as a means of resistance and
defense against external forces that (sub)consciously seek to harm members of the
collective. From an intergroup perspective, Black women within the collective share
a gendered racial identity, which means that we can be considered members of an
in-group while non-Black women constitute the out-group. In-group members have

an intrinsic motivation to strive for a positive social identity. Thus, members of the collective likely enhance the undesirable characteristics of an outgroup, particularly groups with societal privilege, that contributes to Black women's subordination within the United States and a history of discriminating against Black women (e.g., white women, Black men). For example, when a collective assembles, they might verbally derogate a racist white woman colleague or a dishonest Black male romantic partner. Derogation is one way Black women can (indirectly) confront individuals who pose harm to their members. However, Black women do not need an identifiable human target to retort with confrontational messages. The United States is structured in such a way that gendered racism against Black women is systemic and institutionalized (Collins, 2000), which means that members of the collective have an ever-present hostile force to retreat from and confront.

While the theory, and strength regulation more specifically, indexes the notion that strength is functional, it also recognizes that strength is equally problematic as it encourages many Black women to maintain a façade of emotional fortitude even in situations when emotional expression is warranted and necessary. For women who identify with and embody the SBW image, expressing emotions may be considered the antithesis to strength (Abrams et al., 2019; Jones et al., 2021). To that end, the SBWC theory posits that strength regulation is a barrier to Black women exploring the full range of our humanity. For example, Black matriarchs may label a younger family member as "weak" or even communicate messages such as "if our ancestors can make it through slavery, then you can make it through anything" in response to that family member crying because she is overwhelmed, seeking help for a personal hardship, or failing to exhibit other characteristics that are associated with the SBW image. Matriarchs might make these comments as a form of "tough love" that attempts to backfill the critical resources for that woman to survive in a cruel and discriminatory society. But these messages are also invalidating and can prompt its recipient to feel as though she is less of a Black woman for exhibiting behaviors that contradict strength. In sum, the theory posits that when women attempt to regulate each other's strength, they also stymie each other's emotional maturity, intelligence, and health.

Research and Practical Applications of Strong Black Woman Collective Theory

Research on the SBWC theory is far-reaching and can span across relational types and contexts. In regard to relational types, members of the collective can have relationships that are characterized by intimacy and closeness, such as sistah friendships or blood-linked kinship. For instance, strength regulation and the subsequent outcomes and implications might take the form of racial socialization by primary socializing agents who shoulder the responsibility to prepare loved ones for racial discrimination in the United States. Black mothers along with Black female older siblings and aunties might carve out time during a family gathering to teach a young girl in their family how she can defend herself at school. These messages can constitute lessons on how to talk, dress, or even quick quips that the young girl can communicate. This process of strength regulation can also occur among Black women with a limited relational history (e.g., members of a historically Black sorority).

The communication context for the collective can also vary; viable contexts may include social support and communal coping, as well as racial-gender socialization, group decision-making, group therapy, communication within sports teams, and even collective bereavement. While there are various contexts in which this theory can be applied, one of the most viable is social support and coping. Strength may be considered a culturally nuanced form of support that Black women communicate to a sistah in distress (see Davis, 2019), and it is likely that Black women might regulate strength in each other because it is a dependable and effective quality that squelches distress. In this way, regulating strength as a form of support may help a woman cope with a devastating event or loss. For instance, a woman may have learned that her child was murdered by the police and gathers with her sistah friends to process the loss. During the conversation, the friends might encourage the woman to get herself together and be strong for her other children. The friends may also advise the woman to shift her energy to suing the police department and fighting for justice. In this way, the sistah friends might bolster the woman's strength as a communicative response to a momentary lapse in her strength performance, even if the lapse occurred during a devasting life experience.

Continuing the Conversation

The SBWC theory makes numerous contributions to the field of communication as well as research on the SBW image in other fields. Chief among them is that it is one of the first frameworks to theorize that *strength is functional*. While research in the field of psychology illuminated the possibility, this theory is one of the first (to our knowledge) to make this assertion. Second, the theory is predicated on honoring and validating Black women's agency to self-define strong Black womanhood, convene in meaningful ways, and actively resist and retreat from oppression. The theory illuminates that controlling images, specifically, and oppressive stereotypes, broadly, are not entirely "doom and gloom." Black women can intervene and disrupt these oppressive forces in ways that facilitate our survival. This kind of theorizing shifts the focus about Black women from a deficits-based approach to a strengths-based approach (literally and theoretically). Too often, our ways of being are pathologized, but this theory contrasts this paradigm through its presentation of an ethical, validating, empowering, and people-oriented communication framework about how Black women respond to oppression. Moreover, through its relational communication focus, the theory builds upon what is already known about the implications of the SBW image at the micro level (e.g., psychological distress; Abrams et al., 2019) by considering how Black women collectively make sense of macro-level issues, such as gendered racial oppression, at the meso level. Finally, and germane to this textbook, the SBWC is a specific and unapologetic communication theory about Black women's relational encounters. Difference matters. Thus, scholars should lean into the notion that co-cultures need frameworks that make sense of our unique communication behaviors without consideration of what it means for other cultural groups. Nevertheless, the SBWC theory may inspire the development of new companion theories to explain how other racialized groups of women or men communicate and regulate cultural demands during relational encounters.

The SBWC is ripe for scholars to examine its tenets in future research. One consideration for research might be to examine when (and to what extent) each of the theoretical tenets occurs; it may be the case that strength regulation centered on racial-gender socialization most commonly emerges among a collective of close-knit Black women, whereas social support may emerge among any collective (e.g., Black women acquaintances). Also, the external hostility that the collective contends with can emerge in the form of a connection with an individual of which there is no relationship (e.g., a celebrity), a preexisting relationship (e.g., non-Black woman classmate or coworker), or even a distal relationship with a nonhuman entity (e.g., breast cancer, misogynoir, anti-Black racism). Therefore, another empirical consideration may include an exploration of how the collective (differentially) contends with each of these external forces.

While the theory is applicable to Black women across ages and generations, future scholars may also examine emotional constraint and self-silencing among younger generations of Black women who recognize that emoting is necessary and healthy, yet pathologized by others in U.S. society including older Black women (see Abrams et al., 2019; Jones et al., 2021; Nelson et al., 2016). Within- and cross-generational examinations can reveal how Black women's perception of strength, and its functionality, has shifted over time. Not to mention, they will reveal if the communication of strength and the process of strength regulation have evolved to become more nuanced than originally theorized (Davis, 2015). This timely avenue for future research reveals an immediate next step for the theory, which is an inductive analysis of interpersonal interactions among Black women to illuminate the explicit and implicit natures of strength regulation through concrete, empirical examples. Needless to say, research on each of these topics constitutes important paths for the refinement of the SBWC theory.

Summary

The Strong Black Woman Collective (SBWC) theory is one of the first frameworks to consider strength as a fundamental component of the SBW image and functional resource that help Black women navigate systemic gendered and racial oppression, thereby shifting scholarly discussions about strength from good/bad to functional. This chapter reviewed the theory by discussing how Black women reappropriate the dominant SBW image and employ certain communication behaviors to affirm strength in each other. By exhibiting these behaviors, Black women delineate a safe space to promote solidarity and pride within the group and confront oppressive forces from outside the group as a collective. While reinforcing such behaviors as a collective enables resistance against external hostilities and validates Black womanhood, it may also impede sharing vulnerability and emotionality. Future scholars can use this theory to make sense of the way Black women use communication in sistah spaces to help one another maneuver gendered racial oppression in the U.S. social realm.

FOR FURTHER THOUGHT AND REFLECTION

1. What are some real-world examples (i.e., personal experiences, television shows, news stories) of Black women who are communicating strength?

2. How (if at all) can others encourage Black women to utilize strength *without* stifling their vulnerability and emotionality?

3. How do you think the strong Black woman image has evolved as new generations of Black women age?

4. Does contemporary U.S. society allow Black women to deviate from the strong Black woman image?

5. What methods can scholars use to study the strong Black woman image? Can you design a study that would allow scholars to examine the image using the strong Black woman collective theory as a theoretical lens?

STORIED REFLECTION
Making Ourselves Visible

Nickesia S. Gordon
Rochester Institute of Technology

"I am not here to colonize your minds," was the most profound statement I heard during my high school years. It was delivered, with much passion, and just a hint of annoyance, to my history class by a then new teacher who was abrasive and most disagreeable (or so we thought). As it turned out, she wasn't so bad after all. In fact, she was the best teacher I ever had. Her teaching style and accompanying passion had a lasting impression on me. She was passionate about knowledge and teaching, but most importantly, she was passionate about creating an environment that would stimulate independent and critical thinking. It was the best lesson of high school and a lesson for life.

This seed that was planted so many years ago inadvertently guided my journey into academia both as a scholar and educator. It has fueled my appreciation and love of critical communication theories, particularly those that decenter Western philosophical approaches to academic inquiry. Specifically, postcolonial studies resonate strongly with my scholarly interests and represent a school of thought with which I feel a deep kinship. The connection I feel to postcolonial theories is partly engendered by my so-called "third-world" upbringing and encounters of intellectual imperialism as both an international student and scholar in the United States of America, whose work focuses on phenomena from the geopolitical Global South. There is a certain ethnocentric monoculturalism (Sue, 2004) that guides the reception of scholars such as myself, given the imperial eye through which our contributions are often evaluated. This is a lens through which we are sometimes held as intellectually suspect based on our origins.

As a result of these experiences, especially those from earlier in my career, critical/postcolonial studies have been powerful directives in my scholarly pursuits. The work of scholars such as Edward Said, Chandra Mohanty, Edward T. Hall, and others have provided me with the theoretical tools through which to endure academically under Western eyes (Mohanty, 1984). For scholars who are not Euro-American, postcolonial studies have empowered us with the theoretical scaffolding to "make ourselves visible within our own light" (Braithwaite, 1974, p. 55) and to confidently resist academic colonization.

Regarding my pedagogy, critical studies have also been influential. I firmly subscribe to the idea that education is an instrument that should be used to liberate minds and to integrate individuals into society as creative and "woke" participants. "Woke" individuals are those who are alert to social injustice and who are socially aware. Hence, I do not see it as my duty to "colonize" students' thoughts but rather to engage and stimulate critical consciousness, especially in a field where knowledge production is reified as the province of White scholars (Chakravartty et al., 2018). Students are continuously exposed to a system of education that devalues the contributions of nonwhite scholars and establishes traditional communication scholarship as singularly authoritative. Framing my pedagogy through a critical lens helps to foster a dialogic classroom environment within which such assumptions may be interrogated.

This philosophy resonates with Brazilian thinker Paulo Freire's concept of education. In his book *Pedagogy of the Oppressed,* Freire (2014) observes that there is no such thing as a neutral educational process. What I believe he meant by this is that education, and by extension, knowledge, is powerful and can either be used to create or proliferate conditions of oppression or to liberate and create transformation. I am perhaps sensitive to the potential intellectual prison that higher education can create based on my background, where a colonial educational system was geared towards perpetuating intellectual dependence.

In closing, I reflect on the poem "Love after Love" by West Indian poet and Nobel laureate Derek Walcott (1987). In it, Walcott relays to the persona that "the time will come" when they will welcome themselves, "arriving at [their] own door" (p. 328). In this moment, the persona also sees themselves in their "own mirror." For me, the poem invokes experiences of liberation, affirmation, and self-discovery. It captures what critical and postmodern theories have affirmed for my scholarship, namely the value of non-Western epistemologies in the academy and the continued decolonization of my own thinking through inquiry grounded in this positionality.

CHAPTER 10

Theory of Differential Adaptation

Antonio Tomas De La Garza

California State University, San Marcos

W hat if assimilation was not a self-evident good? What if someone moved into a new society that contained hostile or toxic cultural elements with whom migrants should avoid assimilating? These where the primary questions that my coauthor and I sought to understand when we began to develop our differential adaptation theory (DAT). Differential adaptation is a "non-universalist framework that acknowledges the radical diversity of immigrants' experiences, immigrants' agentic efforts to navigate pressures to assimilate, and the potential they have to reshape subjectivities, culture, and society" (De La Garza & Ono, 2015). DAT was developed to provoke a discussion in the field, one we believed to be long overdue, about how structural racism and academic imperialism influenced the field's understanding of the migrant experience. As our critique of traditional theories of adaptation deepened, we realized that insights from postcolonial and critical race theories provided a much more nuanced language for theorizing the immigrant experience.

Differential adaptation theory is organized across two dialectics. The first is the tensions between universality and specificity in the immigration experience. Far too often, researchers produce flattened depictions of "the other" in search of a universalist framework for theorizing the migrant experience. DAT addresses that failing by reorienting the researcher to the historical, political, and discursive context that will shape an individual immigrant's experience of a new culture. Doing so allows scholars to attend to the tactical choices migrants make about when, to what extent, and how to adapt to a new culture. The second dialectic is the tensions that exist between an individual and a society. DAT recognizes that immigrants move for different reasons, have different agendas, and may experience the new culture in radically different ways. Furthermore, the "adaptation process immigrants employ can be either contested or supported by the host culture, and the interplay of contestation and support structures adaptation" (De La Garza & Ono, 2015, p. 270). By situating the society and the individual in dialectic tension with each other, DAT highlights the interplay of agency, power, and discourse that may facilitate or hinder a migrant's adaption. Though still in the early stages of development, DAT produced space for thinking differently about the immigrant experience and is being adopted by scholars around the world.

Intellectual Tradition of Differential Adaptation Theory

Scholars in disciplines ranging from anthropology, sociology, psychology, and communication have developed theories to explain how and why individuals alter their behavior subjectivity to thrive in a new culture. In particular, research in the area of adaptation or acculturation "comprehends those phenomena which result when groups of individuals having different cultures come into continuous first-hand contact, with subsequent changes in the original cultural patterns of either or both groups" (Redfield et al., 1936). This anthropological definition has been adapted and modified for use across disciplines to theorize the experiences and, to a lesser extent, the wellness outcomes of migrants. Prior to the development of DAT, the focus of the scholarly inquiry was on acculturation, which is best exemplified as "an adaptation process occurring when individuals from one culture are in contact with a host culture. By this process, individuals adopt characteristics of the mainstream culture and retain or relinquish traits of their traditional background" (Salabarría-Peña et al., 2001).

A handful of theorizations recognized and included some contextual factors, such as citizenship discourse, as pertinent to research on immigration. However, many of these studies were siloed as not part of the "intercultural subfield," which resulted in them having a limited impact on intercultural scholarship. Prior to DAT, most research in the field of communication placed the responsibility on the individual immigrant and judged the success of their migration on how they accommodated the host culture without ever critically reflecting on pressures exerted by the host culture, which may be racist, sexist, nationalist, colonialist, or in other ways harmful. When scholarly models did account for both the perspective of new and old cultural groups and the individual, they often assumed two mutually exclusive groups, a unidirectional flow of change and adaptation, flattened depictions of non-U.S. cultures, and a static theory of identity formation. According to DAT, the migrant and the host culture relate to one another through a series of negotiations informed by fluid and hybridized interpretations of identity and culture. As a result, DAT provides intercultural scholars with a language to describe behavioral, communicative, and sociocultural changes in both the migrant and the host culture that may lead to mutual accommodations, subversions, conflicts, and adaptation by both the migrant and the host culture. Adaptation, assimilation, and acculturation each pertain to the predominant models used to assess the psychological adaptation of immigrants in the host society. Central to this adaptation process are one's ability and desire to communicate in accordance with the norms and practices of the host culture and continuous and active engagement in the interpersonal and mass communication activities of the host society.

However, as a theoretical construct, acculturation theories tend to oversimplify the adaptation process and have historically been bereft of tools to account for concepts such as power, migrant agency, conformity pressure, immigration policy, and cultural hybridity. Previous theories failed to account for individual/community relationships, missing the nuances that arise when the individuals in question are refugees, colonized, people of color, voluntary immigrants, or forced (trafficked) immigrants. DAT was developed in opposition to three prevailing assumptions guiding adaptation research. The first was a lack in accounting for immigrant agency. The second was a lack of attention to barriers faced by immigration and the third was the omission of contextual factors that particularize a migrant's experience. The conclusions drawn from not accounting for these gaps subtlety reenforced xenophobic and nationalistic attitudes about immigrants and provided scholarly backing to critics of immigrants for choosing not to speak or learn English, choosing to wear the Hajab, or choosing to maintain grooming or hygienic practices from their home culture.

In this same vein, racial battle fatigue (De La Garza, 2015) can be a consequence of abusive immigration rhetoric and is a chronic stressor, which is correlated with an increase in depression symptoms and stress-related illnesses. Furthermore, racist nativism (De La Garza, 2019; Pindi & De La Garza, 2019), structural racism, and immigration discourse can serve as barriers to immigrant assimilation and adaptation. Taken together, these findings suggest that researchers should move towards a theory of adaptation that considers perceptions, attitudes, and behaviors from both the host society towards the incoming group or individual and vice versa. According to DAT, the migrant and the new culture relate to one another through a series of negotiations informed by fluid and hybridized interpretations of identity and culture. As a result, DAT provides intercultural scholars with a language to describe behavioral, communicative, and sociocultural changes in both the migrant and the new culture that may lead to mutual accommodations, subversions, conflicts, and adaptation by both the migrants and cultures.

Adaption, assimilation, and acculturation each pertain to the predominant models used to assess the psychological adaptation of immigrants in the host society. Central to this adaptation process are one's ability and desire to communicate in accordance with the norms and practices of a culture and continuous and active engagement in the interpersonal and mass communication activities of the society. Yet, often previous theories of adaptation fell into the trap of undertheorizing migrant agency and assumed that migrant assimilation was a self-evident good. In contrast, DAT suggests that migrants may adapt in a variety of ways that do not assimilate to or accommodate pressures presented by the larger society they have joined, and that maintaining aspects of the home culture, language, and identity may produce better outcomes in terms of physical and psychological well-being.

Main Goals and Features of Differential Adaptation Theory

To account for the complex social and political realities that shape an immigrant's adaptation experience, DAT reinterprets and centers the agency that migrants have in their own process of adaptation. To break with the essentialist traditions that so deeply influenced past intercultural scholarship, DAT includes interdisciplinary epistemologies like critical race theory and postcolonial theory into its theoretical paradigm. Moreover, because both authors come from families whose immigration and adaptation would be considered outliers and have not been accurately represented or theorized in previous intercultural scholarship, we were intentional about producing a theory of adaptation that allowed us to feel seen and assimilate our own experiences.

DAT acknowledges there is not a singular or universal experience of immigration, even for people from the same home culture. DAT may not always account for general trends in immigrant adaptation; however, this is not a weakness of the theory. Instead, DAT was developed to show how and why individuals from similar cultures might experience and react to the assimilative forces of culture in different ways. The wide reception of DAT and its increasing relevance in the field of intercultural communication suggests other scholars were seeking a finer, more nuanced set of tools to illuminate intercultural dynamics.

The borderlands theory first articulated by Anzaldúa (1999) became an import source of inspiration for differential adaptation. Borderlands refers not just to geographic locales like those that separate the United States from Mexico but also to psychic spaces, the in betweenness and sense of being "out of place" that describe the subjective experience of migrants as being outside of and yet belonging to a new culture. Anzaldúa (1999) describes this as an uncomfortable even painful sensation. At the same time, Anzaldúa (1999) argues that this space is also transformative and generative because that discomfort once confronted produces new subjectivities and cultures. Drawing on Anzaldúa's theories allowed my coauthor and me to move away from the assumption that migrants would inevitably assimilate into a homogeneous society. Instead, DAT provides a framework for investigating how migrants interact and adapt to new surroundings while simultaneously changing and influencing their new locale. Migrants can and do make intentional interventions to change their adopted country and create hybrid cultures. Moreover, a recognition that migrants might make tactical choices about how and when they assimilate also distinguishes between their own personal process of adaptation and external pressures to assimilate.

While grand theories of human behavior can be useful and are often considered the "holy grail" of social sciences, DAT may be conceptualized as being more interested in understanding the outliers, the exceptions, and the divergent. DAT was intentionally developed to give communication scholars tools to investigate migration experiences and behaviors that were not addressed or ignored by the scholarly mainstream. Thus, DAT is best deployed to understand the messiness and particularity of the immigration experience. To accomplish this, we drew heavily on critical border studies, the concept of *nepatntla* (Anzaldúa, 1999), or being caught between ways. This focus is useful not only for scholars but also for students. As an educator, it was important to me that the theory be culturally validating and reflective of the diverse experiences of my students.

While developing this theory, I evoked the mechanical differential in a car, which takes power from the engine and uses a series of gears to change the direction and speed of that power. DAT posits immigrants "as engaged in parallel processes by emphasizing relationality, the role of power in immigration, social, historical, political, and cultural context, and the concrete effects of ideological and material forces that both enable and constrain social adaptation" (De La Garza & Ono, 2015, p. 270). When immigrants engage with their new culture, they must tactically navigate networks of power and discourse that shape their experiences in the world. Rather than portray immigrants as agentless victims of circumstances beyond their control, DAT flips the paradigm and posits immigrants as powerful agents, not only capable of making choices about the speed and extent to which they adapt or assimilate to a culture but also of being powerful agents capable of influencing that culture. Further examples of how DAT is being incorporated into the field include primary attention focused on how DAT can help scholars make sense of identity formation and negotiation among migrants.

Research and Practical Applications of Theory of Differential Adaptation

Rather than reify cultural stereotypes, DAT validates that "the diversity of immigrant experiences provides opportunities for intercultural scholarship to recognize and emphasize that difference is an essential, incontrovertible component of the social world" (De La Garza & Ono, 2015, p. 278). Take, for example, how immigration policy endangered the lives of asylum seekers during the first year of the COVID-19 pandemic. Under the Trump administration's Migrant Protection Protocols (MPP), Central American refugees who were legally seeking asylum were forced to wait in border towns in Mexico before they could make their case for asylum. Some migrants were forced to wait indefinitely, many losing their place in line or their chance to be heard through no fault of their own. They were stranded without support, in a society that discriminates heavily against Central Americans, and lacked the ability to legally work in Mexico. Many of these refugees became easy prey for cartels who shifted their income streams to human trafficking due to shrinking drug profits during the pandemic. It is estimated that "through December 2020, there were at least 1,314 publicly documented cases of rape, kidnapping, assault, and other crimes committed against individuals sent back under MPP" (The "Migrant Protection Protocols," 2021).

The first step of a DAT analysis of this case study is to look at the contextual factors that structure a migrant's experience. An example of these factors includes immigration policies like the MPP. The MPP gives discretionary power to Customs and Border

Patrol agents to decide who will be returned to Mexico under MPP. The process is so arbitrary that "in some situations, this has led to families being separated at the border, with one parent sent back to Mexico and the other parent and the child allowed to enter the United States" (The "Migrant Protection Protocols," 2021). Officially, the MPP is designed to "protect" people seeking asylum in the United States; the policy discourse suggests that potential asylees are "safer in Mexico" and that the Mexican government will provide material and legal support. According to the state department, border towns like Tijuana pose the same risk to U.S. government personnel as war zones like Syria and Afghanistan. At the same time, the COVID-19 pandemic led to tightening control of cross-border traffic, drastically reducing international donations of food, clothing, money, and volunteer aid at a time when that aid was most needed. Refugees, mostly from Haiti, El Salvador, Guatemala, and Honduras, found themselves living in close quarters in the El Chaparral migrant camp while a deadly and infectious disease spread through their community.

Tijuana is ranked as the most dangerous city in the world, and I was living there and working with a refugee organization during the pandemic. I watched as people who had been waiting years for their asylum hearing were denied entry, were provided with out-of-date and inaccurate information from U.S. Customs and Border Patrol, had their paperwork misplaced, and lost their position in the metering system. At the institutional level, it became very clear that the U.S. government was dispossessing potential asylees of their legal rights while attempting to appear as if it was complying with international laws, such as the 1951 Refugee Convention and the Universal Declaration of Human Rights, both of which require nations to accept refugees. U.S. immigration policy provides an example of how the tensions between the individuals and cultures influence a migrant's ability to adapt or even enter a host culture.

Abandoned by both the U.S. and Mexican governments during the pandemic, fleeing refugees seeking safety were subjected to medical neglect and state-sanctioned violence. The Tijuana Municipal Police are notoriously corrupt. They shake down tourists for bribes, often work as enforcers for cartels, and exploit refugees as free labor. The Tijuana Municipal Police engage in stop-and-frisk procedures to establish the residency status of people living in Zona Norte, one of the poorest and most violent neighborhoods in Tijuana. The shakedown is simple: if you are unable to provide proof of citizenship, you may pay a bribe of around 500 pesos, be arrested and released on a $1,200 bail bond, or serve a 72-hour hold, which can be reduced by a few hours for doing janitorial work at the police department. Sometimes people taken for work don't ever return—they disappear as so many others do by the confluence of narcoterrorism and institutional corruption.

Under these conditions, potential asylees from Haiti and Central and South America find themselves unwanted, ineligible for asylum, and expendable. To survive, these people—mostly single mothers and young men—are forced to adopt behaviors and tactics that keep them alive but that also further alienate them from U.S. and Mexican culture. These tactics include learning how and when to bribe the police, engaging in survival sex, adopting a Mexican name and accent to avoid appearing out of place, and learning to navigate the close-knit politics of the sex and drug trade that are the economic pillars and major employers of Zona Norte Tijuana. Previous theories of assimilation would call the behaviors "maladaptive" and the people who practice them "functionally unfit." From the perspective of DAT, the behaviors adopted by the refugee community of Zona Norte can be read as effective, if unfortunately necessary, survival strategies that highlight the ingenuity and complexity of migrant agency in the face of horrific violence. Applying DAT to the lived experiences of people living in Zona Norte during the pandemic enabled an examination of the ways that policy and culture have dispossessed refugees of their fundamental rights, leading to conditions for human trafficking, exploitation, and disappearance. The theory also shows the complexity and ingenuity of migrants' agency as they find ways to survive and resist government and cartel violence. By applying DAT to migrant experiences during the COVID-19 pandemic, I was able to understand how and why migrants might choose to resist or subvert U.S. and Mexican law.

Continuing the Conversation

Chen and Lawless (2018) use DAT to push back against model minority discourse surrounding Asian Americans and extrapolate the notion of "micro/macro-adaptation" among three dynamics: negotiating foreign-female body politics, navigating paradoxes of adaptation, and deploying strategic ambiguity. This research advances DAT by providing an example of how the theory can be used to understand migrant subjectivity and the tactical and negotiated process of adaptation to a hostile cultural environment. Martinez (2017) explores depression and treatments among U.S.-born Mexican Americans using DAT and a culture-centered approach prioritizing *voz* and intersectionality, demonstrating the importance of making migrant agency and voice central in the understanding of the complex issues regarding immigrants' experience and treatment-seeking behaviors. Furthermore, the study highlights how racism, toxic masculinity, and a well-earned distrust of the U.S. medical establishment serve as barriers for immigrants seeking health care, demonstrating the value of attending to cultural and individual dialects in how they shape adaptive behaviors. In both studies, DAT facilitates understanding the complex interplay of migrant agency with racist nativism and how cultures may even actively inhibit healthy assimilation.

Despite the growing use of DAT in the field of interculture communication, there are still several parts of the theory that need to be tested and developed. The two dialectic tensions that structure DAT universality/specificity and individual/society require further investigation and testing. Of particular importance to the development of this theory will be research that explores how a culture might engage in practices that act violently towards migrants or inhibits their successful transition into a new culture. Doing so will be the first step to using DAT to create interventions in policy and practice that can address the trauma that is all too often part of intercultural transitions.

Summary

By developing a theory of the outlier, the particular, and the divergent, DAT theorizes migration as transformative for both the individual and the new culture. Identity and culture are dynamic and often contested; thus, intercultural scholars, whether they draw on quantitative, qualitative, or critical paradigms, must find ways to account for "the diversity of each immigrant and the unfettered potential for multiple, hybrid, fluid, and even contradictory experiences" (De La Garza & Ono, 2015, p. 280).

FOR FURTHER THOUGHT AND REFLECTION

1. Suppose you were assigned to help a new immigrant adapt to culture in the United States. What social, political, and cultural U.S. norms would you consider essential? Why? Can you envision ways that those norms might hinder or harm a new immigrant's ability to thrive?

2. What research projects or paradigms might be a good fit for this theory? Which approaches to the study of intercultural communication would not benefit from incorporating differential adaptation theory?

3. What parts of your home culture (language, gender performance, values, ideologies, etc.) would you be willing to give up to successfully integrate into a new culture? Why? What parts of your home culture would you be unwilling to surrender, despite conformity pressure? Why?

PART IV

Leadership and Organizations

L eadership communication and organizational communication are unique sub-disciplines of communication as they draw from *intra*personal, *inter*personal, and relational communication, yet they apply many of these ideas to an organizational context. Leadership communication focuses more on the dynamics between followers, employees, and decisions made on behalf of the organization's members and external stakeholders. Organizational communication is best explained as processes, channels, and forms of communication that occur within organizations, such as corporations, nonprofits, healthcare settings, and governmental bodies to function, grow, and contribute to their members and society. Much of previous research was skewed towards organizational climate, networks, performance feedback, message flow, profit, retention, and the like from a top-down and Westernized perspective, disregarding the agency, experiences, and influence of an organization's members from underrepresented communities.

As the times changed, so did the research focus of many leadership and organizational communication scholars to a more interpretive and critical approach that took into consideration organizational culture and critical notions of power, politics, agency, and identity. This change was necessary as Parker and Grimes (2009, p. 298) argue organizational and leadership theories tend to "discursively erase the racialised and colonising histories that connect them to white middle-class norms, values, and experiences, casting others as deficient, devalued, or non-existent." Thus, critical theorizing is applied as a liberating influence that disrupts the silence around racialized experiences and better accounts for the realities of all organizational members. In this introduction, first, we elaborate on four foundational theories to organizational communication: two micro level theories and two critically informed macro level theories. Next, we provide an overview of the three theoretical contributions and three storied reflections found in this section.

Existing Canonized Theories

Sensemaking and leader-member exchange are two micro-level organizational communication theories with an emphasis on the leadership-followership relationship. Sensemaking is the way people retrospectively assign meaning to events, experiences, decisions, actions, and choices and then becomes a springboard for future action (Weick et al., 2005). Sensemaking usually occurs continuously and beneath our conscious awareness, until uncertainty, ambiguity, and anxiety arises, then sensemaking slows down and becomes observable. At the micro level, this is an opportunity for leaders to step in and add meaning or frame the narrative in a way that helps followers reach anodyne (i.e., coping) and develop shared meanings or beliefs. Leader-member exchange (LMX) describes the close or distant relationships between the leader and their members (Graen & Uhl-Bien, 1995). Leaders tend to have two types of relationships: high LMX, which are relationships high in trust and obligation, or low LMX, which are relationships low in trust and obligation (Graen & Uhl-Bien, 1995). These high and low LMX relationships are determined by a process of role negotiation initiated by a leader offering bids (i.e., opportunities) to the members and evaluating their performance, then placing them either in the in-group (i.e., high LMX) or the out-group (i.e., low LMX). Sensemaking and LMX are both void of an explicit elaboration on how racial, cultural, and gendered identities can influence the susceptibility and outcomes of the theories.

Scholars have made significant contributions to how identity impacts organizational interactions and the leader-follower dynamic. Cultural approach to organizations and critical theory of communication in organizations are two organizational communication theories with a focus on macro-level organizational change that focuses on identities of the organization and its members. According to Geertz and Pacanowsky (1988), organizations are described as having their own corporate culture, consisting of the organization's image, character, and climate. This culture is learned through the telling of three types of stories: corporate (i.e., information from management to employees), personal, (i.e., personal accounts from employee to employee), and collegial (i.e., stories that employees tell about other employees). Taking a more explicit approach to marginalized identities in organizations is Deetz's critical theory of communication in organizations. At the heart of Deetz's theory (2005) is a focus on communication as a means of exerting control and power in decision making. Deetz contextualizes managerialism (e.g., leadership) as following a set of routine and systematic practices that value control over all other concerns, including those of their followers. Though Geertz, Pacanowsky, and Deetz take critical approaches and center culture in organizations, there is no explicit racial or ethnic focus in their theorizing.

Overview of Chapters

In Part IV, *Organizations and Leadership*, we continue with Geertz, Pacanowsky, and Deetz's critical approach to organizational communication and highlight two models and one theory that draw attention to leadership and organizational interactions that address issues of privilege, prototypes, exploitation, misrecognition of interests, and cultural exclusion. These contributions challenge the intertwined processes of capitalism and colonialism while acknowledging a new conceptualization of leadership-identity development and health-related interactions. No longer privileging the values of white culture as normative and universal, this section values unique standpoints, cultural traditions, and racialized experiences of marginalized people as positioned in the forefront of these theoretical frameworks that are situated in organizational contexts. In addition to our three theoretical contributions, we spotlight three storied reflections from new and tenured communication scholars. These vivid and engaging stories suggest that we are not alone in wanting and needing to see ourselves and our communities in leadership and organizational communication theorizing.

Chapter 11 answers the question "What does a leadership model that centers racial and ethnic identities as an important consideration look like?" Authors Jeanetta Sims and Ed Cunliff answer this question by proposing their four-faceted model of accelerating leader identity, which emphasizes the cultural selves of racial and ethnically diverse leaders. This model disrupts the narrow prototype of a U.S. leader as white, heterosexual, and male, and identifies the potential of a leader's identity as grounded from within based on one's dynamic racial and cultural characteristics. This disruption of the prototype is important because many leaders exhaust valuable time comparing and molding themselves into the prototypical leadership framework, instead of looking inward and becoming the leader that is unique to their own identities and experiences. In this way, the model is designed to assist leaders "in becoming more of who they are sooner and owning this identity for a very long time" (Sims et al., 2018, p. 194). Sims and Cunliff identify the four facets of the model as having a spirited sense of self (e.g., grounded, reflective), an in-process-oriented life (e.g., learner, engaged), a no-gritch mentality (e.g., steadfast, challenges), and a work-infused journey (e.g., meaning in work, sacrificial). As the four-faceted model grew out of the various divergent cultural experiences shared in semistructured interviews, in this chapter, Sims and Cunliff apply aspects of their model to written excerpts from those participants. Overall, Sims and Cunliff encourage a new prototype for leadership, one that is varied, culturally and racially informed, and not one-size-fits-all.

Chapter 12 is authored by Mohan Dutta, a world-renowned health communication scholar whose program of research is focused on culture-centered interventions in health communication contexts. Dutta's culture-centered approach (CCA) to health communication situates communities at the margins into the center of health-related interventions and community-led well-being. Giving a voice to the silenced, the CCA to health communication turns to health meanings at the intersections of culture and agency, both of which are traditionally erased from dominant approaches to healthcare and health communication. This chapter is organized into three main sections. In the first section, it situates the CCA in the critical tradition, interrogating how whiteness is used as a lens to conceptualize health and solutions to health—specifically, how individualism, cognitivism, and reductionism are strategies that engage in the erasure of contexts, collectives, cultures, and communities that constitute health. In the second section, Dutta describes the key theoretical tenets of the CCA, focusing on culture, structure, and agency, along with their interplays and communicative inequality as it pertains to representation, voice, and decision-making in health contexts. This is followed by the third section, an overview of research applications and a look at the future of the CCA in relation to socialist futures, antiracist interventions, and anticolonial imaginaries. In sum, Dutta's culture-centered approach to health communication attends to cultured, raced, classed, ability-based, and gendered processes of disenfranchisement and builds infrastructures to give voice to locally situated interpretations and solutions created by individuals and communities at the margins.

Elaine Hsieh authors the ideal Chapter 13 to follow Dutta's chapter 12. Hsieh brings us from the health communication and organizational level that Dutta elaborates on, broadly, to the specific interpersonal interactions in cross-cultural care. Hsieh's bilingual health communication (BHC) model centers on interpreter-mediated interactions in health contexts. Hsieh describes eurocentric approaches to health communication work as distance between the medical expert and the communities at the margins, as requiring interpreters to have a neutral, invisible, and passive presence in provider-patient interactions. The BHC model disrupts this approach and offers agency to negotiate and adapt the prescribed passive role and actively intervene in the content and process of provider-interpreter-patient interactions. In addition, Hsieh makes a great point about the underutilized professional interpreters due to availability and the reliance on a wide variety of nonprofessional interpreters (e.g., family interpreters and bilingual staff) and their limited language proficiency in cross-cultural care. Therefore, the BHC model poses and answers the question "How do different participants coordinate with each other during the communicative event of provider-patient interactions?" Within this answer, Hsieh elaborates on individual-level constructs of communicative goals, individual agency, system norms, quality and equality of care (QEC), and interpersonal-level constructs of trust, control, power. She also includes specific examples throughout the entire chapter to keep the reader engaged. In sum, the BHC model utilizes the individual interpreter's adaptability based on competing and/or emerging goals and Hsieh encourages these interpreter-mediated medical encounters to become more collaborative.

Overview of Storied Reflections

In addition to the main theoretical contributions, this section offers three storied reflections from Tianna Cobb, Scott Branton, and Wilfredo Alvarez. Cobb, a post-doctoral fellow at George Mason University, reflects on her years as a student and about how her identities as a Black woman who identifies as gay were underrepresented in classroom material. Yet, Cobb's vigor to take an active approach in combatting the standard of representation in curriculum began after having students of her own. Cobb realized that the ease in which she critiques theories (i.e., the leader-member-exchange theory) and filled the gaps in organizational communication literature with her and other marginalized identities became her greatest asset in forming her identity as a scholar activist to ensure *representation is coming*. Branton, a doctoral candidate at the University of Pennsylvania, reflects on *the push and pull of connection making* between himself and the material he engaged with in graduate school courses. Branton reflects on how communication theory can be applied to his experiences with social work and reflect his standpoint as a gay identifying, black, neurodiverse male. Branton passionately identifies his body as a "disruption" to predominantly white theorists and theorizing and acknowledges important Black, Indigenous, or People of Color (BIPOC) scholars in the organizational communication field that helped him realize he could find himself reflected back in scholarship. Wilfredo Alvarez, associate professor at Utica College, applies *Tus Zonas Erróneas*, the celebrated self-help book, to his experiences as an outsider and double outsider. Constantly asking and answering renditions of the question "What is wrong with me?" Alvarez views the academy as a place where he, a nonwhite Caribbean immigrant, does not belong. Eventually, through a path of discovery as told in his reflection, Alvarez finally received external affirmations that communicated that nothing is wrong with him—he is enough, just as he is.

CHAPTER 11

Four-Faceted Model of Accelerating Leader Identity

Jeanetta D. Sims

University of Central Oklahoma

Ed Cunliff

University of Central Oklahoma

The rapidly changing demographic composition worldwide calls into question the relevance of leadership models that historically have omitted ethnic and racial groups (Chin et al., 2018, p. xvii).

What does a leadership model that centers racial and ethnic identities as an important consideration look like? This chapter answers this question and addresses the need for leadership models, which embed the cultural selves of racial and ethnically diverse leaders. After introducing the four-faceted model of accelerating leader identity, we share the ways it guides professionals in developing an internal sense of identity emanating from the lived experiences of their cultural framework.

We begin with the origin of the four-faceted model, which probes leader identity by drawing from the intersection of three interdisciplinary bodies of literature—authentic leadership, relational dialectics, and organizational diversity. We continue by describing the key components of the model. Then, we share examples of personal leader identity reflections to demonstrate how the model has been applied in the development of future leaders. The chapter concludes with a discussion of the contributions of the model and areas for future research.

Inherent in cultural understanding is the notion of norms—that certain elements are normative and others lay outside of the norm. A full consideration of a culture must include considerations both inside and outside of those norms. This more holistic view of normative and non-normative is needed for an appreciation of the breadth of leadership inquiry. Currently, the vision of leaders is contained within a narrow, normative sphere. For example, U.S. leaders mirror our dominant population majority of white, heterosexual, Protestant males. Though more racial and ethnic minorities are entering leadership positions, the dominant coalition within U.S.-based organizations remains quite homogeneous (Chin & Trimble, 2015). As U.S. demographics shift, the focus on leadership too needs to shift from a very narrow orientation to a more co-cultural frame of reference. The changing contexts of the 21st century (Chin et al., 2018) signal the importance of our attention to not only diversity in the ranks of leadership but also in leadership models.

Leadership is "human communication which modifies the attitudes and behaviors of others in order to meet group goals and needs" (Hackman & Johnson, 1991, p. 11); leadership involves both individuals aspiring to lead and those inspired to follow. The four-faceted model of accelerating leader identity emerged from semistructured inteviews with racial and ethnically diverse leaders as well as their follower colleagues and mentees. The model is designed to assist leaders "in becoming more of who they are sooner and owning this identity for a very long time" (Sims et al., 2018, p. 194). The model helps leaders accelerate into their own leadership persona by looking inward, rather than attempting to mold themselves into some external framework. This internal sense of identity, called leader identity, also shapes leader behavior throughout challenges faced in their career. Leader identity can be accelerated in four areas that we call facets. While these facets are present across racial and ethnically diverse groups, they manifest themselves differently given the cultural background and stuational contexts of the leaders.

This section offered the model's development and how it emerged from probing leadership through the experiences of leaders with racial and ethnically diverse backgrounds. In this next section, we begin by summarizing the intellectual traditions that prompted the model's development.

Intellectual Tradition of the Four-Faceted Model of Accelerating Leader Identity

The four-faceted model of accelerating leader identity stems from a sociocultural theoretical lens and draws from three bodies of literature. *Authentic leadership* focuses the genesis of leader development on the selves of racial and ethnic leaders. *Relational dialectics* and *organizational diversity* account for the need to acknowledge complexity and depth when approaching leadership from racial and ethnic leader perspectives.

Authentic Leadership

Authentic leadership assumes leadership conversations begin internally and eventually lead to interactive processes. One of the salient features of the authentic leadership framework is its attention to both *intra*personal and *inter*personal perspectives. The intrapersonal view is consistent with the humanistic sense that leaders look inside and examine self as a foundation to their behavior in leadership roles. The interpersonal view acknowledges that leaders interact with and influence followers. Authentic leaders are those who lead with conviction and originality (Northouse, 2016).

George (2004) contributed greatly to the study of authentic leadership by offering the following five basic characteristics of authentic leaders: knowing purpose, strong values, trusting relationships, self-discipline, and acting from the heart. Though present, these characteristics as convictions of salient personal identity may be invisible to followers. Each of those characteristics is fundamental to the four-faceted model for those looking to grow their leadership. The understanding that leadership is less about self-promotion and more about serving beyond self is parallel to Greenleaf's servant leadership model (1977), which is also a leadership framework that influenced the creation of the four-faceted model.

Relational Dialectics

Relational dialectics offers an explanatory view of how the self is influenced by and influences the other through dialogue. A view of the other within this framework can be organizations, ideas, or people. Dialogue is to be interpreted as contradictions rather than casual conversations (Baxter & Montgomery, 1996). Examining the deep involvement of opposites and inconsistencies is integral to understanding relational dialectics. A view of "the 'both/and'-ness of relating" (p. 6) is also important.

Combined with authentic leadership and viewed through the lens of relational dialectics, leadership is not an end state to be obtained; instead, leadership involves a process where leaders negotiate a series of internal and external struggles between themselves and other people, ideas, and organizations. For example, Sims (2020) offers three dialectics (*included/excluded*; *certain/uncertain*; and *self- and other-weighted/ self- and other-liberated*) in describing an African American woman's administrative journey. Through relational dialectics, we can understand how experiences of racial and ethnically diverse leaders are riddled with inconsistencies and contradictions.

Organizational Diversity

Though numerous definitional approaches exist for organizational diversity, identity is at the heart of these definitions. Nkomo and Cox (1996) summarized diversity research orientations with a particular focus on the experiences of different identities in the workplace. Different identities are often based on characteristics like age, race, ethnicity, sex/ gender, religion, sexual orientation, physical ability, and other dimensions of self-identification. Identity is often influenced by social groups, and individuals may consider themselves to be similar or dissimilar to other identities. Focusing on identities as different and similar permits a both-and orientation (Allen, 2011), which is aligned more closely with relational dialectics.

Each of these theoretical traditions contributed to the need to probe leadership through a racially diverse and inclusive perspective. The four-faceted model of accelerating leader identity emerged from the lived experiences of culturally diverse leaders themselves. Examples of the array of racially diverse leader experiences include: cultural exclusion of women in tribal leadership, the importance of community and cultural paternal groups, and reconciliation of religious beliefs amid racial inequities. The four-faceted model grew out of the various divergent cultural experiences shared in the semistructured interviews.

Main Goals and Features of the Four-Faceted Model of Accelerating Leader Identity

Like Parker's (2005, p. 27) work, leadership can be regarded as a communicative process of mutual influence that needs to "theoretically accommodate the multicultural, racialized, often contradictory viewpoints and paradoxical situational challenges of 21st century organizations." Rather than seeking to distill the experiences of a particular cultural group (e.g., African American women executives), the four-faceted model begins first with leader identity and stimulates leader development through beginning with one's cultural self.

Leader identity is self-defined, varied, and complex (Chin & Trimble, 2015). Figure 11.1 illustrates our core assumptions of leader identity, which is viewed as the starting point of the leadership process. Communicative interactions exist between leaders and followers who are themselves social and cultural beings. Approaching leadership requires an examination of the self through leader identity. Both historical and current elements of identity must be accounted for in the leadership process.

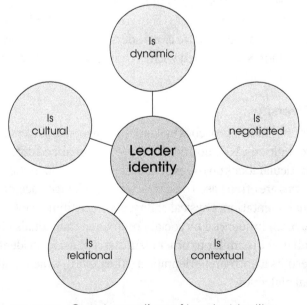

FIGURE 11.1 Core Assumptions of Leader Identity

1. *Leader identity is dynamic.* It is not static, nor permanently situated. Leader identity changes across the span of one's career, job duties, and life span.

2. *Leader identity is negotiated.* It is evaluated based on perceived expectations and obligations from the standpoints of self, and others. Leader identity is steeped in proclivities that constrain, compel, and inspire.

3. *Leader identity is contextual.* It is constrained not only by people but also by situations, environments, and institutions. Leader identity may manifest itself differently across a variety of contexts.

4. *Leader identity is relational.* It is communicatively constructed in connection with others. Leader identity is expressed with followers through verbal and nonverbal communication.

5. *Leader identity is cultural.* It is influenced by the most salient aspects of one's cultural background. Leader identity is shaped by racial, ethnic, religious, gendered, national, and other identities.

As explained in Sims et al. (2018), the four-faceted model of accelerating leader identity emerged from nearly 300 pages of transcript data analyzed using grounded theory. In general, the four-faceted model affirms that leaders are guided by an internal sense of identity, which develops and grows from their lived experiences. The four facets of the model are: a spirited sense of self, an in-process-oriented life, a no-gritch mentality, and a work-infused journey. Table 11.1 features a description of each facet along with key words relevant to the facet's meaning.

Facet One: A Spirited Sense of Self

The spirited sense of self is connected to George's (2004) work, where leaders are viewed as being guided by qualities of the heart. This internal orientation is a sense that comes from within. It is an ability to be unapologetically descriptive of oneself and one's lived experience, and it is not something that can be readily adopted from external sources. This facet manifests itself in a persistent self-confidence founded on self-reflection and discovery. Leaders find this through looking inward and being confronted with questions that only they can answer. Leaders are not willing to be pushed into others' misguided or undesirable portrayals of their efforts or identity.

TABLE 11.1 Four-Faceted Model for Accelerating Leader Identity (Sims et al., 2018)

Facet Name	Facet Description	Key Words Associated With Facet
A Spirited Sense of Self	Participants knew who they were, were content with themselves, and were grounded in an informal process of self-discovery from youth or adolescence	• Grounded • Reflective • Self-Discovery • Passionate
An In-Process-Oriented Life	Participants had a commitment to life-long learning rather than perfection and were more interested in being active, engaged, and in-process rather than achieving a destination	• Active • Learner • Engaged • Permanent-Beta
A No-Gritch Mentality	Participants sought opportunities rather than leadership and service rather than titles; they preferred challenges for growth and botched experiments for greater learning	• Steadfast • Challenges • Opportunities • Obstacle-Free
A Work-Infused Journey	Participants talked about their work more than their titles or their leadership; they were not workaholics, they were work-infused (meaning and purpose)	• Meaning in Work • Sacrificial • Deliberate • Articulation

Note: The term *gritch* was created for this model and refers to speech acts that include complaints, excuses, griping, blaming, or whining.

Facet Two: An In-Process-Oriented Life

An in-process-oriented life is connected to the internal view that a leader has of their efforts, which involves growing, pursuing, and moving. Life-long learning or perpetually developing is most closely aligned with this facet as the leaders display energy, agility, and adaptability in their movement. Similar to relational dialectics, this facet has no fixed goal that can be achieved or accomplished; instead, the orientation is focused on negotiating tensions while moving toward growth and progression goals that are more akin to milestones on a journey. Achievements and continual growth are blended and accommodate each other. Leaders exhibit an appreciation for the process and its essence rather than having a focus on the journey's end.

Facet Three: A No-Gritch Mentality

A no-gritch mentality refers to the leaders' view of challenges, failures, and obstacles. Leaders face setbacks without "gritch," which is a term created by the authors to describe speech acts that include griping, blaming, whining or making excuses. When leaders are presented with obstacles, their perspective on the difficulties overshadow the challenges themselves, which creates a flow that seems to carry the leaders around or through the obstacle. This facet acknowledges that leaders often reframe or sidestep challenges in order to persist more. Leaders seems to thrive by walking against a tide—the tide is there and is forceful, but the movement does not stop. Like the other facets, this mindset is cultivated from within.

Facet Four: A Work-Infused Journey

A work-infused journey acknowledges that meaningful work and personal sacrifices are associated with the journey, though the line that might divide work and play disappears. The boundaries of "after hours" and weekends are often blurred not in a compulsion but in a passion and appreciation for the work itself. For leaders, the work has a meaning that partners with the soul and interests of the individual. Some leaders might suggest this as a calling, while others deliberately articulate a devotion to their work. While the work may take time away from families or significant others, leaders view this as a simple limitation to the hours in a day rather than a negative notion that is regrettable. Leaders find meaning and purpose in their work.

The four facets represent an internal fortitude that is drawn from individuals rather than prescribed for individuals to fit. Through a process of self-appreciation, leaders can assess their position within each facet to accelerate their sense of leader identity using their own cultural framework. Starting with self and acknowledging the leader within is the accelerant. The model offers a new avenue for approaching leadership among racial and culturally diverse leaders beyond the prescriptive approaches present in the literature. Drawing from authentic leadership, relational dialectics, and organizational diversity, the four-faceted model provides a mechanism for self-discovery of the complexities and opposing tendencies often present in the leadership experiences of racial and ethnically diverse leaders.

Research and Practical Applications of the Four-Faceted Model of Accelerating Leader Identity

For racial and ethnically diverse professionals, the four-faceted model of accelerating leader identity provides an avenue that encourages and especially affirms their personal/cultural identity. Over the past four years, the model has been flexible in its adaptation for stimulating leader identity development among hundreds of students and professionals. Through assigned reflections, the model has been embedded in higher education instruction for Leadership and Organizational Communication (graduate education course), Business Leadership and Identity (undergraduate business course), Leadership Development (graduate MBA course), and Black Women in Leadership (undergraduate course) and is a required component in first-year experience courses. With professionals, the model has been a cornerstone of workshops for the Greenleaf Center for Servant Leadership and Higher Learning Commission conferences. Table 11.2 offers excerpts of written reflections where prompts associated with each facet were used to stimulate leader identity development.

TABLE 11.2 Application of the Four-Faceted Model in Leader Identity Development

Facet Name	Excerpts of Written Reflections From Students and Professionals Based on Facet-Associated Prompts
A Spirited Sense of Self	"My leadership … is based on inclusivity, equity, and service. I love to see everyone's ideas reflected and find ways to integrate them. … I know that I have a passion to fight for others who are sometimes overlooked or misrepresented." ~ *Ben* "A leadership selfie of me will have my arms extended and my hands open, reaching out to those in need. Providing any help that I can, while bending down to listen to what's on the hearts of people with empathy and respect." ~ *Sue* "I am most passionate about my family and career … I love children, and I love the law. The best way to fulfill my dream is to become a Child Advocate Attorney." ~ *Louisa*
An In-Process-Oriented Life	"I like to get feedback … of my program regularly from my subordinates, peers, and supervisors. I solicit feedback from the trainers on ways I can improve and things we can improve about the program." ~ *Terry* "Little did I know that [leadership] comes in different forms. … I've learned … to be comfortable with not knowing everything but having the right people around you to help you find the answers." ~ *Amir* "My leadership qualities are constantly under construction. I'm always looking for ways to motivate my students and myself." ~ *Roman*

(continued)

TABLE 11.2   Application of the Four-Faceted Model in Leader Identity Development

Facet Name	Excerpts of Written Reflections From Students and Professionals Based on Facet-Associated Prompts
A No-Gritch Mentality	"We greatly emphasize the need for integrity and not making excuses or blaming others for anything. We practice extreme ownership for our mistakes at work and readily fall on our sword to admit to any wrongdoings." ~ Jackie
	"I have faced many obstacles since returning back to school with a GED, and I graduate in May. I persist because I believe everyone that I come into contact with should feel love, appreciated, and supported." ~ Remy
	"I typically flourish in the face of misfortune. I credit my resilience to the many examples of strong women in my family. These women have served as living examples." ~ Shala
A Work-Infused Journey	"I build the future of our department, and I see the job as an awesome responsibility that I greatly enjoy." ~ Dan
	"One must love their job because there are lives at stake. We sacrifice our weekends and our own time. … Although this may sound heavy, I love my job and I love the impact it has on students' futures." ~ Lily
	"Although I do tend to work well past 40 hours per week and miss out on spending quality time with my [family], it is fully worth it to me." ~ Jeff

Note: Excerpts are taken from students' and professionals' written reflections following prompts completed for stimulating leader identity development. Pseudonyms are used to protect their identities and approval was secured prior to publication.

As demonstrated in the sample excerpts, the model uniquely enables leader identity development with racially diverse and inclusive leaders. The individuals need not engage in leader identity alignment with a set of external personality traits or characteristics; instead, through reflective prompts, the four facets permit leader identity clarification. Through the model, the breadth in scope and relevance of salient racial, ethnic, and cultural experiences can be illuminated rather than ignored or marginalized. The manifestation of salient aspects of the leader's identity emanates from within the leader.

Continuing the Conversation

The four-faceted model offers a new understanding of leaders. In particular, it is uniquely poised to reveal the selves of culturally diverse leaders. The model permits leaders to begin their leadership journeys from self-reflective spaces rather than from places that problematize their lack of alignment with a set of personality traits, with white male-dominated approaches, or with historical European American–culture leadership themes.

The four-faceted model was invited for a featured discussion in the International Leadership Association summer 2021 newsletter. Though first published in 2018 and applied in classes, workshops, and institutes, the heuristic promise is present but not yet fully realized. The four-faceted model lacks maturity in garnering community agreement from within the broader leadership landscape and communication discipline.

The four-faceted model is value-laden. It encourages that diverse leaders spend time first in self-discovery. Through the model, leaders are charged to reflect on how they remain actively engaged in learning, how they approach setbacks, and how they find meaning and purpose in their work.

The model's aesthetic appeal is affirming and aspirational, particularly as a framework for coaching racially and ethnically diverse leaders in leadership development. While leader examinations within each facet can be multistranded and complex, the model is parsimonious.

Though the four-faceted model lacks a robust reform of society and social change, it does have practical utility in corporations and organizational settings where needs are great to carve out space for the cultural selves of leaders amid organizational climates that may be exclusive or toxic.

Existing research on the four-faceted model has focused primarily on current and future professionals from racially and ethnically diverse backgrounds in academic, research, and higher education settings. The four-faceted model has implications for and may be applied to other areas of nonprofit and corporate settings. Future research can probe the facets through the lens of lower socioeconomic levels and intersectional identities. Also, future research can examine the extent to which the facets maintain cultural measurement equivalence beyond the racial and ethnic groups (e.g., African American, Native American, Asian American, and European American) included in past research.

Summary

This chapter offers a four-faceted model for accelerating leader identity, which draws from individuals' personal, cultural, and lived experiences. It may be considered an intrapersonal development process set within the individual's experience that has implications for interpersonal relations. It is a self-reflective leadership model that does not require the adaptation of an external list of characteristics and instead accelerates leader development by starting within.

FOR FURTHER THOUGHT AND REFLECTION

1. The four-faceted model is based on an understanding that there is first a leader within rather than outside of oneself. How do you think leader identity and leadership should be approached? How do you understand these concepts in relationship to your own cultural identity and leadership development?

2. Who are the leaders you know that are authentic? Who are those that appear to have embraced a façade? What differences do you see in regard to their effectiveness as leaders and communicators?

3. If you were to self-assess within the context of the four facets, what would be your strongest area? What would you see as areas for continued self-reflection?

4. How might the facets manifest themselves differently across contexts and across different racial, ethnic, and cultural groups?

STORIED REFLECTION
Representation Is Coming

Tianna L. Cobb
George Mason University

When I first began learning about theory, I did not pay much attention to whose lives they represented. As I read more, it became usual for me to insert [in addition to] and extend theories to represent my own life as a Black woman who identifies as gay. It was customary for me to accept "white" as the standard of representation within the classroom. I learned this much from grade school and my life experiences of being immersed in white spaces. Our education system trained me to accept what was and what others taught me ought to be. It was not until I began having students of my own that I took a more active approach to combat the "standard" in classroom material. I started looking more carefully at the knowledge I shared with my students and analyzed how I wanted to shape minds. This mindset bled into my identity as a scholar. It led me to develop courage and find my voice as a critical communication scholar to push back against the privileged nature of communication theory that further marginalized my identities.

When I first practiced thinking critically, it was not with the theories themselves but rather the studies that used them. My master's program trained me to identify gaps in the literature and critique our course readings. Identifying gaps came relatively easy for me in comparison to my peers. One day, one of my classmates approached me about this same experience in our offices and asked me why it was easier for me to identify gaps in our readings. I did not understand why it was more difficult for them to identify gaps or instances in which the findings would not be supported or representative. I then realized the studies themselves were more representative of my classmates' lives—not mine. Therefore, it was easy for me to identify and critique arguments because I was extending or filling the gaps with my own experiences. This practice drew me to notice a pattern within our course readings; almost all the participants within the studies were white. I began questioning why researchers did not get Black, Indigenous, or People of Color (BIPOC) representation in their participant pool. Then I realized that most of the researchers themselves, at least in the syllabi I was given, were white. This correlation reminded me of the "seat at the table" metaphor all over again. Well, I was about to earn my seat. Representation was going to come one way or another.

My first time critically challenging and exposing a communication theory's underlying privilege was during my first semester in my doctoral program. The leader-member exchange theory had become one of my favorites. I did appreciate the concept of the theory and how it somewhat included more than just the leader's perspective. What captured my interest the most was the applicability of the theory. The theory itself is prescriptive in that it identifies which behaviors would most likely lead to more desired outcomes for both organizational leaders and members. In my organizational communication course, I raised a concern that the theory did not consider agency on behalf of the organizational member. The theory assumed that all members wanted to be in the ingroup with their leaders when that may not be the case. My professor was intrigued that I noticed such a taken-for-granted assumption of this prominent theory. Honestly, that thought process was second nature to me. Being immersed in certain white spaces throughout my life, I had my fair share of moments when I needed to distance myself from leadership for my sanity and mental health. It was not due to ill intentions but instead to the expectation of me assuming such behaviors of "normalcy" when, in actuality, I was masking parts of myself to appease others.

At this point, I was comfortable identifying gaps in articles and extending theories to represent my culture. It was not until my third semester in my doctoral program that I became comfortable speaking for the importance of critical theories. This was challenging because, throughout the semester, I was arguing in opposition to my professor. Based on her arguments, she did not see the validity in critical theories. To me, critical theories were representative of my life and those I love. Critical theories exposed the problematic nature of current systems. Critical theories appeared to be the only frameworks in academia that fought for the rights of my people. Critical theories and theorists taught me that these gaps in theory do not have to exist. So, I earned my seat at the table. I continue to use my agentic power to find my place and voice as a scholar. Representation is going to come, one way or another.

CHAPTER 12

Culture-Centered Approach to Communicating Health

Mohan J. Dutta

Massey University

C hallenging the prevailing approaches to health communication theorizing that define health through the ideology of the colonizing white culture (predominantly in the United States), the culture-centered approach (CCA) to health communication situates health amidst the everyday meanings that individuals, households, and communities construct (Dutta, 2004). Attending to the raced, classed, gendered, and ability-based processes of disenfranchisement, the CCA builds registers for conceptualizing the health of individuals, households, and communities at the margins, voiced through locally situated interpretations. The health meanings draw from cultures, the matrices of values, beliefs, norms, habits, and rituals that are held in communities. At the same time, meanings are created through interactions, contributing to the fluidity of cultures. Health is situated in contextually situated interpretations of cultural interactions; this forms the basis for recognizing the active role that individuals, their families, and communities play in making sense of health and in negotiating health in their everyday lives. This capacity of individuals and communities to make sense of their everyday lived experiences, described as agency, is traditionally erased from dominant approaches to health communication. Whiteness, the cultural values of the dominant white culture, are established as universal, shaping theories that position themselves as health-promoting based on these culturally located white values.

The CCA seeks to intervene into this erasure through the creation of theoretical articulations that are built by communities voiced through their lived experiences, through their negotiations of health and through their struggles to secure health and well-being. As a meta-theory that is embedded in and emergent from lived experiences at the raced, classed, gendered margins of neocolonial structures, the CCA is committed to the practical politics of developing social change processes that challenge structures (Dutta, 2011, 2020). This chapter is organized into three key sections. In the first section, it situates the CCA in the critical tradition, interrogating hegemonic health communication theories. In the second section, I describe the key theoretical tenets of the CCA. This is followed by an overview of research applications. I wrap up by discussing some of the ongoing conversations in CCA scholarship.

Intellectual Tradition of Culture-Centered Approach to Communicating Health

Emergent from and located within the Cold War ideology of the United States invested in serving its capitalist and security interests, the dominant approach to health communication theorizes communication as a technology of social change, producing health behaviors in the target audience through the promotion of communication technologies (Dutta, 2008). This context that anchors health communication theorizing focuses on the creation of effective messages that would produce the desired effects on the target audience. Constituted broadly under the umbrella of health communication campaigns, theories focus on specifying the characteristics of effective messages. The underlying ideology of whiteness that privileges the values of white culture as universal shapes how health is conceptualized and the solutions to health that are proposed. Whiteness works through the active process of establishing the values of white culture as universal while simultaneously devaluing the knowledge systems of cultures and communities that are marked as lacking in health (Dutta, 2004). As an instrument of the colonial project, whiteness in health communication has historically constructed communities in colonized contexts and cultural values of enslaved peoples as in deficit, with the goal of health communication theorizing then to produce the necessary belief, attitude, and behavior change to promote health. The overarching values of individualism, cognitivism, and reductionism shape the dominant approach to health communication theory.

Individualism

Placed within the individual, health is conceptualized as a product of beliefs, attitudes, and behaviors (Dutta, 2004). The atomization of health, reducing it to the smallest components of human life, is central to the development of health-promoting solutions. The individualism of health communication theories shapes their treatment of the individual as the site of message targeting. Specific features attached to the individual are extracted, isolated, and categorized to shape the development of health messages. The turning of the individual as the unit of analysis then shapes how information around health is gathered in the form of data assembled, evaluated, and turned into policy. The lived experiences of colonized and enslaved peoples, seen through the lens of individualism, are constructed as primitive characteristics to be targeted through health communication messages. Consider, for instance, that the hegemonic literature on violence prevention, constituted in the ideology of individualism, projects Indigenous communities and Black peoples as deviant, perpetuating the colonial processes of oppression by upholding the racist prison industrial complex.

Cognitivism

Cognitivism refers to the privileging of belief as the basis for conceptualizing health behaviors and shaping behavior change campaigns of health communication. The definitions of what is rational are shaped by the overarching ideology of whiteness, with the conceptualization of health communication as delivering messages directed at changing the underlying beliefs of targeted communities. For instance, communities bearing disproportionate burdens of cancer risks are marked as needing health information on the benefits of eating five servings of fruits and vegetables (Dutta, 2008). Cognitivism conceptualizes behavior change as a linear progression from knowledge through attitudes to the formation of behavioral intentions to the adoption of the recommended behavior. The colonizing framework of cognitivism erases the emotions, feelings, experiences of trauma, and the contextually embedded struggles that are often the basis for negotiating health at the margins.

[handwritten margin notes: rationality is shaped by overarching ideology of whiteness]

[handwritten margin notes: health comm directed at changing underlying behaviors]

Reductionism

Tied to the individualism of the hegemonic approach to health communication, the whiteness in conceptualizing health and communication is reductionist. In other words, it turns the object of analysis (in this instance health and communication) to the smallest possible unit that can be isolated and placed under scrutiny. The reductionism of health communication perpetuates the values of a prevailing white culture, with its methods held up to erase contexts, collectives, and communities that constitute health. The reductionist approach holds up the capitalist conceptualization of health delivered through the market while simultaneously obfuscating the structures that fundamentally shape health at the margins. Therefore, African American communities negotiating racism and poverty are told to eat five servings of fruits and vegetables, while keeping intact the violent racism in U.S. society that fundamentally threatens African American health (Dutta, et al., 2017). Even as critiques of this reductionism of health communication have been offered, the concepts of culture and participation have been co-opted by dominant health communication approaches while simultaneously rendering invisible the contexts that shape the negotiations of health.

Main Goals and Features of Culture-Centered Approach to Communicating Health

The CCA conceptualizes health inequalities as products of a racist, capitalist, and colonial system that expels communities at the margins from their places of livelihood and simultaneously incorporates them as profitable resources. These twin forces of expulsion and exploitation produce unhealthy environments, health-threatening workplaces, and depleted spaces of living. In this backdrop, the CCA conceptualizes erasure, connecting structural inequalities (in the distribution of material resources) to communicative inequalities (in the distribution and ownership of communicative resources). These communicative resources extend beyond the resources of information technologies to resources for participation in decision-making processes, representation, and voice. Seeing health inequalities as reproduced through the erasure of the voices of the margins, the CCA seeks to co-create a practical theory of building registers for voice in communities at the margins through which they own the health solutions addressing their needs and build anchors to theorizing health and communication rooted in their lived realities. Culture-centered interventions, rooted in community voices, have been carried out across spaces in the Global South and the South in the North for almost two decades, offering examples of academic-community-activist relationships that build infrastructures for voices of the margins to articulate meanings of health and well-being, to build registers for changing the unequal structures based on these meanings, and to sustain spaces for the voices of the margins (Dutta, 2008, 2018; Dutta et al., 2019).

Culture-Structure-Agency

Culture, structure, and agency are the key tenets of the CCA, centering health meanings articulated in voice infrastructures amidst their interplays (Dutta, 2008). The turn to health meanings at the intersections of culture, structure, and agency shapes culture-centered interventions that are designed and owned by communities at the margins. The participation of communities at the margins foregrounds locally embedded meanings in co-creating solutions for achieving community-led well-being (Dutta & Thaker, 2020). Culture reflects "shared values, practices, and meanings that are negotiated in communities ... culture is both static and dynamic; it passes on values within a community and at the same time co-creates opportunities for transforming these values over time" (Dutta, 2018, p. 241). Situated with the local context of community life, it is dynamic, fluid, and heterogeneous, negotiated through the meanings that community members make of their lived experiences. Culture exists in the rhythms of daily lived experiences (Dutta, 2020). Culture is intertwined with the knowledge held by communities, embedded in community life, and the basis for everyday negotiations of health (Dutta, 2004).

The intertwined processes of capitalism and colonialism have historically erased cultural claims to health, pathologizing cultures of enslaved and colonized peoples while simultaneously erasing the cultural values of whiteness by treating them as universal

(Dutta, 2004; Elers et al., 2021). In hegemonic health communication theory and practice, culture is conceptualized as a characteristic of the other, driving health campaigns seeking to change culture or incorporating key cultural characteristics to enhance the message's effectiveness to the targeted community. Dutta (2020) explains that the configuring of cultural messages further erases the margins of the margins by co-opting experts or role models as the key creators, drivers, and disseminators. In so doing, the margins of the margins of communities are again positioned as problematic, passive recipients of communication targeted at them (Dutta, 2004). Interventions seek individual-level behavior change to produce healthy citizens, simultaneously erasing the structural contexts of capitalism-colonialism that threaten human health and well-being. Conversely, centering culture as a site for social justice communication, the CCA provides alternatives to a neoliberal, hegemonic paradigm by engaging and foregrounding community articulations of health meanings as the basis of creating meaningful social transformations (Dutta, 2008). In its explicit commitment to mobilizing culture as a site for resisting the interplays of colonialism and capitalism, the CCA challenges the essentialism of elite-driven culturalist logics that prop up culture to consolidate oppressive systems (Dutta, 2020).

Agency is the enactment of everyday choices and decisions by community members. It draws on cultural contexts and is expressed through the meanings that individuals, households, and communities make of their health and well-being (Dutta, 2020). The agency of community members at the "margins of the margins," expressed through their voices, offers discursive registers for dismantling the whiteness of the dominant approach to health communication (Dutta, 2020). Cultural meanings are reflected in the agentic expressions of community voices, serving as the basis for negotiating health amidst inequalities and for organizing in communities to transform unequal structures. Agency is both individual and collective, tied to the culture of a particular community and the basis for creating health solutions that challenge the dominant frames of health (Dutta, 2008). The turn to the expression of community voice as the basis of creating, leading, and owning community-led solutions disrupts the hegemonic power configurations in health communication, dismantling the entrenched power held by expert academics, nongovernmental organizations that assume the mantle of representing community voice, private corporations, and government sectors pushing top-down agendas of health.

Structure reflects the underlying political economy of capitalist-colonial societies, referring to the entrenched network of organizations that direct the flow of resources (Dutta, 2008). Access to health resources is controlled by the interplays of capitalism and colonialism. In health, some of these structures can be medical services, including provider-organized transportation services to health facilities, community health organizations, and spaces for health and exercise; shelters; food banks; collectives; communication forums, including media; government social service agencies; transnational corporations that engage in health promotion; and general global health organizations. For communities at the margins, health communication messaging and access to health resources are shaped by institutional whiteness, deepening the experiences of marginalization (Elers et al., 2021). In a culture-centered study, 36 in-depth interviews were conducted across locations amongst Māori, Pasifika, and Refugee communities to accentuate their voices about negotiating health amidst the COVID-19 lockdown in the settler colonial state of Aotearoa New Zealand during 2020 (Elers et al., 2021). This research draws attention to communities already facing multiple socioeconomic challenges of everyday living and survival and the ways in which these structural challenges created further hurdles to negotiate during COVID-19 lockdown. This study depicts the patterns of marginalization across diverse cultural communities produced by whiteness that constitutes the structure of Aotearoa. Similarly, the structures of extreme neoliberalism in Singapore, projected as a model of Asian development, work through the exploitation of low-wage migrant workers elsewhere in Asia, breeding and reproducing health risks. The COVID-19 outbreaks in dormitories housing low-wage migrant workers in Singapore are situated amidst these structures of exploitation (Dutta, 2020).

Communicative Inequality

Communicative inequality reflects the inequality in the distribution of communication resources (Dutta, 2020). Whereas the dominant approach to health communication conceptualizes inequalities in terms of distribution of capitalist technologies and health information disseminated top-down, the CCA conceptualizes communicative inequalities in the context of the resources of representation, voice, and decision-making in addition to information resources. Moreover, information resources are conceptualized in terms of resources about health preventive behaviors and information about structurally constituted health resources. Culture-centered studies of health at the margins have documented the erasure of the infrastructures for voices of communities at the margins. Take, for instance, one of the earliest applications of the CCA within the context of indigenous health among Santalis in the Jangalmahal area of West Bengal, India (Dutta, 2004). The voices of Santali participants situate their negotiations of health amidst the ongoing violence of erasure of their voices from hegemonic spaces of health communication. These erasures are tied to the everyday practices of development as capitalist expansion that threaten Indigenous livelihoods and continue to displace indigenous people from land. The inequality in distribution and ownership of communicative resources plays out in the policies and interventions that sustain and reproduce inequalities. Without their participation in communication infrastructures where their voices matter, communities at the margins are often erased from policy-based decisions (Dutta, 2008, 2011, 2020).

The privatization of health as a commodity mediated through the free market has been accompanied by the increasing uses of participation within dominant health communication projects, co-opting community participation into existing top-down, expert-driven agendas. Even as neoliberal health policies have worked alongside racist policies and practices to perpetuate the ongoing marginalization of the margins, the engagement industry has proliferated (Dutta, 2020). Critically interrogating participation as an instrument of the status quo lies at the heart of co-creating spaces of community democracy where the voices of those at the margins matter.

The work of building communicative infrastructures alongside communities at the margins serves as the basis for voicing health as the right to land, anchoring health in Indigenous claims to repatriation of land (Elers et al., 2020). Similarly, communication infrastructures co-created in African American communities amidst the racist structures of U.S. society attends to everyday racism as the key challenge to cardiovascular health (Dutta et al., 2017). Through their participation in processes of health advocacy, communities seek transformation in the racist social spaces of everyday life. In the negotiations of health amidst low-income households in Singapore, participants foreground the extreme inequalities in Singapore, their challenges with hunger, and hunger as the axis to meanings of health (Tan et al., 2017). From these experiences of hunger and lack of adequate economic resources, an advisory group of households in poverty co-create the "Singaporeans left behind" campaign (Dutta et. al., 2019).

Research and Practical Applications of Culture-Centered Approach to Communicating Health

The decolonizing framework of the CCA, rooted in community voice, reimagines the nature of work performed by the health communicator, shifting this work from one of designing effective messages targeted at communities to one of working alongside communities at the margins to agitate for transformation of racist, colonial, and capitalist structures. The question of research applications therefore turns toward health communication as activism, as crafting authentic friendships with communities at the margins in seeking to transform structures. Two concepts, the body on the line and solidarities, offer conceptual anchors to thinking through health communication methods.

The turn to the structural contexts of health reorganizes the nature of health communication, turning the work of health communicators to challenging structures (Dutta et. al., 2019). Placing our bodies as academics and practitioners of health communication, located in structures of privilege, on the line translates into the work of locating the body amidst struggles for social change. For instance, amidst state repression and tactics of stigmatization to delegitimize the work of the Center for Culture-Centered Approach to Research and Evaluation (CARE) in Singapore, the organizing work of researchers turned to working alongside activists to build public registers for making visible the oppressive practices perpetuated by the state (Dutta et. al., 2019).

The colonizing approaches to health communication scholarship work through the production of distance between the academic expert and the communities at the margins. Even as health communication scholarship discusses health disparities, it does so in a disengaged form, often removed from the work necessary to dismantle the unequal structures. The concept of "body on the line" makes visible the risks that are embodied in the labor of seeking to bring about changes on racist, capitalist, and colonial structures.

For instance, in the placing of the "body on the line" amidst the struggles of low-wage migrant workers, the authoritarian structures of the state that work alongside the interests of capital must be questioned. Agitating to bring about changes to these structures places the body amidst worker struggles. Contrast this to disengaged theorizing on migration and health that produces theoretical articles on the struggles of the low-wage migrant workers without ever stepping into the struggle that is necessary to address the structural contexts of migrant health. As structures respond to the struggles for voice through surveillance, threats of incarceration, stigmatization, and fabrications, commitment emerges as the vital basis for the ongoing work of health communication, turned into ongoing labor of co-creating infrastructures for community voices.

As such, creating solidarities with communities at the "margins of the margins" reworks the role of the health communicator, from one delivering top-down solutions to communities to one working alongside communities in their struggles against hegemonic structures. The nature of solidarity calls for the health communicator to walk alongside communities in their struggles against colonialism, racism, and capitalism. To walk alongside is to craft friendships that are rooted in authenticity and committed to the struggles for voice.

Continuing the Conversation

The frontiers of the CCA explore the intersections of socialism, antiracism, and decolonization as the basis for securing the health and well-being of communities at the "margins of the margins" across the globe.

Socialist Futures

The insistence among voices at the "margins of the margins" that health inequalities are shaped by the neoliberal political economy creates the communicative register for the agentic work of building socialist futures (Dutta, 2020). These socialist futures are organized through the foregrounding of health as a universal human right, placing it in the realm of the collective commons held by communities. For instance, in their voicing of their health challenges amidst the COVID-19 outbreaks in dormitories housing low-wage migrant workers in Singapore, the workers foreground their universal labor rights that form the basis for laying claims to health. Collective organizing in the form of labor unions, emergent from the voices of precarious migrant workers who have migrated from different parts of Asia to Singapore, challenge the hegemonic cultural narrative of "Asian values" that is deployed to attack labor organizing in the authoritarian capitalist state. In turn, narratives of labor organizing from spaces of the Global South across Asia foreground socialist possibilities rooted in the transformation of structures, ensuring the rights of workers to the fundamental conditions of safe workplaces, decent housing spaces, and access to good quality food. The emergent culture-centered activist intervention created and owned by the workers, "respect our food rights," challenges the neoliberal ideology of labor organizing in Singapore that deny the fundamental rights to organizing among migrant workers (Dutta et. al., 2019).

Antiracist Interventions

The co-creation of voice infrastructures at the "margins of the margins" builds on the recognition that racism underlies the large-scale health disparities we witness across the globe. The devaluing of the right to health of Black, Indigenous, and peoples of color is shaped by the ongoing discursive construction of communities as deviant (Dutta, 2008). Antiracist health interventions therefore make visible the racism of whiteness that perpetuates the processes of devaluing cultures (Dutta, 2004). Vital to this confrontation of racism is the dismantling of the narratives and rules of civility established by the structures of whiteness (Dutta et al., 2017). Simultaneously, building solidarities with activists and social movements seeking to dismantle racism is recognized as the work of health communication scholars and practitioners.

Anticolonial Imaginaries

That colonialism as the theft of Indigenous land is the fundamental threat to human health and well-being serves as the basis for anticolonial imaginations (Dutta, 2020). Health communication as anticolonialism is actively placed amidst the struggles for Indigenous land rights and sovereignty. That decolonizing health communication is about land rights translates into the organizing work with Indigenous communities on re-turning Indigenous land and on retaining sovereignty over Indigenous land. Health communication as anticolonialism resists the frontiers of neoliberal extraction across the globe.

Summary

In conclusion, the CCA foregrounds the role of voice infrastructures at the "margins of the margins" as the basis of addressing health disparities. That communicative inequalities are intertwined with structural inequalities forms the basis for building health communication as advocacy and activism directed at dismantling colonialism, racism, and capitalism as organizing features of global societies.

FOR FURTHER THOUGHT AND REFLECTION

1. Reflect on your own health experiences. Can you identify examples where your interactions with medical professionals were based on individualism, cognitivism, and reductionism?

2. Select a health-related issue that has gained media attention recently (e.g., Black women's maternal health) and critically analyze it through the concepts of culture, agency, and structure.

3. Can you identify threats to human health that are informed by racist, classed, gendered, and ability-based disenfranchisement? How might some of these problematic issues be dismantled through culturally centered health communication?

4. What are the ways in which the culture-centered approach is useful in reshaping your understanding of health communication and health disparities? What are some examples of how you might put your "body on the line" to confront problematic interactions, policies, and health-related messages?

STORIED REFLECTION
The Push and Pull of Connection Making

Scott E. Branton
University of Missouri

One of the reasons I pursued a second graduate degree in organizational communication was to gain a stronger theoretical background that coincided with the applied nature of social work. However, my motivations shifted after my first semester in graduate school where I would describe my experience with communication theory as one constituted by tensions. During my second semester, one of my favorite classes—Democracy, Power, and Voice—opened my eyes to the communicative processes that enable and constrain organizing. After learning about strategic ambiguity and concertive control, I realized it explained so much about what I had experienced in social work. At the same time, it left out so much. I remember thinking, *what is missing here? How do differences such as race or sexuality affect these processes?* For a field that is uniquely concerned with voice, there seemed to be very little attention outside of gender. As such, I sought to change that.

For the sake of standpoint, I identify as gay, black, neurodiverse, and male. Unsurprisingly, I rarely found my experiences located in theories and concepts that I was reading. When I did, it was merely a mentioning of those experiences. In fact, it wasn't until I was writing my thesis that I was finally exposed to organizational Black, Indigenous, or People of Color (BIPOC) scholars such as Brenda J. Allen, Diane A. Forbes, Patricia Parker, and Dawna Ballard. I distinctly remember reading Allen's (1996) article exposing the neutrality within Jablin's model of organizational socialization. *Why had I not read this in my courses? Why had connections to these scholars been left out of my experiences?* These thoughts eventually led me to my thesis, which centered on the tensions and contradictions that diverse faculty experienced with diversity communication. It was here that I learned that I was not alone and that this tension would always exist.

When I first entered my doctoral program, I remember telling my advisor that I wanted to do a piece on the push and pull of whiteness. She said, "I think that's a great idea!" It never materialized. I found myself feeling increasingly apprehensive. I was falling back into the traps of normativity and succumbing to the expectations of being one of the few people who looked like me in organizational communication. After reflecting on this, I believe this apprehension stemmed from the internalized stigma associated with studying race, diversity, and difference, or that I was *expected* to study these areas. I felt the tension between addressing these questions around race and sexuality and the desire to prove to myself and to others that I was intelligent, that I understood the work of scholars like Weick, Giddens, Mumby, and Cooren, and that I studied more than just *difference*. For example, in my communication theory course, I turned down the opportunity to read and present on Cornel West's (2001) *Race Matters*. Instead, I read Anthony Giddens's (1984) *The Constitution of Society* because it was more closely linked to organizing but also because it helped me fit in. I firmly believe that imposter syndrome is a product of normative practices of whiteness, and its effects were acutely felt.

Flash forward, during my comprehensive exams oral defense, I was asked what I would say to those who might ask about the tension from using predominantly white theorists such as Barad and Derrida to study diversity and difference in organizing. And I couldn't deny it. It was palpable. I took a deep breath and said, "That is an ongoing tension. ... However, my body in and of itself is a disruption, based on the fact that I was asked this question."

Now, as a fourth-year doctoral candidate, I'm in the midst of writing my dissertation. I've embraced the tensions that accompany BIPOC and queer scholars in organizational communication. I've also given myself grace. I've connected more with myself, with BIPOC and queer scholars like Cruz, Gist-Mackey, Compton, and McDonald. I've also recognized that learning and unlearning is a mutual process of possibility. Now my efforts are centered on creating more equitable encounters and more connections. I've learned that tensions are merely the push and pull of the relations and connections that constitute everyday life. That tension is a sign there is much work to be done in our field, and we should be doing that work *together*. To quote my mentor, while our journey is our *own*, we are not *alone*.

CHAPTER 13

Bilingual Health Communication Model

Elaine Hsieh

University of Oklahoma

T he bilingual health communication (BHC) model is a communicative model
that explains how interpersonal dynamics can shape the process and content
of interpreter-mediated interactions in cross-cultural care (Hsieh, 2016). The BHC
model views interpreter-mediated interactions as a socially constructed, goal-driven
communicative activity that requires multiparty coordination on the meanings and
processes of healthcare delivery. I use the term *multiparty* (as opposed to *triadic*)
to highlight that interpreter-mediated medical encounters may include other participants (e.g., nurses and family members) in addition to providers, patients, and
interpreters. By adopting heuristic and ecological approaches to communication, the
BHC model recognizes that when patients and their providers do not share the same
language, their communicative challenges are not limited to language barriers but
also include differences in social norms, cultural knowledge, and system-level infrastructures. The BHC model argues that individuals' ability to negotiate, coordinate,
and collaborate with one another to achieve mutually agreeable solutions presents
the best opportunities to achieve quality and equality of care.

Intellectual Tradition of the
Bilingual Health Communication Model

When providers and patients do not share the same language, language brokers
often are viewed as the standard solution to address communicative challenges.
Although translators and interpreters are both language brokers, they work in different domains. Translators primarily work with texts; in contrast, interpreters

transfer oral or signed information from one language to another (e.g., from Chinese or American Sign Language to English). The BHC model centers on interpreter-mediated interactions in health contexts.

The literature, however, suggests two puzzles. First, healthcare interpreters often deviate from the interpreter-as-conduit model, a default role prescribed by interpreters' codes of ethics (Hsieh, 2016). By requiring interpreters to adopt a neutral, faithful, and passive presence in provider-patient interactions, the conduit model casts interpreters as invisible linguistic machines that transfer information from one language to another. However, despite their training, professional interpreters are found to regularly deviate from the prescribed passive role and actively intervene in the content and process of provider-patient interactions. Second, despite state mandates for and availability of professional interpreters, providers consistently underutilize professional interpreters (e.g., on-site interpreters and telephone interpreters) and rely on a wide variety of non-professional interpreters (e.g., family interpreters and bilingual staff) and their limited language proficiency in cross-cultural care (Hsieh, 2016).

The BHC model addresses these two puzzles by adopting a normative approach to theory development. Goldsmith (2001, p. 530) explained,

> A normative theory poses questions such as the following: When a social actor wishes to accomplish some purpose in a particular kind of social context, what are the constraints to accomplishing that purpose, what are the discursive resources that are available for addressing those constraints, and what are the evaluative criteria by which the effectiveness and appropriateness of the actor's efforts may be judged?

The BHC model is a theoretical account designed to predict and explain the meanings and evaluations of communicative responses during interpreter-mediated medical encounters. Rather than focusing on the accuracy and fidelity of interpreted texts or interpreter behaviors, the BHC model asks, "How do different participants coordinate with each other during the communicative event of provider-patient interactions?" By assuming individuals coordinate their competing goals through communicative practices, the BHC model argues that certain practices can be more effective and appropriate than others due to the unique values and preferences within specific contexts, including clinical contexts (e.g., end-of-life care), sociocultural contexts (e.g., organizational hierarchy and cultural preferences), and sociopolitical environments (e.g., attitudes toward noncitizens in the host society).

Following the traditions of dialectic theorists (e.g., Bakhtin, 1981), the BHC model conceptualizes interpreter-mediated medical encounters within the contexts of potentially conflicting goals and the dilemmas these goals can create. By recognizing that each participant in an interpreter-mediated encounter may have distinct goals regarding tasks, identity, and relationships and that these goals are often (a) implicitly coordinated between participants and (b) mediated by an interpreter, the BHC model explores situations in which the tensions between individuals' management of these goals are high to understand how communication serves as a way to manage these competing goals.

This line of questioning presents two major shifts in research focus, moving away from the text-oriented, interpreter-centered analysis to an investigation of multiparty interactions in cross-cultural care. The first shift is to focus attention not simply on the frequency of individual communicative behaviors (e.g., interpreter alterations and mistakes) but also on the meanings of such practices. The end goal of a normative approach is to account for judgments that some communicative practices in interpreter-mediated medical encounters are "better" than others. The second shift in research focus is to move from a linear, positivistic view in prescribing appropriate behaviors in interpreter-mediated medical encounters to an interpretive, heuristic approach to predict and explain evaluations of behaviors as more or less appropriate and effective.

The BHC model does not aim to define, identify, or regulate the behavior that is deemed appropriate or effective in a given provider-patient interaction in a top-down manner. Rather, the BHC model explains why certain behaviors are evaluated more favorably than others by examining how well these practices adapt to the potentially conflicting values emerged in provider-patient interactions.

Main Goals and Features of the Bilingual Health Communication Model

By adopting a heuristic approach, the BHC model conceptualizes interpreter-mediated interactions as an interactive, goal-oriented communicative activity that is situated in the larger communicative event of cross-cultural care (for more details, see Hsieh, 2016). The next sections elaborate on the individual-level and interpersonal-level constructs of the BHC model, followed by the propositions of the model.

The Individual-Level Constructs

Individual-level constructs are factors that shape individual behaviors and evaluations of the interpreter-mediated medical encounter. The four individual-level constructs under the BHC model are: communicative goals, individual agency, system norms, and quality and equality of care (QEC; see Figure 13.1). All four constructs are applicable to all participants.

COMMUNICATIVE GOALS

All participants in interpreter-mediated interactions, including the interpreter, have communicative goals. The communicative goals may be inherent in the communicative activity but can also emerge during the dynamic discursive process. Although individuals in interpreter-mediated interactions may share some goals (e.g., improving a patient's health), they also have unique individual goals. For example, providers may hold specific interpersonal goals (e.g., developing trust and rapport) in addition

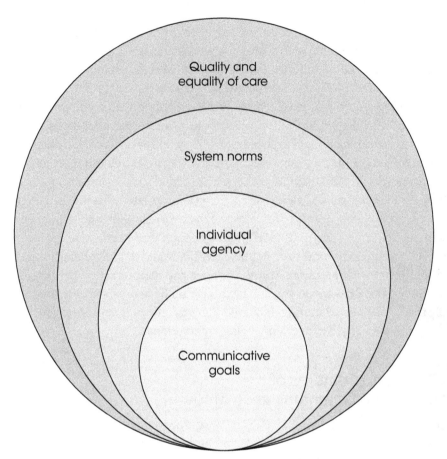

FIGURE 13.1 Individual-Level Constructs Within the Bilingual Health Communication Model

to their therapeutic goals. Individuals' multiple goals may not be compatible with each other or with others' goals. For example, patients may wish to receive Western biomedical care without giving up their cultural health practices (e.g., taking herbal medicine). Alternatively, providers may prefer interpreters who adopt an invisible role to facilitate provider-patient bonding, but interpreters may recognize that they can significantly improve the quality of care if they interject their knowledge and experience to facilitate provider-patient communication (Hassan & Blackwood, 2021).

An individual's ability to fulfill their communicative goals may be dependent on their and others' communicative competence as well as other contextual factors during the communicative event. For example, an interpreter who believes that the quality of interpreter-mediated communication is dependent on a passive, neutral conduit interpreting style may feel frustrated when a provider lacks sufficient intercultural competence to "ask the right question" (Hsieh, 2006, p. 724). When a provider responds to a Jehovah's Witness's refusal of blood transfusion by saying, "When the time comes, if the patient will die if he does not receive the transfusion, *we are not going to allow it and we are going to do it anyway. But you tell them that's okay,"* an interpreter is put in an impossible position to honor provider-interpreter trust without compromising patient autonomy and informed decision-making (Hsieh, 2006, p. 723). Alternatively, interpreters may alter others' narratives to provide culturally appropriate empathic communication, offer topics for information-seeking, and facilitate understanding (Hsieh, 2016). From these perspectives, interpreters' alterations to others' narratives are not mistakes but purposeful activities to achieve specific goals.

INDIVIDUAL AGENCY

Individual agency is a necessary condition for individuals involved in a medical encounter to pursue their communicative goals. From an institutional perspective, individual agency can be shaped by power structures, institutional hierarchy, access to resources, and professionalism. For example, physicians are likely to have more individual agency than nurses because they are the head of a healthcare team, imbued with higher institutional power. In contrast, compared to nurses, interpreters may have even less individual agency as they do not always have an institutionalized office (e.g., interpreter services), can be outsourced to external agencies, or are considered to be low-priority workers. As a result, physicians are likely to exert their own communicative goals over those of an interpreter when their goals conflict with one another. On the other hand, because interpreters are often trained to assume a neutral, passive presence in provider-patient interactions, an interpreter may actively refrain from intervening in the medical discourse even when they have observed problematic interactions (Hsieh, 2008).

At an individual level, individual agency can also be derived through individuals' educational background, self-efficacy skills, communicative competence, emotional status, and motivational relevance. For example, a family interpreter who also serves as the primary caregiver is motivated to ensure the patient gets quality care and may be more likely to intervene in the provider-patient communication and exert their communicative goals than a telephone interpreter at a remote location. At an interpersonal level, individual agency can be shaped through interpersonal relationships, social obligations, and interactional dynamics. For example, a provider may feel reluctant to rely on a family interpreter when working with a new patient with advanced cancer due to concerns about the quality of interpreting. However, the same provider may feel comfortable relying on a family interpreter in a simple follow-up visit with a long-time patient with arthritis. Or a provider may feel pressured to use a family interpreter because the patient shows extreme anxiety in a new environment and resists sharing his/her medical information with a professional interpreter who belongs to the same small immigrant community as the patient. Finally, at a system level, individual agency can be influenced by cultural norms and social expectations. For example, in cultures that adopt the family-centered model (i.e., medical decisions are jointly determined by the patient and her support network) rather than the patient autonomy model (i.e., medical decisions are made solely by the patient), a patient may purposefully rely on supportive others "for information-seeking and health decision-making as these actions are essential to their understanding, performance, and fulfillment of their social roles" (Hsieh & Kramer, 2021, p. 178). In short, individual agency is not just an inherent or fixed ability that a human agent holds but is also a quality that can be interactively negotiated and socially enacted.

SYSTEM NORMS

According to the BHC model, the system includes social systems and cultures in which there are specific norms, values, and worldviews that are imposed upon individuals. Individuals interpret meaning through the system to which they subscribe. For example, providers' understanding of illness is based on the culture of medicine, which may conflict with a patient's cultural illness ideology (e.g., an illness caused by spirits stealing one's souls). Because system norms guide the behaviors of individuals within the system, individuals' behaviors are always coherent and consistent within the meaning structure of the system. However, because individuals in cross-cultural care are not necessarily regulated by the same systems and the systems involved may not be compatible with each other, individuals may struggle to (a) identify the systems at play during a medical encounter and (b) prioritize and negotiate the systems that give meaning to the current interaction. For example, patients may choose to ignore a provider's treatment recommendation if they believe the provider has failed to provide an accurate diagnosis. Just as a U.S. patient may scoff at a shaman's effort to dispel an evil spirit, a Hmong parent who believes that his child's epilepsy is caused by a lost soul is unlikely to accept a U.S. physician's explanation that the illness is caused by an electrical storm in the brain (Fadiman, 1997). However, in the United States, providers can contact child protective services and remove a pediatric patient if they suspect that the parent has endangered the child by providing substandard care (Fadiman, 1997). In other words, not all systems are of equal footing.

The identification and prioritization of systems may prompt individuals to ignore or overrule other participants' needs and preferences. An interpreter may choose to editorialize other participants' narratives if they feel obligated to act as institutional gatekeepers to conserve limited resources, moral mediators to ensure the quality of care, or patients' health literacy guardians to avoid ill-informed decision making (Hsieh, 2016). By aligning themselves with a system of higher power/value (e.g., moral values and ethical standards), those with a lower institutional ranking (e.g., nurses and interpreter) may feel legitimized to adopt behaviors that override the values of other systems (e.g., organizational guidelines) or attitudes of superior others (e.g., physicians). Miscommunication due to incompatibilities between systems can result in problematic outcomes, including intense conflicts.

QUALITY AND EQUALITY OF CARE (QEC)

QEC is the overarching value of the BHC model—an all-encompassing value that integrates differences between systems, providing an ultimate value that guides the interpretation of competing systems in cross-cultural care. Even though QEC cannot escape the influences of (cultural) systems, individuals within different systems can learn to recognize and acknowledge its transcending values. For example, a provider can recognize and respect a parent's desire to provide the best care for a child patient, despite their disagreement on the treatment procedures. Similarly, interpreters can educate providers, patients, and their family members about the cultural differences in the meanings and functions of truth-telling in end-of-life care, allowing all participants to become aware of other participants' legal and social obligations.

The BHC model argues that individuals from different (cultural) systems can generate an integrated value of QEC. As such, the BHC model adopts the integral fusion approach delineated by Hsieh and Kramer (2021) as parties of a communicative event resolve potential differences and conflicts through developing mutually agreeable consensus and solutions. Within the integrated value meta-system, values within different systems (from the participants) are not always consistent or compatible with each other. Thus, QEC is neither a fixed nor universal value. Rather, QEC is always contextually situated, interactionally managed, and locally defined in the communicative process. It allows individuals with competing system norms to acknowledge others' perspectives and forces all participants to subject themselves to the meta-value of quality of care that is co-constructed by all involved in the medical encounter. Such an approach also echoes the argument that interpreters' and providers' practices should be guided by valued principles situated in interactional contexts, rather than a set of predetermined, context-free rules.

All participants collaborate to develop a prioritized list of diverse values, accessing resources to strengthen their claim and control over the definition of QEC. For example, a U.S. physician may adopt different disclosure strategies for a poor prognosis with a German patient versus a Japanese patient in response to differences in the patient's cultural norms. In addition, a U.S. physician may have different communicative patterns when talking to a Japanese patient who has lived in the United States for decades, a German exchange student on a summer program, or a Syrian refugee who recently arrived in the United States out of fear of genocidal threats. Differences in providers' communicative behaviors are not causes for inequality in healthcare delivery (i.e., treating everyone the same does not equate to quality care). Rather, a physician's ability to understand, empathize, adapt, and respond to a patient's unique needs and expectations can give the provider more resources to provide QEC. This requires a provider to be mindful of the specific criteria and contexts that shape a patient's understanding of QEC.

The Interpersonal-Level Constructs

While individual-level constructs shape individual behaviors and evaluations of interpreter-mediated medical encounters, interpersonal-level constructs delineate the dimensions through which these individual-level constructs operate.

TRUST-CONTROL-POWER

As a theoretical dimension, trust-control-power shapes how participants negotiate the various individual-level constructs with one another, reflecting individuals' efforts and competition in defining their interactional (and professional) boundaries. This can be particularly tricky in cross-cultural care, as the boundaries of medicine, language, and culture are often overlapping and blurred (Hsieh, 2010). In addition, the three components (i.e., trust, control, and power) are interdependent and intertwined with each other. For example, as an interpreter develops more trust with the provider, the interpreter will have more power to control the process and content of provider-patient interactions. On the other hand, a provider who insists on maintaining absolute control over the interpreter-mediated interaction can develop a utilitarian view of the interpreter's role and function in which even the interpreter's interpersonal care (e.g., emotional support) is viewed as a tool for the provider's therapeutic objectives (Hsieh & Kramer, 2021). In other words, even interpreters' communicative goals are subject to providers' control.

TEMPORAL DIMENSION

Time is an important dimension in any system. Most systems are open systems that develop adaptive changes in response to outside influences as well as internal tensions. Because interpreter-mediated provider-patient interactions involve several different systems, each of which entails its own unique values and norms, the participants are likely to face tensions, challenges, and conflicts due to their diverse systems, including practices and values. However, time as a dimension makes integration of diverging systems possible at individual, organizational, and even cultural levels.

The Propositions of the BHC Model

Based on the individual- and interpersonal-levels constructs proposed in the BHC model, I offer the following general propositions that guide the understanding and interpretation of interpreter-mediated medical encounters:

1. Successful BHC is dependent on individuals' ability and agency to negotiate and adapt to competing and/or emerging goals. Moving away from the focus on interpreter performances, this proposition views interpreter-mediated medical encounters as a collaborative achievement among all participants.

2. The desired interpreting style is dependent on contexts. Rather than adopting a positivist stance on pursuing the ideal interpretation through equivalences between two languages, the BHC model acknowledges that contexts are essential in participants' understanding and preference of interpreting performances. The contexts include but are not limited to clinical, interpersonal, and sociocultural contexts.

3. Evaluation of the appropriateness and effectiveness of interpreters' interpreting strategies requires consideration of the corresponding short-term and long-term

impacts. One strategy may have desirable short-term impacts in clinical care but problematic consequences for long-term provider-patient trust.

Continuing the Conversation

As a normative model, the BHC model provides a basis for recommendations about how communicators can achieve desirable outcomes. Thus, the BHC model is applied with a focus on problem-solving in real healthcare settings. In language-concordant provider-patient interactions, desirable outcomes are not necessarily predetermined or universal for all patients. Rather, desirable outcomes are emergently negotiated and continually (re)evaluated during the evolving, dynamic, and emergent process of a patient's illness event. Similarly, in interpreter-mediated medical encounters, desirable outcomes are not fixed targets to be achieved but are socially constructed through meaningful interactions among all participants. By recognizing that the communicative process, the meaning of an illness event, and even the quality of care are socially constructed, the BHC model provides multiple opportunities and entry points for theory development and practice implications.

A challenge faced by a normative model is that it is often regulated by sociocultural norms. As such, it can be vulnerable to the social injustice and inequality that are embedded in the social norms of a particular community, time, or place. Nevertheless, a unique aspect of the BHC model is its recognition of interpreters' agency and responsibility in addressing social injustice and protecting patients' voices and perspectives. Such an attitude has been reflected in the current literature, which recognizes the needs and values for interpreters to serve as patient advocates and system agents. In other words, interpreters are expected not to blindly reinforce the existing unbalanced or unjust process of provider-patient communication. The BHC model expects a skillful interpreter to have high individual agency in providing all participants with equal access to and effectiveness of clinical and interpersonal care.

Some may argue that conceptualizing interpreters as social agents who are obligated to protect individuals' equal access to and effectiveness of bilingual health communication may appear to be a Western value because not all cultures believe that all individuals should have equal footing in a communicative event. In this regard, I view interpreters as being essential in ensuring freedom of expression, a fundamental human right delineated in the UN's Universal Declaration of Human Rights. This obligation to human rights transcends any cultural/system norms and is essential to the communicative process in healthcare settings. The common denominator is our shared humanity.

Summary

The BHC model demonstrates how communication theories and practices can accommodate an existing dominant system (e.g., Western biomedicine and bioethics) without compromising minority or marginalized perspectives (see also Hsieh & Kramer, 2021). Rather than seeking conformity to a predetermined value, individuals with different perspectives negotiate, coordinate, and collaborate with one another to generate a mutually agreeable consensus (e.g., QEC). Through the process, the parties of a communicative activity are transformed into a team—a community with shared goals and values. The fairness and equity of the process can be safeguarded at both individual and system levels (e.g., institutional policies and human agents). Each team member is empowered to voice their perspectives *and* to respond to emerging challenges. Because all parties' perspectives are incorporated into the problem-solving process, the desirable outcomes are always responsive and inclusive to those involved. In addition, because communication is always ongoing and never-ending, the BHC model recognizes that the "perfect" solution is not achieved by a final result but rather is reflected in the *process* — all parties are committed to listen to others' differences and to generate an integrated value system that respects and accommodates all who are involved.

FOR FURTHER THOUGHT AND REFLECTION

1. To ensure the quality of interpreter-mediated interactions, healthcare institutions are typically focused on limiting interpreters' interference to provider-patient interactions. In what ways does the BHC model provide new opportunities and intervention points to improve the quality of care in interpreter-mediated medical encounters?

2. Although the BHC model appears to be specific to interpreter-mediated interactions, can you think of other communicative activities or research projects that can benefit from adopting a multiparty, goal-oriented approach to communication?

3. Does the BHC model provide more insights into communicative activities of interprofessional teams? Is it possible to develop transcending values to guide the conflicts of competing systems or communicative goals? How? Is it always possible to create an integrated value system?

4. The BHC model adopts a normative approach to predict and explain the meanings and evaluations of individuals' communicative behaviors. What are the strengths and weaknesses of a normative model?

STORIED REFLECTION
Grappling With My *Zonas Erróneas* as a Double Outsider

Wilfredo Alvarez
Utica College

Erroneous: Containing error; mistaken; incorrect; wrong; straying from what is moral, decent, proper, etc. ("Erroneous," 2021)

When I was a child in the Dominican Republic, I remember my parents' excitement about the book *Tus Zonas Erróneas*. The celebrated self-help book was about "bold, but simple techniques for taking charge of your unhealthy behavior patterns" (Dyer, 1976, front cover). It was around this time that I recall wanting to become a psychologist. Like my father, I wanted to help people communicate more effectively about their individual and relational struggles. Those days represent the beginning of my musings on human behavior's complexities and perhaps my complicated relationship with communication theory.

Tus Zonas Erróneas was about self-awareness, establishing a deeper appreciation for, and healthier relationships with, ourselves and others. These concepts later became central to my postsecondary education journey in the United States. It was in hindsight that I discerned a central theme was driving my academic aspirations: *self-understanding*. However, that was also a tumultuous time in my life. I was having challenges communicating with my mother. I thought, "Why do we struggle so much to communicate? *What is wrong with me?*"

My poor communication with my mother became a catalyst for my intellectual pursuits—and also an intense period of self-definition. One of the ways that I defined myself was as an *outsider*. During this time, I perceived myself to be not only an outsider but also a *double outsider*. I perceived my burden as an immigrant to be both linguistic and cultural, which manifested relationally. For example, when an acquaintance responded viciously to something I said (cultural), and *how* I said it (linguistic), it included criticism, *"What the hell is wrong with you?"*

Grappling with my perceived double burden as an immigrant fueled my desire to understand myself, and others, which led me to an undergraduate interpersonal communication course. We studied classic theories like social penetration theory and uncertainty reduction theory, but I felt distanced from them. Largely, during that time, when I reflect on my relationship with communication theory, *disengaged* is a word that comes to mind. I could not place my disconnect anywhere, and to aggravate things I remember seeing some of my colleagues revel in their "theoretical epiphanies." Once again, I found myself contemplating, *"What is wrong with me?"*

It was not until the latter part of my doctoral program that I connected with co-cultural theory (Orbe, 1998). I thought to myself, "Finally, a communication theory that speaks to me! A theory that seeks to illuminate and elevate the voices of nondominant group members' communication experiences! I have to reach out to the author!" Subsequently, I sent Mark Orbe an email saying, "Thank you for doing this work!" For the first time in a long time, I considered a shift in my internal narrative, *"Maybe there isn't anything wrong with me."*

I view the academy as a place where I do not belong. My status as a nonwhite Caribbean immigrant made it imperative to find meaningful theories for me to "exist" in the academy. Co-cultural theory gave me the voice to speak to and about the experiences of the marginalized, the disqualified, and the f***ed-up members of society who are rarely centered in academic discourse. As such, co-cultural theory inspired my dissertation topic on the communication experiences of Latin American immigrant janitors. This project became somewhat cathartic for both the janitors and me (Alvarez, 2013). Giving theoretical life to my and the janitors' voices was a transcendental revelation and a moment of intellectual self-discovery that I relish.

My communication experiences in/out of the academy inform my self-definition as a *double outsider*. I still grapple with heeding *Tus Zonas Erróneas's* advice—learning to accept who I am without complaint. I feel displaced as I still seek connection with/in the academy. My turbulent relationship with communication theory is perhaps a corollary of my perceived state of dislocation. However, co-cultural theory helped me shift my internal narrative and planted the seed for a more confident scholarly voice. This hopeful happenstance became a catalyst for me to begin to take charge of my unhealthy communication behavior patterns. As a result, I am now more open to receiving external affirmations that communicate, *"You're enough just as you are"* (Greenfield-Sanders, 2016).

PART V

Public Rhetoric and Influence

The previous part examined the pervasiveness of the communication process as it functions in leadership and organizational environments. Now we shift the focus to an area that is equally pervasive—the power of public rhetoric. While the history of rhetoric extends beyond the 2000-plus-year mark, rhetorical theory is just as vibrant and important as ever.

A traditional approach to rhetoric accounts for influence as present in nearly every human communication interaction—even if indirectly and whether publicly articulated, this view suggests individuals are constantly shaping meaning, strengthening understanding, seeking change, or clinging to avoid change. Given the range and complexity of these aims across a myriad of everyday situations, some argue (e.g., Gass & Seiter, 2003; Miller, 2002) we are unable to avoid influence attempts. However, others (e.g., Gearhart, 1979; Foss & Griffin, 1995) contend "this conception is only one perspective on rhetoric and one … with a patriarchal bias" (Foss & Griffin, 1995, p. 2). These scholars have called for a new invitational rhetoric that defies the underlying values of domination and control embedded in the approach to traditional rhetoric and replaces them with basic principles (e.g., equality, immanent value, and self-determination) that invite understanding.

In Part V, we ground contemporary theorizing of diverse racial and ethnic scholars with arguably the oldest form of communication study—rhetoric. In doing so, we acknowledge that traditional rhetorical scholarship has been "concerned almost exclusively with citizen discourses, mostly from white men in public" (Chávez, 2015, p. 163).

Existing Canonized Theories

The tradition of public rhetoric extends back to Ancient Greeks and especially to the work of Aristotle (1932). Though other ancient Greeks (e.g., Cicero, Corax, Tisias, Gorgias, Plato, etc.) contributed, Aristotle "provided the first comprehensive theory of rhetorical discourse" (Dillard & Pfau, 2002, p. ix). He laid out three forms of rhetorical proof (ethos, pathos, and logo) as the means available for an orator to persuade, and he introduced one of the earliest categorization schemes for public speaking (forensic, deliberative, and epideictic). Another example is Bitzer's (1968, p. 2) view of rhetorical situations; he asserts that "no major theorist has treated rhetorical situation thoroughly as a distinct subject in rhetorical theory; many ignore it." This realization prompted Bitzer to declare that rhetorical situation alone, "not the rhetor and not persuasive intent" (p. 6), controls a rhetorical response. Bitzer identified three main areas of a rhetorical situation: exigence (an obstacle marked by urgency and capable of being acted upon); audience (persons who function as real change agents), and constraints (e.g., beliefs, attitudes, documents, etc. that influence decision and action). We note that competing perspectives exist on the extent to which rhetorical discourse is active versus reactive and on whether audiences are real or imagined.

Burke's work (1966, 1969a, 1969b) is perhaps the most cited among contemporary rhetorical theorists. His theory of dramatism emphasizes the role of language as a symbolic act and man-made invention. Language induces guilt, which can be viewed as tensions or grief ameliorated through public speaking. From a dramatistic perspective, Burke (1969a) contributes the pentad, which consists of five rhetorical elements (scene, purpose, agent, agency, and acts) employed by a rhetor. The pentad offers a framework for examining the motives of a speaker and for critiquing the interrelationships between rhetorical elements. Burke's (1969b) theory of identification (establishing common ground between a rhetor and the audience) is a cooperative precursor to persuasion. Burke suggests: "You persuade or communicate with a man only insofar as you can talk his language by speech, gesture, tonality, order, image, attitude, idea, *identifying* your ways with his" (1969b, p. 55). Burke noted that *consubstantial* is the way in which two individuals share a common substance.

We note two canonized theories of persuasion and social influence in acknowledgement of a communication science perspective. First, Petty and Cacioppo's (1986) elaboration likelihood model (ELM) is worth highlighting for its dual process of persuasion. According to ELM, influence occurs through two routes (central and peripheral) that work simultaneously. Central route processing occurs as individuals scrutinize message content (e.g., message evidence and information, etc.), and peripheral route processing occurs as individuals weigh factors related tangentially to the message (e.g., number of arguments, length of message, etc.). Second, McGuire's inoculation theory (McGuire 1961, 1962), which has been advanced by Pfau and colleagues (e.g., Pfau, 1992; Pfau et al., 1997), focuses on resistance to influence. Along with the core mechanisms of threat (perceived attitude susceptibility) and refutational preemption (weakened counterattitudinal arguments that are refuted with stronger arguments), scholars have identified additional avenues by which inoculation confers resistance through research that has spanned more than six decades. While some research within these theoretical frameworks occasionally incorporate or examine aspects related to culture, their central aims do not situate our understanding of influence from diverse racial and ethnic perspectives; therein lies the value of the voices offered in this part.

Overview of Chapters

Within Part V, our aim is not to share a singular rhetorical view or approach to influence; instead, our desire is to offer room for a multiplicity of perspective. Though we offer an array of theories, commonalities do exist in this part for approaching rhetoric and influence. We simultaneously feature theoretical frameworks where perspectives agree to disagree and boldly juxtaposition their presence in communication inquiry—all in the same book. We empower scholars with salient racial and ethnic identities as they discursively make space for their own pursuit. And we center marginalized stories and ways of knowing in rhetorical discourse with theories capable of helping us see more clearly what is perhaps in plain view—the need to address racism, the quest for finding a home, and the hidden wisdom of diverse communities.

Chapter 14, which opens Part V, focuses on complicity theory, which is uniquely and appropriately situated for this part and for this time in U.S. and academia history, given the exacerbated racial tensions persisting amid the pandemic and protests. Mark McPhail, in this chapter, lays out complicity theory as a distinctive vehicle for addressing adaptive problems like racism and poverty. McPhail draws from the theory's rich heritage, which is informed from the ancient Greeks, Buddhism, philosophy, and colonial studies to provide a refined understanding of the rhetoric of racism. Through complicity theory, the role of persuasion in improving race relations is interrogated, challenged, and questioned. McPhail weaves together powerful examples that enumerate how complicity theory reveals the inequity in impulses of domination and how oppression occurs in oppositional discourse. McPhail's contribution positions complicity theory as an alternative epistemology and a fitting lens for viewing matters pertaining to rhetoric and race.

Womanist rhetorical theory is the topical focus of Chapter 15. Dianna N. Watkins-Dickerson illuminates this rhetorical theory from her powerful perspective. Watkins-Dickerson offers the distinctions among feminism, Black feminism, and womanism, cogently explaining how and why womanist rhetorical theory stands alone at rendering Black women's truths. With stylistic headings descriptive of Black culture and brief pieces of womanist rhetorical analysis, Watkins-Dickerson traces the origins of womanist rhetorical theory centering the meaning and methods of Black female rhetors to share their truths on their own terms. Womanist rhetorical theory provides great value as a window to the embodied accounts of oppression, disrespect, and despair experienced uniquely among Black women. Watkins-Dickerson showcases the discursive practices of Black women, while demonstrating the breadth and scope of

Black women's speech acts. We agree with Watkins-Dickerson that womanist rhetorical theory is uniquely situated to affirm Black women's marginalized voices without apology or permission.

In Chapter 16, we focus on the positive deviance approach. Arvind Singhal provides an overview of this theoretical framework and shares how some realities may be hiding from us in plain sight. Through a view of wisdom as improving well-being, Singhal demonstrates how the positive deviance approach shifts theorizing within social influence and offers a new framework for intervention approaches. The positive deviance chapter reveals the ways in which expertise and ability can function as constraints placing existing and uncommon wisdom out of purview. Singhal offers two useful case studies that focus on ethnically diverse communities—malnutrition in Vietnam and childhood obesity among the Latinx population. With clarity, Singhal illustrates the utility of the positive deviance approach, which extracts and amplifies solutions along the upstream and downstream continuum directly from the communities seeking to be served. In this way, Singhal delivers on the promise of sharing how communication intervention approaches and influence efforts can reside in communities of color in plain sight.

Overview of Storied Reflections

In addition to the main theoretical contributions, this part offers three storied reflections from Virginia Sánchez, Alberto González, and B. Liahnna Stanley. Sánchez, an assistant professor at Auburn University, shares her *connections and disconnections* with communication theory by retelling family interactions and academic experiences. Starting with her initial frustrations from data collection practices and applicability of theory, she recounts the familial tensions resolved through engaging with communication theory. Her journey crystallizes the importance of persisting to capture lived experiences in communication research, while expecting gaps that may exist. As he *hovers about prevailing theories*, González, a distinguished university professor at Bowling Green State University, reflects on his experiences writing about "otherness" and venturing out into the white world. He recalls his desire to have names and language with Spanish origins appear in communication journals, and he offers a key realization learned through his first publication in the field. González explains the challenges in using Western theories of culture as starting points and shares the importance of pushing beyond what prevails to arrive at a theory perspective. Stanley, a doctoral student at Arizona State University, offers her personal narrative of *returning home*. Through questioning the compatibility of theory with Indigenous ways of knowing, this doctoral student guides us to her arrival at a nuanced understanding of home—home as locating oneself *within a process rather than a place*. Stanley's reflective account speaks deeply to those who seek to resist assimilationist and colonial logics, to those who desire to honor Indigenous brilliance, and to those who yearn to draw strength from their ancestors.

CHAPTER 14

Complicity Theory

Mark Lawrence McPhail

Indiana University Northwest

C omplicity theory was introduced to the discipline of communication in 1991 as an approach to theorizing interracial and intercultural conflict and its resolution. Complicity is described by Anderson (1996, p. 92) as an "activative" model that "forces the recognition that inquiry is not a method of discovery or a critical analysis but instead a complicitous partner in the meaningful systems in which we live." The theory examines core assumptions and beliefs about rhetoric and race as manifestations of an unchanging and essential reality and domination and subordination as problems of human nature or structural conflict. The theory explores the role of rhetoric in the social construction of difference and identity, challenging the belief that persuasion can address or ameliorate racial conflict and division. The theory advances the position that the epistemological assumptions at work in traditional views of rhetoric are grounded in the oppositional logics of reason and rationality, which limit language to the role of representation and marginalize its generative and constitutive potential.

Intellectual Tradition of Complicity Theory

Complicity theory draws upon perspectives advanced in the fields of rhetoric and philosophy, Buddhism, contemporary physics, and colonial studies to offer an approach to human communication that examines the ways in which seemingly divergent or antithetical positions are implicated in each other (for more information on the intellectual influences of Buddhism and quantum physics, see McPhail, 1994). This approach is expressed in the *dissoi logoi* or antilogic, and the theory of the opposite party of the Greek Sophists is signified by the *Tai Chi* symbol of Eastern spirituality and philosophy and is imagined in the possibility of an implicate order emergent in contemporary quantum physics. In relation to the study of race and racism, it is expressed in the analyses of colonialism offered by Albert Memmi and Vincent Crapanzano, both of whom amplify Franz Fanon's exploration of the ways in which the oppressed and oppressor are implicated in systems of domination, both symbolically and psychologically.

For Memmi (1965, pp. 130–131), the complicity of the colonized is manifested in the embrace of racial reasoning: "All racism and xenophobia consist of delusions about oneself, including absurd and unjust aggressions toward others. Included are those of the colonized—the more so when they extend beyond the colonizers to everything which is not strictly colonized." While the colonized become implicated in their own oppression by embracing the racial reasoning of the colonizer, Memmi points out that the roots of such reasoning rest with the oppressor. "When, for example, they [the colonized] are carried away by enjoyment of the misfortunes of another human group simply because they are not in slavery they are guilty of xenophobia" (p. 131). For Memmi, "the colonized's racism is the result of a more general delusion: the colonialist delusion" and that "the colonized end up accepting this Manichean division of the colony and, by extension, of the whole world" (p. 131). The core of the colonialist delusion is the impulse to dominate, and complicity theory maintains that this impulse inevitably implicates the targeted in systems of structural inequity and inequality through oppositional discourse. Whether the rhetoric of protest or the critical interrogation of oppression, oppositional discourses are grounded in the epistemic foundations of argumentative inquiry, its privileging of reason over affect, and its essentializing of intellect as a vehicle for emancipatory action.

By recognizing that rhetorical responses to, and critiques of, racism and other discourses of negative difference implicate their agents in the systems and positions they oppose, complicity theory attempts to uncover the adaptive impulses of discourse that facilitate the substitution of one oppressive discourse for another: a theory of the opposite party. Memmi (1984, p. 6) expresses the same recognition in noting that "the colonized imitate and often admire those who have colonized them; but that does not mean that they consent to domination. Such behavior is even a sign of the contrary, of their refusal to give that approbation." The *character* of this refusal is a central concern of complicity theory, as is the question of whether it resists or reinforces domination. Memmi reminds us of the seductiveness of dominance, a seductiveness embedded in the oppositional impulses that generate and sustain the colonized's complicity, a complicity that Vincent Crapanzano (1985) identifies as a consequence of essentialism.

Crapanzano argues that the critique of racism "masks other classifications that have the same epistemological roots and permit the same social and psychological tyranny" (p. 20). Like Memmi, Crapanzano recognizes and acknowledges the structural forces that inform racial consciousness and action and similarly explores the individual and psychological impulses that symbiotically sustain negative difference. Crapanzano addresses rhetorical and epistemological dimensions of racial reasoning, observing that while "racist and other essentialist social categories—when they exist—enter the rhetoric of domination and subordination in hierarchical societies, they are not as freely manipulated by the dominant, the possessors of power, status, and wealth, as is popularly thought" (p. 20). The rhetoric of racism cannot, for Crapanzano as for Memmi, be adequately addressed or understood in the black and white terminology of race, which is itself rooted in essentialist epistemological assumptions and practices.

Complicity theory's exploration of rhetoric and race aligns the concerns of cultural scholars such as Memmi and Crapanzano with research articulating alternative epistemologies that challenge essentialist conceptions of language, life, and method. Originally envisioned as a restorative approach to racial transformation and reconciliation, the theory's development over time has led to a revising of its initial reading of the rhetoric of racism. Complicity theory's evolution has been further influenced by rhetorical scholarship that questions the efficacy of persuasion for achieving racial reconciliation, as well as the work of philosophers of race and the epistemologies of ignorance they interrogate. These influences have prompted a reconsideration of complicity theory's original conceptualizations of rhetoric, rationality, and racism.

Main Goals and Features of Complicity Theory

Rhetoric's reemergence as a productive art that creates as well as represents reality begged the question that complicity theory attempts to answer: what kind of reality is created by language limited to argument and persuasion? The answer offered by the theory is that racism and other forms of oppression are embodied expressions of the dualistic and oppositional assumptions at the core of the dominant theories of knowledge that shape Western intellectual and social culture. These same assumptions have historically limited and defined the identity and scope of rhetoric, relegating it to a subordinate role as a functionary of reason and logic—at best a servant to philosophy. Complicity theory intuits that the subordination of rhetoric by philosophy rests upon the same epistemological assumptions that generate race, racism, and the oppositional discourses that sustain them.

The focus in complicity on the implicative character of racism and its critique of essentialism have evolved since the theory appeared, as has the theory's optimistic investment in the reconstructive potential of a rhetoric of dialogic coherence. James Golden and Richard Rieke's exploration of African American rhetoric, and Aaron David Gresson III's work on the rhetorics of minority epistemology, racial recovery, and atonement, contributed significantly to a theoretical shift of emphasis from rhetorical coherence to racial (re)signing and resignation. Golden and Rieke (1971, p. 6) offer a provocative theorizing of rhetoric's efficacy in matters of race and racism: "The study of the rhetoric of black Americans suggests the possibility that the rhetorical goal—communicating with white men about their beliefs and attitudes regarding black men—may be more a psychiatric than a persuasive problem." Their analysis suggests that racism's immunity to the available means of persuasion might be rooted in deeper impulses and anxieties: "When the black speaker tells his white audience to look deep inside their own belief system and purge their racist ideas, he is confronting the most central, the most ego-involving of all attitudes of the listener" (p. 7).

Their theoretical insights are supported by the experiences of Black psychiatrists who attempted to have extreme racism classified as a form of mental illness by the American Psychiatric Association. "The association's officials rejected the recommendation, arguing that since so many Americans are racist, racism in this country is normative—a cultural problem rather than an indication of personal pathology," recalls Alvin F. Poussaint. "But this position is ill founded. Extreme racism is a serious mental illness" (Poussaint, 1999, p. A21). Poussaint and his colleagues produced a significant amount of research to support their position, illustrating both individual and institutional manifestations of racism in psychiatry and society. Yet the APA's officials did not view racism as a "more than expectable and culturally sanctioned response to a particular event" or the "manifestation of a behavioral, psychological, or biological dysfunction in the individual" (p. A21). This disavowal, predicted by Golden and Rieke, is also anticipated in Aaron Gresson III's writings on minority epistemology, racial recovery, and the pedagogy of healing.

Gresson (1977, p. 247) points to the complicity of traditional views of rhetoric and race in the establishment and maintenance of systems of domination and inequality. "The problem is that rhetoricians, like dominant social orders, generally operate under the assumption that whatever change is sought takes place within existing paradigms, according to scientific principles and their rhetorical equivalents, the inherited canons of 'good rhetoric.'" He extends his analysis of rhetoric and race in his examination of racial recovery narratives, illustrating how the complicitous acceptance of essentialized notions of difference redefines notions of racial power and privilege. "In short, white recovery accounts for the diffidence of racism rhetoric" (Gresson, 1995, p. 12), he explains.

But other forces are at work here as well: whites have not been the only opponents of seeing systemic racism as the lens for understanding human relations or the primary force blocking various groups from achieving greater human rights. Nowhere, in fact, is this dampening more evident than in Black-on-Black conflict and communication (p. 12).

Gresson suggests that racial recovery narratives exhibit a possessive investment in "*rhetorical reversal*, or persuasion through reversed meanings" (1995, p. 12). Rhetorical reversals normalize discourses of "duplicity and dishonesty" and "lessons of self-deception." "It is for this reason, in part, that the 'racialized other' in each of us stands in need of 'atonement.' But this fact does not negate the need for real, painful, racial atonement by the perpetrators of individual and institutional racism" (Gresson, 2015, p. 230).

Like Memmi and Crapanzano, Gresson recognizes the complicitous character of dominance without equating implicature with agreement and resituates racial recovery in the realm of everyday life and individual agency. Gresson resists the essentializing impulses of oppositionality in his discussion of "the postracial," offering an alternative possibility for engaging the idea. "Yet, among the arguments that have been made for the present time as 'postracial,' I would add one more: we are living in an aggressively and non-apologetically *existential moment*: a time/place that is meaningful and vital right now to those who want to be agents, be active *and* effective. This is, I believe, the degree of truth to the idea of the 'postracial'" (2015, p. 231).

The "postracial" signifies for Gresson not an attempt at lazy absolution but rather an opportunity to engage the deeper impulses that fuel complicity in systems of oppression. "Of course, this has very little to do with racism—structural, individual, corporate, or global. It has everything to do with the 'liberation' of the affective, the various forces that undergird our emotions, feelings, and ways of seeing ourselves in the world" (2015, p. 231). From the point of view of complicity theory, emotional liberation has *both* little *and* everything to do with racism, for it offers a coherent path of resistance and reflection for engaging the "epistemologies of ignorance" that motivate individual, intellectual, and ideological investments in what Charles Mills calls the "Racial Contract."

Mills (1997) argues that the social contract assumes an abstract moral neutrality while the Racial Contract is realized in "a moral psychology (not just in whites but sometimes in nonwhites) skewed consciously or unconsciously toward privileging [Europeans and their descendants], taking the status quo of differential racial entitlement as normatively legitimate, and not to be investigated further." The Racial Contract is a complicitously sustained "dominance contract" that "prescribes for its signatories an inverted epistemology, an epistemology of ignorance, a particular pattern of localized and global cognitive dysfunctions (which are psychologically and socially functional), producing the ironic outcome that whites will in general be unable to understand the world they themselves have made" (p. 20). Mills argues that "mapping an epistemology of ignorance is ... a preliminary to reformulating an epistemology that will give us genuine knowledge," (2007, p. 17). He positions the Racial Contract not as an oppositional refutation of Western moral philosophy but as an elaboration and correction of its imperfections as they are expressed in the lived experiences of exigencies of "systematic social oppression" (Mills, 2007, p. 19).

The primary agents of this correction, Mills maintains, are persons of African descent: "The white delusion of racial superiority insulates itself against refutation. Correspondingly, on the positive side, the route to black knowledge is the self-conscious recognition of white ignorance (including its black-faced manifestation in black consciousness itself)" (Mills, 2007, p. 19). Mills links this recognition to Du Boisian double-consciousness and excavates the historical amnesias, psychic projections, and rhetorical reversals that are symptomatic of white ignorance and injustice. "White ignorance has been able to flourish all of these years because a white epistemology of ignorance has safeguarded it against the dangers of an illuminating blackness or redness, protecting those who for 'racial' reasons have needed not to know," he concludes. "Only by starting to break these rules and meta-rules can we begin the long process that will lead to the eventual overcoming of this white darkness and the achievement of an enlightenment that is genuinely multiracial" (2007, p. 35). Mills suggests that a "re-signing" of the Racial Contract can be achieved through a "black radical liberalism that is true both to the (idealized) liberal tradition, the liberalism that *should have been*, and respectful of the black diasporic experience in modernity, victims of the liberalism that actually was and is" (2007, p. 215).

The restorative project Mills proposes for philosophy is motivated by many of the same critical impulses that informed the *Rhetoric of Racism* in both its earliest and later editions. Yet, while Mills remains optimistic that the Racial Contract can be (re)signed and that the consequences it creates for its beneficiaries, signatories, and targets can be critically interrogated and ameliorated, complicity theory offers a less sanguine reading of the (im)possibility of racial reconciliation. The essentializing of reason as emancipatory, which sustains Western moral philosophy and its contractarian values, is identified in complicity theory as an *adaptive dominance contract*: similarly, what Mills describes as an "epistemology of ignorance" is in complicity theory embedded in the essentializing impulses of rational philosophy.

Research and Practical Applications of Complicity Theory

As initially conceived in *The Rhetoric of Racism*, complicity theory proposed a nonoppositional rhetoric of dialogic coherence as an alternative way of knowing and a fitting response to exigencies of race matters. The theory evoked mixed responses. Nikitah Okembe-RA Imani (2000) views the theory as "a valid and accurate critique of Western essentialism and its materialism" but dismisses its critique of Afrocentricity. Detine Bowers suggests that the theory is little more than an integration of Afrocentric and Burkean theory. Ines Miyares characterizes the theory naïve, and complicity theory has also been described as a critique of "Black racism." Subsequent essays have addressed these concerns through reexaminations of the rhetorics of Afrocentricity and the Black Islam, reconsiderations of dialogue's efficacy in addressing racial divisions, and reinvestigations of rhetorical and philosophical critiques of racism that explore the psychological dynamics of race and reconciliation (for more on critiques of complicity theory and responses, see McPhail, 2004, 2018). The result has been a revisiting of the theory's epistemological roots and an amplification of the role of reason in the perpetuation and maintenance of systems of symbolic, psychological, and material domination.

The theory has been utilized by African American communication scholars to examine the complexities of black nationalism and black masculinity as well as notions of racial difference and identity. The theory has also influenced scholarship in whiteness studies, queer studies, media studies, educational diversity, interspecies communication, and racial reconciliation. In each of these areas, complicity theory offers a useful lens through which the complex character of discursive resistance and reification can be analyzed and explicated. Whiteness studies examine how racial blindness sustains white privilege and ideological innocence; queer studies situate complicity at the intersection of Christianity and sexuality; media studies have used complicity theory to explore the transformative potential of media to address racial differences and divisions; educational research has examined the contradictions between policy and practice in affirming diversity values: and human-animal communication scholarship has drawn upon the complicity theory to destabilize the anthropocentric foundations of knowledge.

Beyond the discipline of communication, scholars in the fields of law, international relations, women's studies, and the social and behavioral sciences have found the theory agreeable. Theories of complicity have been also advanced in literary, cultural, and rhetorical studies that focus on the symbolic creation and maintenance of oppression and the ways in which individuals are implicated in systems of domination by oppositional discourse and critique. Within rhetorical studies, the theory's most sustained applications have been its use as a critical heuristic in debates exploring the problems and possibilities of racial reconciliation. These debates have significantly influenced the transformations the theory has undergone since its original conception, shifting the focus from how the dominated are implicated in systems of domination to the conceptualization of reason itself as a dominance discourse.

Continuing the Conversation

While complicity theory has maintained its initial intuitive assumptions, the influences of Golden and Rieke, Gresson, and Mills have significantly reshaped the theory of negative difference into a revised reading of the rhetoric of racism. Understanding racism as a psychiatric problem, theorizing rhetorical recovery as affect and intentionality, and reengaging the epistemic conception of ignorance in the conflict between rhetoric and philosophy reframes the rhetoric of racism as "adaptive." Richard Perry characterizes modern racism as adaptive, arguing that racism is sustained by a rhetoric of "protective coloration through semantic camouflage" (2007, p. 16), while Ronald Heifetz (1994) recognizes that adaptive problems such as poverty and racism resist the technical remedies offered by rhetorical, political, or material forces. Both point to the (im)possibility of reconciling racism through traditional means and call for new paradigms and perspectives for addressing adaptive problems. Complicity theory represents one such perspective.

Complicity theory's original insight, that oppositional discourse implicates us in systems of domination and oppression, remains an important consideration for critical scholars of race and philosophy, in particular those concerned with "epistemologies of ignorance." Complicity theory intimates that the very notion of ignorance itself, in both its classical and contemporary manifestations, presupposes problematic binaries that inform and invigorate racial reasoning, rhetoric, and resistance. A revisiting of the roots of epistemology reveals the philosophical and rhetorical resources used to sustain these distinctions since their first articulation in the Platonic definition of knowledge as "justified true belief" and its corollary characterization of ignorance as either "self-aware" or "transferred." Transferred ignorance, which Plato marks as morally problematic, reflects an inability to recognize that one's belief cannot be justified as true, that is, that one's beliefs are "wrong." That inability, and the evil acts it produces, are in Platonic philosophy, the result of ignorance.

Socrates argues in the *Protagoras* that no on intentionally engages in evil acts, and that since it is human nature to be rational, and one's rational self-interest would preclude doing harm to one's self, one would therefore not do harm to others. The position, which forms the foundation for rational epistemology and moral theory, makes an inferential leap between self-interest and the interests of others and invites a disavowal of the evidence of our senses in favor of an *essentially* rational "human nature." The subordination of affect and experience rehearsed in philosophy's domination of rhetoric is the same adaptive impulse that creates and sustains racism as nothing less than an expression of normative sociopathy. Racist rhetoric is characterized by a lack of empathy, compulsive prevarication, disavowal of responsibility and accountability, and *intentionality*. Racial complicity persists in a collective investment in innocence and the belief that racism is a product of ignorance. Yet much of the evidence of our senses suggests otherwise, a reality made empirically and powerfully clear in the year 2020, when rhetoric, racism, violence, and a virus collectively conspired to reveal how far we are as a nation from the possibility of rhetorical coherence, racial reconciliation, or coherent conceptions of identity and difference.

Summary

Complicity theory suggests that we cannot develop solutions for adaptive racism precisely because those solutions are shaped by the essentializing dominance impulses of reason and rationality. It implies that we cannot, as Audre Lorde presciently observed, rebuild the house built with the Master's tools, nor can we escape from it when with the fire next time burns it down around us. From public persuasion to practical reasoning, rhetoric's rational impulses implicate us all in networks of mutuality both good and evil: we cannot have one without the other, and yet we cannot have both. This is the paradoxical understanding of race and racism that complicity theory invites us to address. Just as complicity theory reframed the efficacy of oppositional discourse, the rhetorical theory of adaptive racism has the potential to redefine our understanding of race and racism in provocative ways and radicalize how we understand, enact, and engage race, racism, and the exigencies it reveals in the realms of practical discourse and symbolic action.

FOR FURTHER THOUGHT AND REFLECTION

1. How do complicity theory and rhetorical coherence relate to the idea of a "post racial" America?

2. How might complicity as a theory of adaptive racism be used to understand the "Big Lie" of the 2020 U.S. presidential election?

3. How can a system of education reliant on rationality lead to a just and equitable society if it effectively "educates us out of empathy?"

STORIED REFLECTION
Connecting and Disconnecting Through
Proyectos e Investigaciones

Virginia Sánchez
Auburn University

In an introductory communication theory course, my professor stated for the class, "You all like theory. If you didn't, you wouldn't be here." At the time, I took their words as truth and coped with the fact that I *hated* theory. I felt discouraged by readings that constructed theory using data collection practices based on privilege and was frustrated with being unable to make connections between my experiences and theoretical explanations. However, throughout the semester, I began to understand what the professor meant. Liking theory involved enjoying discovery, forming assumptions, and contributing to our field. While I often felt frustrated with the applicability of theory, I was also being trained to challenge theory, create theory, and mold it in a way that accounted for my experiences and observations. Communication theory, for me, has offered a series of tensions between my familial and academic experiences.

Theory Connects and Disconnects Family

Separation within families is painfully understood among immigrant communities. I have always wished for more time with my grandparents who lived in Mexico. One day, my uncle was struggling to convince my grandmother that he should help her into a new outfit. I had just completed a semester learning about communication theory and how relationships are developed through communication. We had also learned several theories of persuasion that helped me understand how difficult it would be to convince her to do the very thing she didn't want. I wasn't confident in being able to help her change her clothing, so I decided to try to persuade her instead. I approached and said something along the lines of *"Abuela, este vestido se me hace muy bonito. Puedo ver como se le ve puesto?*[1] To my surprise, she said yes. Although physical distance, and now age, prevented us from making memories, that small moment of brief connection was invaluable. This moment was made more meaningful when contrasted with the struggles to communicate about theory with family.

I've never really told my family the specifics of my work. They know I am a professor (though not necessarily an assistant professor), I teach, and I need to complete *proyectos e investigaciones.*[2] But I've never talked to them about the theories I use. As a first-generation college student and the daughter of Mexican immigrants, I've tried to find ways to compare my job to theirs to bridge our occupational differences. My parents understand promotions and finances. So I use these concepts to explain the tenure-track process. However, I haven't found an equivalent to communication theory—an important aspect of my work. I could describe it as an output, similar to the metal casts my dad used to put together at a foundry or the rooms my mother used to clean at a nursing home. But then, what would be the metatheoretical assumptions or the contributions? The lack of an equivalent is frustrating, but not inopportune.

Theory Connects and Disconnects Experiences in the Lived World

On several occasions, I sat in graduate courses trying to find connections between my experiences and theoretical explanations. When professors challenged me to talk about emotional work and labor, I recounted feeling disappointed when I ended up organizing media purchases instead of taking on more field work at an activist organization. When we discussed anticipatory vocational socialization, I shared that I needed to go to college but was unprepared for what I experienced. Although I never felt shamed for or shame in sharing these experiences, there were times when I felt different.

My conversations with other academics have echoed these experiences. I've reflected with others about how theory building often takes a different form when your experiences are not frequently reflected in research. There are days when I worry that I am towing the line between a theoretical contribution and appropriating from my own culture in my own research. Recently I won an award for a project that contributes to research about having a calling. When I talked to my family about my award, they were happy, but they did not fully understand what was "new" about my findings. Knowledge that is "new" to academics has, in many cases, previously existed within less represented communities.

I share these stories to contrast the various ways in which I engage with theory—how I use theory while also struggling to interpret and broker its importance. I acknowledge that while there is strength in knowing what theories worked well, there are also areas of my life that theory hasn't been able to neatly package. Communication theory is *messy*, but it is also ripe with potential.

---

1   "Grandma, this dress is so pretty. Can I see what it looks like on you?"
2   Projects and research.

CHAPTER 15

Womanist Rhetorical Theory

Dianna N. Watkins-Dickerson

University of Memphis

F rom the time Black women's personhood, dignity, and freedom were exploited for profit and ill-gain through the trans-Atlantic slave trade, and their recompense existed only through a hearty welcome of dissonance, discord, and death-dealing despair and disappointment, womanist rhetorical theory has been brewing into a conceptual framework. This theoretical perspective presents itself neither solely dedicated to challenging theories centering whiteness nor embedded in conventional wishes for a project pioneering through a revisionist approach to doing communication theory. Fitting squarely within the scope of this text, womanist rhetorical theory answers the call of this textbook to recenter the intellectual ingenuity and alacrity of marginalized and underrepresented rhetorical perspectives. More specifically, womanist rhetorical theory focuses on the importance of empowering Black-centered, cold, hard truths through the lens of Black women coming to voice in public and private spaces. Led by the culturally specific and linguistically creative chapter headings, this chapter briefly explores the historical, political, cultural, communal, and social focus of womanist rhetorical theory and its scope for doing scholarship beyond normative (read traditionally white and male-centered) communication scholarship.

Intellectual Tradition of Womanist Rhetorical Theory

To be clear, womanism stands on its own logical structure and scope, building her own house without the master's tools (or instruction manual). While there have been instances inside and outside of academic and activist circles where womanism may have been conflated with Black feminism or feminism in general, as a womanist rhetorician, I must clearly state that this is not the case. Historian Karen Offen (1988, p. 123) offers a traditional dictionary-based definition of feminism as: "a theory and/or movement concerned with advancing the position of women through such means as achievement of political, legal, or economic rights equal to those granted men." While there are countless other definitions available, Offen's is quite concise and clear in the scope of what feminism tries to observe and accomplish. Yet, Black women and other women of color have historically been left out of the broader picture and denied seats at the decision table, far too often on purpose. Black feminism, while centering the experiences of Black women, is not entirely dissimilar or divergent from womanism. It does take up the needs of Black women and the communities they represent, but womanism is still more nuanced and distinct. In part, the central commitment of feminism, writ large, is focused on dismantling clashes of class and sexism against patriarchal forces over and against anything else. Even more so, establishing the central, and arguably separatist, stance of rejecting the word *feminist* and instead accepting *womanist* further reifies a decision that is not only important rhetorically but also culturally, politically, theoretically, and even historically.

Much of the basis of womanist musings are still closely committed to what womanist ethicist Stacey Floyd-Thomas (2006) calls the tenet of traditional communalism, highlighted through Alice Walker's (1983) explanation that a womanist has a profound commitment to the liberation of an entire Black folk. Still, the importance of naming likewise highlights what womanist New Testament scholar Stephanie Crowder (2016) outlines in her scope of womanist maternal thought. Due to what she examines as its matrilineal commitment, womanism upholds a considerable amount of pride in naming. Like humankind's quest to travel in outer space, or claim personal territory, naming space for womanism, not simply as ideology but also as an identity driven by relevant everyday experience, serves as a point of privilege. Beyond this, it demonstrates a staunch philosophical stance laying ground toward a right and rite of passage for those understanding the importance and power of what is in a name.

There is a popular African American aphorism that says, "It's not what you're called, but what you answer to." While the call for "all of us to be feminists" is (partially) true in necessitating an innovative rally cry for allyship and advocacy toward women's rights and equal treatment, in the words famously recounted by writer, teacher, activist, and who I would claim a proto-womanist Anna Julia Cooper (1892, p. 31), "only the Black woman can say, when and where I enter." With this in mind, womanists consider themselves naming and claiming space that understands the hypervisibility and invisibility of living in a world where being Black and a woman, automatically insinuates (and unfairly perpetuates) an underclassed caste category or assumption. In worse instances, I have come to hear womanism titled "womanist feminism," which is a truly dangerous manifestation of assumed ownership by white feminists hiding in the social protection of false allyship, particularly in neoliberal academic spaces. In fact, neither of these considerations is true, as womanist thought is its own stand-alone project.

Main Goals and Features of
Womanist Rhetorical Theory

Many Black women felt the need to bridge cognitive dissonance from the women's liberation movement, which rejected the centrality of their experiences of racist oppression in the United States. Black women felt the civil rights and Black Power movements of the 1960s and 1970s neglected the importance of how sexism and misogynoir capriciously built pillars standardizing unattainable expectations of womanhood, femininity, and motherhood against Black women's interest. Out of these experiences of Black women, womanism was born as a distinct category of thought in literary, activist, and academic circles. Misogynoir, a term coined by Black feminist scholar Moya Bailey, is plainly defined as the specifically anti-Black misogynist (thus inherently sexist) violence society holds Black women hostage to perform and suffer from without recourse. Thus, instead of dichotomizing gendered expression and racial uplift only to leave out a portion of the whole self, womanism affords Black women a specific standpoint honoring a worldview that is built by a Black-female-centered real-lived experience. It is equally committed to the vitality and holistic thriving for and by Black women, and Black women only. The concept, already familiar in communal spaces through colloquial phrases such as "you acting womanish," which is to say a girl or young woman is too mature for her age—willful, or even (prophetically even) wise beyond years—to distinctly call one's self a "womanist," was introduced by Alice Walker in 1979 in her short essay *Coming Apart*. In this text, the central character found herself incapable of being accepted wholly by Black men and altogether rejected by white women. Later Walker's (1983) literary work, alongside the backdrop of womanist literary and religious scholars of the 1980s and early 1990s, demonstrates that womanist thought begins and ends by centralizing the ways in which Black women's ontological oppression, rhetorical repression, and social suppression push them to the margins of society and even salvation.

Much of the womanist project was drafted by scholarly research celebrating, as opposed to the typical denigrating, Black life, language, culture, and religion. For instance, beginning in the 1970s, womanist sociolinguist Geneva Smitherman challenged the generally accepted lexiconic structures of (white) English by centering Black English/Ebonics/African American Vernacular English (AAVE) in ways demonstrating that culturally relevant language can be liberative, particularly in a racist-sexist-classist society. Smitherman has upheld the argument that Black women and men have always communicated through Afrocentric patterns, while holding in tension the reality that they must work with added intellectual fervor in communicating in a society that accepts Black culture as *chic*, protects Blackness when uniquely benefiting market capitalism, and otherwise rejecting Black bodies when they no longer benefit white bodies. Much like the other theoretical projects accumulated within this textbook, womanism starts from the margins and works toward centering those voices to get the whole truth and nothing but the truth.

For example, Smitherman (2000) provides a dictionary of Black language that encapsulates culture, faith, education, religion, politics, history, and more with richness and texture traditionally rejected in canonized academic works. She demonstrates the reality that language construction is not only an amalgamation of religious belief, culture, politics, heritage, and beyond, but it is also a theoretical undertaking. It takes skill, invention, and, in the case of Black women and men, a certain level of subversive genius to overcome and outwit the difficulties of surviving while Black in a negrophobic society and the counterculture that *yet* survives the onslaught of never ceasing attack. Likewise, the late U.S. representative Shirley Chisholm, who stated that she wanted to be remembered as a woman who dared to be herself, operated from a rhetorical space and style that was not only capable of using the rhetorical structure and play of the English language to her advantage but was simultaneously conscious of her Black audience along with their priorities, sensibilities, and capabilities. In the same way that Chisholm picked the slogan "Unbought and Unbossed," womanist scholarship is defined by Black women. This is not an exclusionary tactic to marginalize or demean others but is in line with their thoughtfully consistent project toward committing discursive space for all human thriving.

Womanist rhetorical theory takes seriously the meanings, methods, and musings of Black female rhetors and the relationships they maintain as necessary to their spiritual, social, communal, psychological, and intellectual survival and thriving. More than this, womanist rhetorical theory includes an ethic that calls forth a need to assess communication study regarding Black female rhetors through a liberative lens. This means that they are not only the subject matter experts in their own [T]ruth, but they are also the only individuals who can map out the best path en route to their own thriving. Far too often, heteropatriarchal forces push Black women toward the center, only using them when they are beneficial for upholding normative standards of respectability and/or when Black women are tokenized to display diversity, inclusion, and progress. This does not free Black women's bodies. It only further marginalizes them and compromises their personhood. Instead, womanist rhetorical theory centers Black women's ability to analyze their own truths, with their own means, and in their own manner; thus, it is an intervention and earnestly deviates from normative theoretical frameworks. It intervenes on behalf of Black women and is typically and most effectively used by Black women practitioners who celebrate, as opposed to demonize, the intrinsic worth, value, and everyday experiences of Black women.

In many ways, places such as the historical Black church, National Pan-hellenic sororities, women's improvement societies, and social clubs, to name a few, have consistently valued the importance and imperative of centering Black women's experiences and want for social, political, educational, and holistic uplift, noting that some of us have always had to be brave (Hull et al., 1992). To elaborate on this point, womanist scholarship contends with how social and political commentary can thrust Black women into spaces where they are not seen as women but are instead cast into tropes, caricatures, conjecture, and objects to be studied and consumed. This includes critical cultural critique of the times when they not only claim "I was 'missin 'somethin," but know that they were cast as mammy, jezebel, welfare queen, or the like, and forced to assume a strong Black woman attitude because their tears of blood would neither be seen nor considered representing pain, especially when compared to white women (Shange, 1976). For example, a womanist reading of *Jane Eyre* would lift habits and histories discounting Black women's full humanity, in spite of the harsh reality in which she exists. Hidden in the pages of this text, touted as a premiere read for feminist literary scholarship, are anti-Black undertones according to womanist literary scholar Chikenwe Ogunyemi (1985). In this essay, Ogunyemi emphasizes the logical move some Black women academics have made in moving away from traditional feminist perspectives that do not always intellectually serve them and instead toward adopting a womanist frame.

Pitched as an antagonist (against Jane and Rochester), Bertha Rochester is defiled and abandoned by her white counterparts, acquaintances, and husband. Her anger and frustration with the patriarchy leave her nothing outside of the ashes that burn with the estate she torches. To this end, Ogunyemi explains, "[F]or Black women who would be feminists the lesson is simple: in fighting the establishment, the black woman must not be so mad as to destroy herself with the patriarchy" (p. 89). Instead of highlighting Bertha's assault against white male oppression and general denial of respect toward women, the text unravels a history all too familiar with how white women far too often attempt to claim the few crumbs of power from patriarchy in their preoccupation with individual survival ethics, as opposed to communal striving. History has shown that white women's tears and fears of Black men have produced pain through public lynchings, and their strivings toward wholeness stand on the backs of the Black women they posit as impious, sexually capricious and irresponsible, lewd, and licentious. Not only do readings and real-world experiences such as these highlight the difficulty of Black women's ability to find wholeness in their womanhood or align themselves (safely) with white women, but when stranded in a society committed to anti-Black racism and sexism, they find a need to create new options. Womanist rhetorical theory explores such a communicative space for them to do so.

Research and Practical Applications of Womanist Rhetorical Theory

Womanist rhetorical theory has only been mildly introduced into communication studies; nonetheless, there are several women who identify with the perspective and utilize ideas from the perspective in their work. Janice Hamlet (2000) was the first to introduce the term *womanist* or *womanism* in her work. Hamlet noted Black feminist sociologist Deborah King and argued that "[t]he emergence and development of a womanist epistemology and methodology presents African American women and the scholarship about them as distinct subjects of the human family worthy of acknowledgment and study" (p. 421). This exploration of womanist thought and language gave communication scholars, particularly Black women, an opportunity to further explore what it meant to have a mode of theory centering their voices and frames of doing scholarship.

Another critical scholar associated with womanist lineage in communication scholarship is Olga Davis (1998), who asserts that Black women should be able to see themselves as viable contributors to communication methods and theory. In this work, Davis explains "this essay advances the need to validate self as a rhetorical critic in order to re-discover Black women's rhetorical tradition" (p. 77). By arguing this, I contend Davis is openly criticizing the limited spaces for Black women's thought and praxis in the communication canon and how this leaves out a considerable amount of information to be gathered and explored. In this, it also reifies the very point of womanism; Black women hold within their experience rhetorical moments that could be forever lost and perspectives persistently held at bay if they are not endorsed and engaged in academic spaces. While small, there is a clear lineage stemming from the work of Hamlet and Davis outlining the possibility of Black women's theory in the field of communication, whether focusing on rhetoric, pedagogy, health disparities, politics, religion, or more.

While womanist rhetorical theory and thought is still a growing perspective in the field of communication with Toniesha Taylor, Monika Alston, Kimberly Johnson, Annette Madlock Gatison, Cerise Glenn, and others consistently publishing projects to center Black women's narratives, the history of womanism is over 30 years old. Its academic foundations are based in Walker's definition from *In Search of Our Mother's Gardens*, where the term *womanist* is given an extensive definition. From this text, Walker (1983, p. xii) defines womanism as:

WOMANIST

1. From womanish. (Opp. of "girlish," i.e. frivolous, irresponsible, not serious.) A black feminist or feminist of color. From the black folk expression of mothers to female children, "you acting womanish," i.e., like a woman. Usually referring to outrageous, audacious, courageous or willful behavior. Wanting to know more and in greater depth than is considered "good" for one. Interested in grown up doings. Acting grown up. Being grown up. Interchangeable with another black folk expression: "You trying to be grown." Responsible. In charge. Serious.

2. Also: A woman who loves other women, sexually and/or nonsexually. Appreciates and prefers women's culture, women's emotional flexibility (values tears as natural counterbalance of laughter), and women's strength. Sometimes loves individual men, sexually and/or nonsexually. Committed to survival and wholeness of entire people, male and female. Not a separatist, except periodically, for health. Traditionally a universalist, as in: "Mama, why are we brown, pink, and yellow, and our cousins are white, beige and black?" Ans. "Well, you know the colored race is just like a flower garden, with every color flower represented." Traditionally capable, as in: "Mama, I'm walking to Canada and I'm taking you and a bunch of other slaves with me." Reply: "It wouldn't be the first time."

3. Loves music. Loves dance. Loves the moon. Loves the Spirit. Loves love and food and roundness. Loves struggle. Loves the Folk. Loves herself. Regardless.

4. Womanist is to feminist as purple is to lavender.

Most, if not all, womanist scholars cite this definition to explore their own specific fields of study and expound upon it. And while this entry is not an exhaustive explanation about all the ways in which womanist thought is diverse and offers a certain level of fluidity in application, womanist rhetorical theory, at its heart, is primarily regarded as an interactive dialectic invested in the heart of Black women and the communities they love and that love them in return.

Continuing the Conversation

While Aretha Franklin was well known for her 1967 hit "Respect," her life had dark moments with storylines displaying despair, distrust, disloyalty, and denial despite the richness of her talent. A quick womanist analysis of a few words from this hit single demonstrate how little respect is regarded, either in personal or private relationships, or even in public space. The lyrics are almost as if she is belting out a ballad to the ways in which respect must be a formidable start toward continuing any conversation of solidarity, companionship, community, and forward thinking. The lyrics play all too well in the womanist formation of identity in a world accustomed to sentencing Black bodies to the margins or worse. To continue the conversation of womanism inside and outside of the communication classroom, the work must be done with care, justice, and with Black women at the center. Doing this requires scholars, students, and practitioners to exercise due diligence in finding out and respecting what it means to live life through the lens of a Black woman, and how her voice is consistently compromised, and not by her own doing. This does not include speaking for her, but letting her words, ways, and wisdom speak for themselves.

Womanist rhetorical theory serves as an intervention in a white, male-dominated cannon of (assumed) great white scholarship. Far too often, this roster of thought is influenced by (what is often considered strictly) philosophical and civic study seated at the helm of the Greco-Roman empire. Yet, through the slave uprisings in the Caribbean, such as the infamous Haitian revolution of 1791–1804 led by Touissant L'Ouverture, to the shores of Charleston, South Carolina with African Methodist minister Nat Turner, to the thousands of miles traveled by Harriet Tubman, who never lost a passenger on her train toward freedom, Black men and women have utilized all means of physical, mental, spiritual, and emotional energy to overpower and outthink the discursive devices that were used to keep them enslaved. Womanist scholarship serves as a means to give Black women the space to "speak truth to power" and to live beyond the promises of pain the world offers. Even more so, womanism exists in imaginative and very real spaces that uplift the voices, values, and visions of Black women (and the communities that love their full humanity).

Despite what the conventional canon of communication scholarship holds as representative of theory, womanist rhetorical theory exists to offer what theory can be and should be: a space for all to come to voice in a holistic manner that supports and defends dignity, personhood, and Black women's experiences, which can and are worthy to be trusted and believed. A textbook holding space to chart the discursive practices and ways in which Black women center their rhetorical musings from their own position in this world is well overdue. A text is ripe to not simply conquer the plague of whiteness in communication scholarship but to show the breadth and depth of Black women's speech acts in private and public spaces by defining and exploring womanist rhetorical theory.

While I would define rhetoric as the art of authentic voice construction in public and private communicative space, I would define theory as the study of discovering and determining concepts within, or for a community to understand or argue a system of thought. Yet, womanist thought is very specific and particular in its scope. Altogether, womanist rhetorical theory is a call or summons for the centering of Black women's voices, experiences, and bodies (without apology). The goal of this rhetorical theory somewhat broadly excludes those who are not Black women, but unlike normative practices, it is not built by appropriating, discrediting, or undervaluing any human being. Womanist scholarship, in general, is neither committed to nor made famous by oversimplifying and ignoring the intrinsic value of any person; instead, it centers marginalized stories by celebrating, highlighting, and voicing their existence, resistance, and persistence hegemony.

Summary

Womanist rhetorical theory is an intellectual and practical exercise dedicated to illuminating the ways in which Black women discursively exist in this world. It not only centers Black women's discursive insight but also highlights the ways in which they are change agents in their own route toward thriving as they rename and reconstruct worlds of their own that are not dedicated to exploiting and profiting from their pain, but instead celebrating their joy. Thus, womanist rhetorical theory values the speech acts of women in charge of their own rhetorical destiny, healing, and ideological capabilities beyond the constrictive places and spaces that silence their everyday embodied voice.

FOR FURTHER THOUGHT AND REFLECTION·

1. After reading this chapter, how has your understanding of womanism, woman-
    ist thought, and womanist theory, particularly as it applies to communication,
    been expanded?

2. How would you say womanist rhetorical theory can be distinguished from more tradi-
    tional ways of thinking in the communication studies?

3. As a student, how would you apply this theory in your own learning and research, and
    what more would you like to learn? Can you generate one particular aspect of popular
    culture that would benefit tremendously from a womanist analysis? What would it be,
    and what might be gained?

STORIED REFLECTION
Hovering About Prevailing Theories

Alberto González
Bowling Green State University

In 1990, when I wrote about the sense of "otherness" in the poems of migrant farmworkers in
Ohio, I was also writing about the otherness I experienced in my graduate program and later
as an assistant professor encountering for the first time the community of communication studies. I wasn't intimidated; I was simply reminded of the way I felt as a child when my father took
me from the familiarity of home to the strange white world of the supermarket.

I wanted readers to encounter authors like Gloria Anzaldúa, Carlos Fuentes, and Octavio Paz.
For me, they theorized cultural identity and the strategic influences and consequences of discourses as well as anyone. I wanted names with ˜ and ´ and Spanish language terms to appear
in communication journals. So I wrote them in.

Ten Years Earlier

I always had an ambivalent relationship with the prevailing theories in communication studies.
In graduate school in the early 1980s, we were encouraged to pick a theoretical and critical
location. Everyone went somewhere. I hovered about.

While all of the theories and critical options helped me to understand rhetorical and cultural
concerns and processes, I didn't quite connect to any of them. The focus of my master's thesis
and my dissertation involved Mexican and Mexican American residents in Northwest Ohio.
To be true to their voices, I believed that I had to craft a research approach that blended their

views of the world with the scholarly touchstones that my respective committees expected to find in my writing. It was an awkward blend.

In 1980, an event occurred that would establish my approach for decades to come. My dissertation director asked if I wanted to rewrite a class paper for publication. We decided that we were going to explain how Bob Dylan rhetorically moved his fan base from expecting the angst and disaffection of his 1960s songs to accepting the themes of Christian conversion found in his 1980s music. This new paper would include an analysis of lyrics and musical elements of the songs.

There wasn't a lot of literature on rhetoric and popular music, but there were several key sources that we drew upon. Still, there wasn't any theory or theoretical concept that quite explained what Dylan was doing lyrically and musically. So we invented our own term: "rhetorical ascription" (Gonzalez & Makay, 1983). The paper was published in *Quarterly Journal of Speech* (my first publication) and what was equally important was the realization that anyone (meaning me) could contribute a new explanation and give it a name.

Back to the 1990s

The same impulse to see the names of Latinx sources and Black, Indigenous, or People of Color (BIPOC) scholars published under the category of communication studies gave rise to *Our Voices: Essays in Culture, Ethnicity, and Communication*. The sixth edition was coedited with Yea-Wen Chen (González & Chen, 2016). In all the editions, we privileged a narrative way of knowing and sharing. Our central goal was not the advancement of prevailing theories but rather to push the door open to allow access to ignored domains of cultural communication.

Embracing the rupture and lacking humility, I depicted myself as a mutinous fugitive from the mainstream of communication studies. I repeated the "sacred claims" of social constructivism and asserted that, "These claims do not make me sweat, as they once did; nor do they ease my pain, which they never could. Now these claims challenge us to look *beyond* them, and they challenge us to look *before* them" (González, 1997, p. 382, italics in original).

Present Day

Fortunately, there have been many developments in communication theory and criticism. Our field has seen the emergence of critical perspectives in rhetoric and intercultural communication. In our research, we have moved from a reliance on *a* theory to the acceptance of a theory *perspective* within which multiple complementary accounts of communication and culture may cohabit.

As I work on an analysis of the public displays at the Demilitarized Zone that separates South and North Korea, the analysis centers on a rhetoric of *han*, a key cultural concept in Korea. In thinking about the rhetorics of Korean figures such as freedom fighter Kim Koo or labor activist Chun Taeil, Western theories of culture and communication do not work well as starting points. So, I hover about.

CHAPTER 16

Positive Deviance Approach

Arvind Singhal

The University of Texas at El Paso

merican poet Robert Lee Frost, who won an unprecedented four Pulitzer Prizes, deftly and succinctly opined on complex social and philosophical phenomena. One such pithy rendition included, "We dance round in a ring and suppose. But the secret sits in the middle and knows." These two lines capture the discomfort and incertitude that scholars and practitioners of communication and social change face in their quest to address complex social problems. Their unease results from the gnawing dilemmas about the myriad ways in which social problems can be approached, the seeming impossibility of untangling their complex web of underlying causes, and a haunting apprehension that the real solution may exist and yet remain hidden from plain view.

While communication and social change scholars crave the Frostian "secret," they are well aware that the social world is fraught with probabilities, uncertainties, and ambiguities. For instance, solving malnutrition is more than simply producing more food, and reducing school dropouts requires more than just hiring more teachers. For this reason, for millennia, spiritual leaders, philosophers, and intellectuals have tried to discern and dissect what constitutes wisdom—one that "sits in the middle and knows." This love affair with wisdom gave rise to philosophy or *philo-sophia*, literally "the love of wisdom," and various symbolic manifestations—for example, Athena, the Greek goddess of wisdom, and Minerva, her Roman incarnation, are represented by an owl—one able to see in darkness. From "darkness to light" is a common wisdom refrain in the Hindu Vedas, the Christian Bible, and the Islamic Quran.

While elusive to grasp, wisdom is the coordination of knowledge and experience to act purposively and deliberatively to improve the well-being of individuals, communities, and societies. Wisdom is multidimensional and may include contextual problem solving with sustainable actions, value-based actions grounded in ethics, and an acceptance and celebration of life's complexities, ambiguities, and uncertainties.

In this chapter, I interrogate the positive deviance (PD) approach, an innovative conceptualization of communication and social change praxis that lies squarely in the wisdom tradition. The PD approach represents a radical shift in how we theorize communication and social change praxis, believing in the value of local wisdom—that is, the knowledge and vital capacities of ordinary and marginalized groups (Pascale et al., 2010; Singhal, 2021). The PD approach, grounded in ethical, moral, and nonhierarchical actions, turns the classical, expert-driven interventional approaches on their head, offering a radically different framework to tackle the world's most intractable problems (Singhal & Svenkerud, 2018).

In this chapter, I describe the PD approach, detailing its historic application to solve the problem of malnutrition in Vietnam. In so doing, I systematize the key tenets of the PD approach, including a distillation of the six steps that characterize the PD method of identifying and amplify existing and uncommon wisdom. Further, I extend the PD problem-solving frame by interrogating a case involving the double burden of malnutrition—that is, obesity, and analyzing how PD interventions can be situated upstream or downstream. Through these analyses and interrogations, we demonstrate that the PD approach is a radically different way of theorizing communicative praxis and holds valuable implications for communication and social change scholars and practitioners.

Intellectual Tradition of Positive Deviance

To grasp the intellectual basis of the PD approach, let us begin with the invocation of a Sufi tale in which the mystical character Nasiruddin appears on earth as a smuggler (Singhal & Dura, 2009). He would arrive at the customs checkpoint each day leading a herd of donkeys. The customs inspector would feverishly turn the baskets hanging upside down on the donkeys, hoping to nail Nasiruddin in an act of wrongdoing. He, however, never found anything of interest and hence had little choice but to let the smuggler pass through. Months, years, and decades roll by and Nasiruddin's legend as a smuggler grows. The inspector grows increasingly frustrated. One day, after Nasiruddin and the inspector had retired from their respective occupations, their paths crossed. The former inspector pleaded, "Tell me, Nasruddin. What were you smuggling?" "Donkeys," Nasiruddin replied.

Nasiruddin's donkey story holds the key to grasp the key principle of the PD approach. Often the solutions to highly intractable problems stare us in the face but remain invisible in plain sight—outside the gaze of an expert's radar. What prevented the customs officer from seeing Nasiruddin's donkeys? Part of the answer lies perhaps in the bounded rationality of an expert's mind that selectively processes what is meaningful and relevant. Some call this inattentional blindness or trained incapacity, a state where one's expertise and abilities function as constraints. Clearly, the custom officer's frame—guided by selective representations, perceptions, and interpretations of what constitutes "contraband"—delineated the boundaries of what was visible or invisible. The baskets were visible; the donkeys were not!

So how can one purposely discover Nasiruddin's donkeys? The PD approach shows the way. It is based on the premise that every community has individuals or groups whose uncommon behaviors and strategies enable them to find better solutions to problems than their peers, although everyone has access to the same resources and challenges (Pascale et al., 2010). However, these individuals—akin to Nasiruddin's donkeys, are hidden from plain view. Consider a nurse who uses her "knuckle" (not fingertips) to press the hospital elevator button, and a patient who has figured out a way (using winks and nods) to let medical personnel know that they need to wash their hands before touching him. In both cases, these micro-behaviors reduce the risk of spreading deadly infections and saving patients' lives (Singhal et al., 2010; 2014). However, such micro-behaviors are ordinarily invisible to others, especially to expert change agents. The nurse and the patient represent "deviants" because their uncommon behaviors are not the norm; they are "positive" deviants because they have found ways to address the problem effectively, while most others have not. By focusing on "what is working," the PD approach relies on unearthing the wisdom that lies hidden within ordinary people (or "unusual suspects") and amplifying it in a process that leads to sustainable organizational and community transformation.

The section that follows illustrates the six steps in the positive deviance approach by discussing its success in combating malnutrition in Vietnam.

Main Goals and Features of Positive Deviance

In 1990, *Save the Children U.S.* sent Jerry and Monique Sternin to Vietnam to implement a nationwide program to combat childhood malnutrition. Prior to their arrival, the Vietnamese government had learned from experience that results achieved by traditional supplemental feeding programs were not sustainable. When the programs ended, the gains usually tapered off. Thus, the Vietnamese government challenged the Sternins to come up with an approach that enabled the community, without much outside help, to take control of their nutritional status and to maintain it. And, further, the Sternins were asked to show positive results within six months.

From years of studying Mandarin, Jerry knew that the Chinese characters for "crisis" included two ideograms: danger and opportunity. Perhaps there was an opportunity to try something new in Vietnam. Isn't necessity the mother of invention? If old methods of combating malnutrition would not yield quick and sustainable results, the Sternins wondered if positive deviance might hold promise.

The Sternins first learned about the concept of positive deviance from Professor Gretchen Berggren of Harvard University in 1991 when she visited them in Hanoi as

Save the Children's technical health advisor. She urged Jerry and Monique to read the recently published book by Tufts University nutrition professor Marian Zeitlin and colleagues, *Positive Deviance in Childhood Nutrition* (Zeitlin et al., 1990).

Zeitlin broached the notion of PD as she tried to understand why children in some poor households, without access to any special resources, were well nourished. What were the parents of these children doing? Perhaps combating malnutrition called for an asset-based approach: that is, identifying what is going right in a community and finding ways to amplify it, as opposed to the more traditional deficit-based approach of focusing on what is going wrong in a community and fixing it from the outside.

The PD concept appealed instantly to the Sternins for it was proof that solutions to a complex problem *already* existed. Could this be the elusive missing link to sustainable development? They could see that it was practical and possible to find poor families with well-nourished children and then discover what they did that others did not.

PD sounded good in theory, and yet no one had operationalized the construct to design a field-based nutrition intervention. Fortuitously, the Vietnamese Communist government liked the PD concept and gave the green light. However, the Sternins had no road maps or blueprints to consult. Where to begin?

The government assigned the Sternins to work in four communities in Quang Xuong district in Thanh Hóa province, south of Hanoi, where childhood malnutrition rates were especially high. The Ho Chi Minh trail, the major supply route for the Vietcong guerillas during U.S. hostilities in Vietnam, snaked through Quang Xuong, so suspicion of U.S. Americans was noticeably high. The Sternins' first task was to build trust with all stakeholders. The rest would follow.

Building rapport with village elders, and working closely with local health volunteers, the Sternins facilitated a process by which some 2,000 children under the age of three years were weighed and their locations mapped in a participatory mapping exercise. When all the growth charts were compiled for the 2,000 children, the Sternins posed the quintessential PD somersault question: *Are there any well-nourished children who come from very, very poor families?*

The response from the local officials was "Yes." Indeed, some children from very poor families were well nourished. These families who had managed to avoid malnutrition without access to any special resources represented the positive deviants. Through a process of community-led self-discovery, it became apparent that the PD families were practicing a few simple behaviors that others were not:

- Family members collected tiny shrimps and crabs from paddy fields, adding them to their children's meals. These foods are rich in protein and minerals. While these foods were accessible to everyone, most community members believed they were inappropriate for young children.

- Family members added greens of sweet potato plants to their children's meals. These greens are loaded with micronutrients.

- PD mothers and caregivers fed their children smaller meals three to four times a day, rather than the customary two big meals twice a day.

- PD mothers and caregivers actively fed their children, rather than placing food in front of them. Active feeding ensured that no food was wasted.

- PD mothers continued to feed their children when they had diarrhea, rather than the customary practice of limiting food intake during this time.

- PD mothers insisted that their children washed their hands before sitting down for a meal.

After some trial and error, a two-week nutrition program was designed and implemented in the four intervention villages. Caregivers whose children were malnourished were asked to forage for shrimps, crabs, and sweet potato greens. The focus was not on information-transfer but rather on action, practice, and embodied experience. In the company of positive deviants, non-PD caregivers of malnourished children learned how to cook new recipes using the foraged ingredients. These caregivers practiced the behaviors that the PD families had discovered on their own.

Before feeding their children, mothers weighed them. They washed their hands and the hands of their children. No food was wasted as the children were actively fed. Upon returning home, the non-PD caregivers were encouraged to feed their children three or four small meals a day instead of the traditional two meals. Such feeding and monitoring continued throughout the two-week program. Caregivers could see their children becoming noticeably healthier. The scales were tipping in favor of the children! Then the project expanded to another 10 adjacent communities. Community members engaged in a process of self-discovering the PD behaviors, as opposed to importing them from neighboring communities. The process of self-discovery was found to be as important as the actual behaviors that were uncovered.

Research showed that malnutrition decreased by an amazing 85 percent in the first 14 PD communities (Pascale et al., 2010). The program was scaled up by building a "living university" around these 14 PD communities. Teams from other communities with high rates of malnutrition spent up to two weeks directly experiencing the essential elements of the PD process. When they returned home, they would implement the PD nutrition program in at least two local communities. Through this lateral expansion, the PD intervention spread nationally, helping over 2.2 million people improve their nutritional status, including over 500,000 children (Pascale et al., 2010). A later study, conducted four years after the program ended, showed that older children and their younger siblings in PD communities continued to be better nourished, demonstrating the acceptability, affordability, and sustainability of the PD intervention (Mackintosh et al., 2002).

The Vietnam case led to the systematization of the six "D" steps that characterizes the PD approach. See Table 1 for the six "D" steps shared in the positive deviance process in the Vietnam case.

1. *Define* the problem to be solved.
2. *Determine* the presence of positive deviants.
3. *Discover* the uncommon but replicable behaviors of positive deviants.
4. *Design* an intervention to enable practice of these uncommon behaviors.
5. *Discern* effectiveness through community monitoring of progress.
6. *Disseminate* through the principle of "living universities."

TABLE 16.1 The 6 "D" Steps of the Positive Deviance Process in the Vietnam Case

6 "Ds" of PD	Illustrations From Vietnam Case
1. *Define* the problem.	Baseline data provided by Vietnamese officials showed 65% of children were malnourished.
2. *Determine* existence of statistical outliers.	Two thousand children were weighed by health volunteers and community members; some children from very poor families were well-nourished and their locations were plotted on a map.
3. *Discover* uncommon but replicable behaviors and practices.	Community-led self-discovery involved interviews and observations to discover PD behaviors and strategies: What were PD families doing that other families were not?
4. *Design* intervention.	A two-week action-based nutrition program was designed and implemented; PD caregivers taught non-PD caregivers their strategies; non-PD caregivers practiced the new recipes and PD behaviors.
5. *Discern* effectiveness.	Feeding and monitoring continued; caregiver families could see progressive weight gain of their children during the intervention.
6. *Disseminate*.	The project expanded to 10 adjacent communities. Malnutrition decreased by 85% in the 14 PD communities. Over time, the PD intervention spread nationally to 298 communes, helping 2.2 million people (including 500,000 children). Four years later, a study confirmed sustained nutrition status for the children and their siblings.

The systematization of the six PD steps by Jerry and Monique Sternin in Vietnam greatly aided the dissemination of the PD approach to many locations. By 2021, the PD approach had been employed in over 65 countries to solve many intractable problems. These problems include: school dropouts in Argentina; female genital circumcision in Egypt; infant and maternal mortality in Pakistan; hospital-acquired infections in the United States; and teenage pregnancy along the U.S.-Mexico border (Pascale et al., 2010; Singhal, 2021; Singhal & Sowards, in press).

Next, we demonstrate the versatility of the PD problem-solving frame by interrogating a case involving the double burden of malnutrition—that is, being overweight and obese. In so doing, we demonstrate how the PD approach can intervene both upstream and downstream—a testimony to its research potential as well as practical applicability.

Research and Practical Applications of Positive Deviance

The problems of being underweight and malnutrition coexist with being overweight and obesity—commonly referred to as the "double burden" of malnutrition. In 2014, while 462 million people were underweight, more than 1.9 billion adults worldwide, 18 years and older, were overweight, of which 600 million were obese (World Health Organization, 2015). Not surprisingly, both malnutrition and obesity exist in the same community, region, or nation.

As a problem-solving strategy, PD interventions should span the upstream-downstream continuum (Heath, 2020). *Downstream* interventions react to problems once they have occurred—for instance, ineffective management of diabetes by Latinx adults. A PD inquiry, for instance, can ask the following somersault question to *determine* the presence of positive deviants:

Are there Latinx (men, women, and nonbinary persons) over the age of 40, who hail from low socioeconomic status households, with a diagnosis of Type 2 diabetes, with no access to medical insurance or a prescription drug plan, and yet have effectively managed their blood sugar levels over the past 12 months? If the answer is "yes," the next step would be to discover the uncommon and replicable behaviors of these Latinx positive deviants.

Conversely, *upstream* interventions aim to prevent those problems from happening—for example, prevention of childhood obesity among the Latinx population. If one can prevent childhood obesity among the Latinx population and cultivate healthy habits early on, one may significantly reduce incidence of diabetes, high blood pressure, and high cholesterol in later years. By intervening upstream, one may also break the cycle of intergenerational obesity, that is, children who are obese are likely to have one or both parents as being obese.

Foster et al. (2018) carried out a case-control study to identify positive deviance practices among Latinx families whose two- to five-year-old children maintained a healthy weight trajectory over time. A mixed methods analysis suggested that PD families were distinct from controls in several parenting strategies:

- PD families purposely created healthier food environments. They refrained from stocking unhealthy junk foods at home and purposely stacked counters and refrigerators with fruits such as apples, oranges, and grapes. Further, they purposely packed healthy foods (carrots and celeries and apple wedges) during family outings.

- PD parents displayed message consistency: Their children knew what foods they could or could not eat for snacks.

- PD families were more proactive in addressing their child's picky eating habits in contrast to letting it be an ongoing challenge. Rules were set early and reinforced repeatedly.

- PD families made incremental changes for self-correction: They were more likely to reduce availability and consumption of unhealthy snacks rather than trying to eliminate them. Similarly, they were more likely to increase physical activity gradually (e.g., first spending more family time in the backyard before introducing a family walking/biking routine) rather than introducing—abruptly—a new rigorous physical activity.

- PD families took an all-family approach to food and physical activity. Everyone had access to the same food in the counters, refrigerators, and on the dining table. Further, they engaged in more collective physical activity.

- PD mothers were able to effectively change or reign in the indulgent behaviors of grandparents or fathers toward their children (e.g., buying them candy or giving permission to have an extra slice of cheesecake).

Continuing the Conversation

The pioneering PD experience in Vietnam demonstrates the limitations of reifying expert-driven, top-down approaches to address problems and thus, by default, overlooking and rejecting local solutions. Therein lies the greatest potential in future research with PD as evidence of its heuristic value—serving as a vehicle to address contemporary challenges of our time, including for effectively addressing prevention, care, and vaccination challenges of COVID-19 (Singhal & Kim, 2021). The Foster et al. (2018) study demonstrates that a complex social problem lends itself to a PD intervention via multiple entry points, that is, along the upstream and downstream continuum. The PD approach can expand the solution space for intractable issues and be useful in future work dealing with the wellness of families, communities, and organizations.

Summary

By focusing on what is working (local solutions, assets, and resources), rather than what is not working (problems, gaps, and needs), the PD approach identifies the hidden endogenous wisdom of ordinary people, enabling the amplification of culturally appro-priate solutions to community problems.

The PD approach questions the traditional role of external change agent and reframes it as a role of coach, facilitator, and guide. Their role is simply to help the community define their problem, determine the presence of positive deviants, discover their uncommon practices, and design an intervention to act on those practices. PD is a process driven by internal change agents and anchored on endogenous wisdom.

In the PD approach, the PD behaviors already exist and are currently in practice. Thus, the solutions are accessible without delay or access to outside resources. Further, the benefits are sustainable since the solution resides locally.

FOR FURTHER THOUGHT AND REFLECTION

1. What is one complex social problem that you believe could be solved by applying the PD approach locally?

2. To undertake a PD inquiry for the above problem, what question might you ask to deter-mine the presence of positive deviants?

3. When invited to participate in a neighborhood town hall to address police brutality, what "somersault" questions might you pose to inject PD thinking into the conversation and expand the solution space?

4. What might an upstream and downstream PD determining question be to expand the solution space for addressing police brutality?

STORIED REFLECTION
Returning Home

B. Liahnna Stanley
Arizona State University

During the beginning stages of my master's program, I felt like a lost rez dog: a presumed stray grubbing around for resources, not necessarily needing or wanting rescue, but want-ing a home. Being an Indigenous, first-generation college student, I didn't quite understand what graduate school was before entering it, much less have an abundance of knowledge about communication theories. Most theories made sense to me, but they seemed incompat-ible with the complexities of Indigenous knowledges, if not completely excluding them. Only a few professors—primarily Black scholars and scholars of color—would address colonialism in their theoretical critiques and acknowledge the lush intellectual and political systems of Indigenous lands, lives, and relationalities.

Still, I wonder/ed: *Is there space for me here? How will I measure up? Am I an imposter?* I began to feel myself ripping along the seams, with open wounds scarring, old wounds haunting. It wasn't just that I didn't *see* myself in theory, I didn't *feel* myself in theory. I didn't feel myself at all! As I negotiated the disjunct between pride and excitement for "making it" in graduate school and the debilitating feelings of inadequacy and self-doubt, I found comfort in the praise and affirmation of my professors. And so, I succumbed to the toxic pressure to conform and contort my comportment according to neoliberal calibers. In hindsight, perhaps this was a strategy for surviving against the pathologizing nature of the colonial academy, a loud whisper I wish I could pass on to my younger self.

By the second year of my master's program, I found theoretical inspiration in postcolonial and decolonial criticism for both my scholarship and my understanding of the academy more generally. This was also around the time when disciplinary conversations about #CommunicationSoWhite started to surge against the existing structures of domination pervading the field—namely the discipline's historic investments in whiteness and colonial logics. Engaging decolonial and anticolonial theories, alongside witnessing a collective mobilization for transforming the field, I was provided the language to articulate what was deeply subjectively felt and known as well as energizing me to work toward structural change. I also became more attuned to the important reflexive work of undoing my own complicity upholding these structures. These factors were crucial in motivating me to continue my work at the doctoral level.

In the summer before I began my doctoral studies, my cousin back home called me. He lives on the Poarch Creek reservation in Lower Alabama. He called to ask if I planned on visiting before moving to Arizona. With regret in my voice, I told him I couldn't. I was too busy with work, and my wife and I were preparing for a cross-country move. In reply, he joked: "Damn, Li! This academic stuff really has colonized you, huh? Ain't even coming home no more. You got no love for us!" Now, my cousin is always one to tease. But even if shared jokingly, his words struck me. I was so concerned with finding my academic home, so concerned with fitting in, that I let myself become uprooted and forgot my real home: my homelands and community. *I shouldn't have to come home because I should've never left home.* Home, the greatest source of communal power, prayer, resistance, and of course, the poetics of Mvskoke thought, livelihood, and theorization. Home, my greatest teacher.

Taking seriously my cousin's banter, I felt a responsibility to resist my dreamscapes and body being colonized. I carried this responsibility with me into my doctoral program. I committed to refusing the assimilationist and exclusionary logics through which the academy functions and advocating for structural change within and outside the academy. Indeed, schooling has always been a target of colonialism, dispossessing us of ourselves and kinship networks so we learn to forget. I needed to listen to my cousin. I knew I needed to return home and (re)invigorate my spirit.

I'd say returning home is more about locating myself within a process rather than a place. Returning home is realizing I left home, but I've never left home; I am always there, and my relatives are always with me. It is honoring the complexity of Indigenous brilliance to reconceptualize the field against the white Eurocentric mainstream. It is finding strength through embodying the enduring resistance of my ancestors—both past and future—and developing it through praxis-oriented action for change.

Through the process of confronting these truths, I've become inspired by my responsibility to radically unimagine them and enact new worlds into being, worlds that are life-affirming and -sustaining for peoples and relatives at the margins as well as the more-than-human world with which we share time and space. Perhaps I wasn't as lost as I once thought I was. I just needed home.

PART VI

Media and Technology

In previous parts, we have highlighted theoretical frameworks that focus on various aspects of human communication broadly defined. This has included theories centered on the self and identity, interpersonal messages, relationships, organizations, leadership, rhetoric, and influence. The final part of our book takes a new direction and shifts the focus to media and technology. Our specific focal point is to present frameworks that advance our understanding of (1) how messages are communicated via different computer-mediated technologies, and (2) how those messages impact, and are impacted by, diverse human communication experiences.

Media can be defined broadly as the communication tools used to create, deliver, exchange, and store information. More specifically, media refer to the variety of communication technologies that work to extend the range, speed, channels and overall capabilities of human communication. As such, mass-mediated communication is the use of technology to disseminate messages to others. The particulars of specific media (e.g., print media, radio, television, film, social media) influence the message, given their capabilities (e.g., limited text, pictures, graphics, images, interactive features). Other factors—speed of delivery, ease of utility, complexity, usability, visibility, impact/reach, relative advantage, and the like—also influence communication-based decisions surrounding media.

A central idea of media ecology is that changes in technology alter the environment and, in turn, shape human experience (McLuhan & Foire, 2005). Similar human communication behaviors—talking, sharing, teaching, learning, storytelling, persuading, and engaging in social gatherings—existed through time *and* technology as each time period has had a tremendous influence on how those activities were experienced. At this point, it is difficult to imagine a world without media and technology.

The omnipresence of mass-mediated images, (over)reliance on technology, and the pervasiveness of social media regulates such an image to days gone. Media are a powerful presence in our lives: providing information, facilitating interactions with others, supplying a never-ending array of services, offering engaging and entertaining interlinkages, influencing and persuading, cultivating stereotypes, unifying and dividing, and so on. The powerful influence of the media on, and within, the communication process is undeniable. Theoretical frameworks that provide ways in which to understand that influence are crucial to our ultimate negotiation of the role that media play in our lives.

Existing Canonized Theories

Attempts to theorize the intersections of communication, media, and technology have intensified as their role in society became more pervasive over time. In the mid-20th century, the focus of media theories was on effects: How did mass-mediated images impact audiences? Scholars initially situated media images as extremely powerful, believing that consumption impacted our thoughts like that of a "magic bullet" entering human minds. These early attempts to theorize media effects gave way to scholars rejecting initial assumptions; the result was a pendulum swing to an oppositional stance known as limited effects. This body of work criticized earlier theories that regarded media consumers as passive and, instead, prioritized human agency and critical thinking capabilities. The end of the 20th century witnessed an array of media theories that acknowledge the value of both perspectives: media as powerfully influential yet not all powerful in terms of their impact on consumers.

The canon of media theories is best represented by a core of frameworks that seek to explain both media effects and consumer agency. For example, agenda-setting theory is grounded in the idea that the media serve as a catalyst for public opinion. According to McCombs and Shaw (1972), media cannot tell audiences "what to think," yet it does tell them "what to think about." More recently, scholars have also written about how the media, through framing and other covert techniques, do provide guidance on how to think about different issues. Cultivation theory, generated by Gerbner (1998), argues that the media's power is far-reaching and demonstrated through its pervasive effects on people's perceptions and behaviors. It also recognizes the audience as active interpreters who have some agency in the amount and type of media images that are consumed. In short, Gerber believed that media creates images that inform people's perceptions of the world—especially the case for "heavy viewers"—and in doing so, mold society. Uses and gratifications theory (Katz, Blumler, & Gurevitch, 1973) represents a shift from a focus on media effects to one of the media choices of consumers: "what people do with media," rather than "what media does to people." Here the focal point is on the important role that individual motives play in selecting particular media forms, a crucial factor for understanding any potential effects that media has on consumers. While these media theories provide a useful lens to understanding mass-mediated communication, they are limited in their core acknowledgement of the salient role that culture—race, ethnicity, nationality, gender, and the like—plays in the relationship between media, technology, and communication. Absent from these theoretical frameworks is any critical engagement with how the media serves the dominant cultural group, something that marks the prominence of Stuart Hall's work related to cultural studies (the focus of Chapter 19).

In sum, the powerful effects of media are more likely in select situations. According to Ball-Rokeach and DeFleur (1976), media are most influential when individuals cannot rely upon personal experience or sources for information. In other words, we rely especially on media images, and the version of the world's reality that they come to represent, when they capture experiences beyond our own lives. Consider this point as the world grapples with cultural divisions fueled by preconceived notions of racially and ethnically diverse people. We do not recommend that you avoid media at all costs, as if that is even remotely possible in today's world. We do recommend that you engage with the media with an informed, critical eye. The four chapters included in Part VI contribute to such a goal.

Overview of Chapters

Communication-based theorizing of media is in a constant state of playing catch-up in regard to the ever-changing growth of new media technologies. In different ways, the canon of existing theories has implicitly situated majority experiences as universal, and in doing so, failed to consider the perspectives of minoritized group members. So while existing canon of media theories provide some productive insight into diverse mass-mediated experiences of the 21st century, they also oftentimes fall short in engaging the diverse and nuanced communicative realities associated with new emerging technologies. Part VI of the book covers theoretical frameworks that provide a productive lens through which we can examine how racially and ethnically diverse people impact, and are impacted by, media and technology.

We begin the final part of the book with Chapter 17, which describes the significance of cultural studies. Isabel Molina-Guzmán identifies the work of Stuart Hall as instrumental to foregrounding the issues of representation and racial, ethnic, and gender differences and their relationship to economic, political, and cultural power. Hall, a Jamaican-born British sociologist, was a founding figure in what is known as cultural studies—a theoretical framework that continues to provide powerful insight into how media representations matter. At the core of cultural studies is the idea that all media forms are fruitful sites for the study of culture, politics, power, and societal relations. Within this chapter, Molina-Guzmán describes how ideologies are produced through language, rhetoric, popular culture, and media. She also provides insight on how producers and consumers of mediated messages are shaped by their consumption of ideologies, which leads to a range of interpretive decoding possibilities. In doing so, she explains the hegemonic struggle whereby capitalist democracies continue to maintain the status quo in terms of political, economic, and cultural power relations. Through insightful contemporary examples, this chapter makes a strong argument for cultural studies as a lens through which to critique issues of difference, power, and inequality. Highlighting the nuanced ways in which the cultural is always political, this framework interrogates the role that dominant media and popular culture play in maintaining existing economic and political power. Molina-Guzman concludes the chapter by explaining how critiques of media are central ultimately to cultivating more equitable, pluralistic, and democratic societies.

Chapter 18, authored by Catherine R. Squires and Mark P. Orbe, chronicles the emergence of (counter)public sphere theory. It begins by outlining the origins of public sphere theory, a set of ideas conceptualized by Jürgen Habermas, who believed that democracy is maximized when private citizens and engaged thinkers have the opportunity to utilize egalitarian spaces to express, exchange, and develop ideas. Squires and Orbe then summarize the limitations of Habermas's initial ideas as they reflected a privileged perspective based on race, gender, and class. The crux of the chapter is on extensions of public sphere theory, specifically that which highlights the importance of considering social inequality and the copresence and prevalence of counterpublics. The authors argue that recognizing the existence of multiple public spheres—dominant public spheres alongside counterpublics like those created by traditionally underrepresented groups including enclaves, counterpublics, and satellites—is crucial in understanding the diverse ways in which individuals participate in democratic deliberations. Their argument is supported by examples of Black counterpublic spheres: Black print media, radio, civil rights organizations, community and fraternal groups, Black Twitter, Black Lives Matter, and the like. As demonstrated through this chapter, public sphere theory remains a highly relevant frame to study contemporary public discourse, especially that which is facilitated through various mass-mediated platforms. The theory also is an excellent exemplar of how existing theories, while providing some general insight into communication processes, are inherently limited when they do not consider culturally diverse perspectives.

This book is committed to highlighting cutting-edge theories, including those frameworks that reflect the most up-to-date ideas emerging from current diverse standpoints. Our final two chapters epitomize that commitment in beautifully articulated ways. First up is Chapter 19, a description of critical media effects (CME) by Srivi Ramasubramanian. As the world grapples with pandemic inequalities, white supremacy, anti-Black racism, rising fascism, and increasing xenophobia around the world, CME explores how media researchers and practitioners can use the power of media for prejudice reduction, inclusive communication, and favorable intergroup relations. The theoretical framework initially emerged from the realization that mass communication theories mute, marginalize, and minoritize traditionally underrepresented groups. As an alternative to the existing canon of mass communication scholarship, CME framework offers the opportunity to reflect on the ways in which quantitative methods and media effects theories can be used to address critical issues in the emerging sociopolitical and mediated contexts. The framework is grounded in four central pillars that are crucial to that goal: (1) power, (2) intersectionality, (3) context, and (4) agency. Collectively and synergistically, these pillars reflect the core values of mass media research and theorizing that centralize culturally diverse and inclusive perspectives. In short, CME offers communication and media scholars utilizing a traditional social scientific approach the means through which to avoid complicity in reinforcing dominant ideologies. As such, it provides an invaluable launching pad to engage in meaningful conversations regarding media, communication, theory, and methods—in essence, a roadmap that embraces the cultural diversity of our ever-changing world in meaningful, substantial, and inclusive ways.

The final chapter of the book explains an important and emerging theory by Amber Johnson and Jade Petermon—hyper(in)visibility. Chapter 20 captures the essence of the story of how these two scholars, initially working independently of one another, joined forces to make the connection between identity, communication, lived experience, and the media explicit and clear. Throughout the chapter, Johnson and Petermon provided many insightful examples where the theory of hyper(in)visibility provides nuanced insight into local, national, and global events. The theory highlights four layers of visibility: (1) invisibility, signified by a lack of mediated representation, (2) visibility, or frequent and complex representation in the media, (3) hypervisibility, present when mediated stereotypes are so pervasive that they are regarded as more believable than more authentic truths, and (4) hyper(in)visibility, described as a state where people choose to cause others harm based on their association with deeply sedimented stereotypes. In short, minoritized people are more visible in mediated texts than ever before, yet those representations remain stereotypically superficial and lacking in depth, nuance, and complexity. Hypervisibility can lead to hyper(in)visibility, defined through multiple forms of violence, including that which is physical, discursive, legislative, political, and/or economic. However, hypervisibility also can be curbed with meaningful, substantial interpersonal interaction. This is an idea that amplifies that interconnectivity of various communication contexts. So while the theory of hyper)in/visibility is featured in the final part related to media and technology (instead of other sections where it also "fits"), we feature it as the last chapter of the book because of the powerful ways that it incorporates multiple communication contexts simultaneously.

Overview of Storied Reflections

The storied reflections within Part VI feature a diverse set of experiences with theory. First, Catherine R. Squires, a professor at the University of Minnesota, provides a powerful account of how her introduction to theory began with one name, Stuart Hall. Within her short essay, she highlights how her own experiences and engagement with interdisciplinary scholarship led to her own theory-building. Despite this significant accomplishment (see Chapter 18), she was hesitant to describe herself as a theorist—something that theory helped her to understand. The second storied reflection in this part of the book is authored by David Stamps, an assistant professor at Bentley University. Stamps uses his essay to reminisce on the problematic ways in which race was represented during his graduate school experiences. Writing with a sense of cultural humility, he also points to the inherent limitations of scholars and theorists who write about the experiences of groups to which they do not belong. The third, and final, storied reflection is a compelling account of the transformative power of theory. Elizabeth M. Lozano, professor at Loyola University Chicago, artfully describes how theory (and her identity as a theoretician) saved her life. Her journey from a difficult home life in Colombia, to her selection as a Fulbright scholar in the United States, and ultimately a communication professor epitomizes the liberating power of theory. In no certain terms, it captures how we understand the important role of theorizing in the lives of racially and ethnically diverse people.

CHAPTER 17

Stuart Hall and Cultural Studies

Isabel Molina-Guzmán

University of Illinois at Urbana-Champaign

In the wake of global protest against systemic racism and the reemergence of the Black Lives Matters movement, both spurred by the 2020 police killing of George Floyd, the streaming service Netflix changed its opening app banner to "Representation Matters." U.S. protests against systemic racism had reinvigorated cultural activists' calls to change the racial, ethnic, and gender makeup of media representation and production—news, television, film, and streaming. That same call for changes in media production and representation also motivated and shaped the theoretical legacy of the Centre for Contemporary Cultural Studies/Birmingham School of Cultural Studies (CCCS) and the development of the cultural studies paradigm. Within the cultural studies tradition, it was Stuart Hall who foregrounded the significance of studying issues of representation and racial, ethnic, and gender differences and their relationship to economic, political, and cultural power. Today, years after Hall's death, the cultural studies approach he shaped continues to provide a framework to explain why media representations matter, who profits from the representational matters, who gets represented and how matters, and why communication scholars have an ethical imperative to study them.

In this chapter, I first trace the intellectual tradition of cultural studies with a specific discussion of its key concepts and Hall's contributions to their development. Specifically, I discuss Hall's reconceptualization of the concepts of ideology, hegemony, media audiences, and the significance of difference and representation in the study of media and popular culture. I conclude by placing the contributions of the cultural studies in conversation with contemporary intersectional feminist media studies and ethnic studies media scholarship through three case studies.

Intellectual Tradition of
Cultural Studies Theory

The CCCS's approach produced and contributed to a Marxist-influenced model that shifted preexisting theoretical frameworks for studying the media and popular culture away from the Frankfurt School tradition and media effects approaches. This approach became known as the Birmingham School of Cultural Studies, or "cultural studies" for short.

Cultural studies developed in the context of the major cultural and politics forces of post–World War II society. Scholars working within this tradition brought critical attention to the post–World War II rise of popular film and television programs, the emergence of youth cultures such as rock-n-roll, subaltern cultural movements such as punk, and counterculture movements such as the feminist and civil rights movements. Indeed, cultural studies situates all forms of media and culture as fruitful sites for the study of politics, society, and the formation of culture.

Of particular note, cultural studies challenged the intellectual dominance of the Frankfurt School's model about politics and the media. Founded by Theodor Adorno and Max Horkheimer in 1923 Germany, the Frankfurt School produced a model also centered on a critique of post–World War II culture, the easy accessibility of mass-produced media, and the capitalist commodification of culture. Composed of Marxist-influenced interdisciplinary scholars working across the arts, philosophy, economics, linguistics, and sociology, among other fields, the Frankfurt School produced a series of influential articles and manuscripts, such as the canonical "The Culture Industry: Enlightenment as Mass Deception" (Adorno & Bernstein, 2001). Research influenced by this framework continues to present a powerful and compelling theory for understanding the relationship between capitalism, cultural commodification, politics, and the negative effects of the consumption of mass media and popular culture by society.

Decades after the emergence of the Frankfurt School, scholars working within the cultural studies tradition took a radically different and transformative approach to the study of the mass media and popular culture. Equally defined by its interdisciplinarity and Marxist influence, cultural studies challenges the Frankfurt School's theoretical assumptions. Specifically, it questions the premise that mainstream media and popular culture are a prima facie negative social and political force that contributes to the maintenance of dominant economic and political power. Instead, cultural studies shifts the Frankfurt School's development of a more linear relationship between media content, capitalism, commodification, and democracy towards a more open-ended model that positioned audiences as active participants and cultural negotiators, constrained but not limited by capitalist systems of cultural production. That is to say, cultural studies scholarship complicates the role of the media in capitalist society while privileging audiences and minoritized communities' engagement with the media and popular culture to create a diverse set of social identities and narratives.

Main Goals and Features of Cultural Studies Theory

Underlying the cultural studies approach is a commitment to the study of the relationships between the political, capitalist democracies, media, and popular culture. Within this model, the cultural is always political. And the study and critique of media and popular culture are perceived as central to producing a more equitable, pluralistic, and democratic society. In particular, Stuart Hall's theoretical rearticulation of Louis Althusser's discussion of Marx and ideology (1985) and Antonio Gramsci's concept of hegemony (1986) generated two of cultural studies' most significant theoretical contributions to the study of popular communication—a focus on the study of audiences and an emphasis on the study of representations of race and other forms of difference. This section begins with a discussion of ideology and hegemony and concludes with a discussion of the application of hegemony to the study of audiences and representations of race and other forms of difference.

Ideology

Hall defines ideologies as systems of representation through which we create meaning (1985, p. 103). He argues these ideologies are produced through and by a diverse array of social practices—for example, through language, discourse, the media, and popular culture. Important here are two conceptual implications. First, there is not one *ideology* but multiple, conflicting, and convergent systems of representations or *ideologies*. Second, in systems of capitalist democracies, ideologies are located outside of the formal public functions of governments and within the private institutions of civil society, such as the schools, religious organizations, the media, and popular culture. Thus, cultural studies scholars situate the relationship between the ideological, economic, and political as complex and indirect. Cultural studies scholarship avoids a one-to-one correlation between class identity and ideologies and the belief that there is one true, correct, or authentic singular ideology.

One only needs to reflect on the 2016 election of Donald Trump to understand the significance of the cultural studies approach. Support for Trump's economic policies, heavily weighted towards the wealthy, resonated with a mix of poor and working-class white people, middle-class educated white voters, and conservative communities of color. These communities of voters did not make the decision to vote for Trump because of their class ideologies alone. They made strategic decisions to vote for him grounded in a convergence of ideologies represented in part but not exclusively through Trump's rhetoric, news coverage of Trump, and political advertising in traditional and social media outlets. While some of those ideologies were grounded in economic beliefs, other ideologies evoked social and political beliefs grounded in religion, nationalism, systemic racism, and gender bias. Cultural studies scholarship argues against the suggestion that the ideologies of these voters should be reduced to or determined by their economic class alone or that these voters are duped into voting against their economic interest.

Instead, Hall proposes ideologies work in "discursive chains, in clusters, in semantic fields, in discursive formations" (p. 104)—sometimes working in concert and other times struggling against each other to create meaning. These clusters are not floating unattached to the lived conditions of voter, but they are instead anchored in their relationships to the social, political, and economic conditions of voters. It is this struggle over ideologies, representations, and discourse that moves us to the next core concept of cultural studies, *hegemony* or *hegemonic struggle*.

Hegemonic Struggle and Hegemony

Stuart Hall turned to Gramsci to theorize the ideological struggle to create meaning and its relationship to power through the concepts of hegemony and hegemonic struggle. Specifically, Hall engaged these concepts to think through the puzzle of how capitalist democracies stayed in power when they do not control the media or the representations about the state. Hegemonic struggle describes the process by which capitalist democracies, where convergent and competing ideologies are freely produced through the mechanisms of civil society, continue to maintain preexisting organizations of political, economic, and cultural power (Hall, 1985, p. 100).

Focusing on an analysis of a dominant ideology in the media or popular culture, for instance, assumes a direct relationship to the economic and political. Instead, Hall pushed cultural studies scholarship to focus its analysis on the processes by which the relationships between economic, political, and cultural forces produce competing and oppositional ideologies (1986, p. 13). A hegemonic analysis of the media and popular culture identifies those ideologies and explains the political, economic, and cultural conditions under which some are eventually incorporated into dominant ideology and other ideologies remain outside of the dominant, acting instead as internalized and external oppositional-pressure forces.

Hegemony itself is the moment where the process of ideological struggle results in a dominant political, economic, or social group achieving or maintaining economic, political, or cultural power (Hall, 1986, pp. 14–16). Because, as previously discussed, the relationships between the ideological, political, and economic are open-ended, the production and identification of hegemony is historically contingent. Hegemony is internally and incrementally unstable, hard to achieve in the short term, and difficult to maintain over a long historical period of time. Consequently, Hall called for situating hegemonic analysis of media productions, representations, and reception within its specific historical, social, and political context.

Encoding/Decoding and Audiences

One of the most influential models developed out of the cultural studies tradition's approach to ideology, and hegemony is the theory of encoding/decoding (Hall, 1991). The theory directly challenged the Frankfurt School model and communication research on audiences dependent on the dominant linear model of communication of sender-->message-->receiver. Instead, it proposes a more iterative model of communication where media messages, their production, and reception are shaped by the relationships of the economic, political, and ideological as embodied in producers and audiences.

First, the encoding/decoding model proposes the works of mainstream media producers are shaped by their own consumption of ideologies, professional norms, routinized cultural labor, economic constraints, and imagined constructions of the audience among other factors. Producers are encoders and decoders of the world and the ideological messages around them. Second, since the model assumes producers themselves hold a range of ideologies, the work of cultural producers is also characterized by ideological struggle. Finally, audiences are conceptualized as decoders and encoders of media representations. Similar to cultural producers, audiences actively engage their ideologies and social, political, and economic contexts to interpret/decode and act upon/encode those messages in everyday life. Since media messages are composed of a set of ideologies, audiences also have a range of interpretative possibilities. Hall's model redefined the field of communication and its notions about producers, content, and audiences. Since its publication, it has been applied to the study of a wide range of cultural forms, practices, and audience behaviors from fan fiction to language to social media.

Research and Practical Applications of Cultural Studies Theory

Underlying Hall's scholarship is an interest in ideology as discourse, language, and representation, particularly representations of ethnic and racial difference. Ideologies, for him, are networks of "chains" or related discourses defined broadly (symbols, language, images, etc.) and the cultural practices that produce those discourses, such that one link in the chain pulls on other links to create or disrupt meaning. Hall sought to understand why the discursive chains around representations of difference perpetually recirculate ideologies grounded in racism and inequality that reinforce relationships of economic and political power. In this section, I provide three case studies or contemporary signposts for illustrating contemporary cultural studies approaches to difference, inequality, representation, and the media.

CASE STUDY 1: ZOË SALDAÑA AS NINA SIMONE

Hall's cultural studies theories about representations of race and difference trace the cyclical nature of negative/positive binary regimes of representation over time to the continuing struggle over power in the relationships of ideologies, politics, and economics. Typical of hegemonic analysis, the study of representations becomes a relational question over the links of ideologies or discourses at play (Hall, 1992). Representations of difference are core to the formation and maintenance of hegemony, and Hall perceived the inability of capitalist democratic society to live with ethnic, racial, gender, and sexual difference as one of its greatest flaws and profoundly inhumane. Hall's theorization of difference in media representations and its relationship to ideological, political, and economic power spawned another vibrant branch of cultural studies research focused on inequality and race, gender, and sexuality.

My research on representations of Latinidad speaks to the continuing discomfort with difference and its relationship to power (Molina-Guzmán, 2010). For example, the 2012 viral debate and backlash by Black audiences, activists, and scholars over the casting of Black Latina Zöe Saldaña in the biopic of the Black icon Nina Simone, and Saldaña's public claim to having both a Black and Latina identity, speak to the struggle and tension over ethnic and racial ideologies in film and television. The debate speaks to a significant set of issues in the cultural production and reception of popular film and television, among them the racially biased typecasting practices that limit roles for dark-skinned Black Americans and U.S. Latinas; and, a troublesome commitment to authenticity in casting that preserves a binary regime of racial representation grounded on biological difference and colorism. In the context of the media erasure of Black and Latina/o communities and the scarce quality casting opportunities for African American and Latina actresses, all roles, especially those surrounding beloved and globally popular historical figures, are highly contested.

Nevertheless, public calls for "accurate or real" ethnic and racial representations enter the fraught ideological terrain of authenticity or representational truth, a truth that depends on the worth of one community and the devaluation of another (Cacho, 2012). On the one hand, Saldaña's desire to represent multiple ethnic and racial identities (Black and Latina) validates her experience. On the other hand, Saldaña's claim to Blackness devalues the representational erasure of U.S. Black women from Hollywood. To understand the ideological stakes of the debate, it must be situated within the demographic, economic, and political emergence of U.S. Latinas/os and the economic and demographic decline of U.S.-born African Americans. It must also be placed within the dominant practices of media producers who racially homogenize Latina actors and characters as white and rarely Black.

The regime of racial representation embedded in the Saldaña/Simone controversy contributes to the maintenance U.S. racial hegemony. It erases the legacy of multiracial Latina/o Black people (Latinas/os of African descent), and it makes invisible the emergence mixed-race Black Latina/o identities (people of African American and Latina/o descent). By placing both communities outside the dominant white majority/Black minority binary that still defines U.S. racial identity, it contributes to the devaluation of Black women and Black Latinas. Media executives' increasing valuation of Latina/o marketability through racial ambiguity or brownness reinforces the belief that there are few opportunities for cultural or political coalescence between Black Americans and U.S. Latinas/os, specifically

(continued ...)

Black Latinas/os. The disruption of coalitional alliances ultimately maintains the U.S. ethnic and racial hegemony that keeps white men in economic and political control, such as witnessed through the 2016 election of Trump.

CASE STUDY 2: POSTRACIAL CULTURE AND NEOLIBERAL MULTICULTURALISM

Hegemony is not permanently achieved. It changes slowly and incrementally, responding to changes in the struggle over ideologies and their relationships to the political and economic. Critical ethnic studies scholar Jodi Melamed (2011) defines the hegemony of the U.S. post–civil rights period from 1980 to today as neoliberal multiculturalism. This hegemonic period is defined by an increase in global migration and the rapid global restructuring of capitalism, the economic and social consequences of which were evident in the 2008–2010 global recession and most recently in the unequal effects of the Coronavirus-19 pandemic across the United States and the globe. During this period, post-racial ideologies, which assume U.S. racial equality is achieved and no longer requires governmental intervention, moved out of the marginalized sphere of neoconservative discourses and into the cultural mainstream.

Neoliberal multicultural hegemony reached its apex with the 2008 election of President Barack Obama, whose electoral victory served as proof the United States as the flagbearer for democracy and capitalism had finally moved beyond seeing racial difference and its legacy of systemic racism. Twelve years after the beginning of his presidency, it is impossible to deny the very opposite of that observation is true. Indeed, the conditions under which we see ethnic and racial minorities in U.S. media remain shaped by ethnic and racial visuality and inequality under the continuing rhetoric of colorblindness.

One only needs to reflect on the Saldaña case study above or the rampant cultural commodification of mixed race/ethnic women's bodies in film, television, advertising, and politics (think Kamala Harris, Zendaya, and Naomi Osaka) to understand how neoliberal multiculturalism permeates U.S.-based "post-racial" global culture. The most contemporary articulation of neoliberal multiculturalism is as dependent on globally circulating and politically decontextualized performance of Black culture as it is on the fetishizing of mixed-race and Black Latina/o performers. Both illustrate neoliberal multiculturalism's contribution to the perpetual devaluation of blackness and revaluation of whiteness as such performances float between nonthreatening Black and dominant white racial identity.

CASE STUDY 3: MILES MORALES AND *INTO THE SPIDER-VERSE (ISV)*

Stuart Hall challenged dominant theories of audiences that positioned them as passive receivers of the mainstream media's ideological messages. Instead, he reminded scholars that not only are messages complexly constituted, informed by the conflicted subjectivities of the producers, but so are also the audiences who consume them active meaning-makers of the media—resistant and oppositional. So I would like to conclude by returning to Hall's call for the importance of studying representations for the audiences who demand and desire to be fully seen in the stories, narratives, and images that float across our varied screens.

In a recently published essay (Moliná-Guzman, 2021) about Sony's *Into the Spider-Verse (ISV)*, an animated movie featuring the mixed-race, bicultural Black Latino teenaged superhero Miles Morales, negotiated pleasure of recognition is clear. Sony Studios' decision to cinematically develop and commodify the animated character of Miles Morales, who is young, and therefore less threatening, and both Black and Latino, is a financially and culturally safe choice. Latina/o audiences are overrepresented as moviegoers, and Latinas/os have the highest rate of movie attendance among ethnic and racial minority audiences. Indeed, 2018's highest grossing film, *Black Panther*, attracted a record diverse audience with 58 percent of its U.S. ticket sales going to African American, Latina/o, and Native American audiences. Yet, despite increasingly diverse audiences, the major Hollywood film studios have been slow to adapt with slightly less than 20 percent of cinematic leads in 2018 going to actors of color.

Morales's location within the dominant global flow of Black popular culture forms (e.g., hip hop, R&B, graffiti art) positions the movie for global circulation and consumption. And the directors and writers of *ISV* strategically straddle the border between color-conscious and colorblind approaches to developing the character and narrative for the consumption of diverse U.S. audiences. That is, they intentionally develop the character of Miles Morales situated within his Black and Latino identities. But the values and experiences that inform the development of the character are universal and devoid of racial and ethnic specificity.

Regardless of the market and production forces that inform the creation of the film, the affective pleasure of Black, Latina/o/x, and Black Latino audiences to seeing themselves represented as one of the comic book genre's iconic superhero, Spider-Man, is compelling. Black, Latina/o, and Black Latina/Latino audience's reviews, fan blogs, and online commentary remind us of the strength of cultural studies approaches. Together, their responses disrupt the hegemonic ideologies of neoliberal multiculturalism in production of the narrative and character development and (re)imagine the present through the textured convergence of art, science, and technology.

For audiences of *ISV*, the act of seeing an intelligent, compassionate, empowered Black and Latino "self" in the mirror is the powerful ideological moment. A commenter's response to a podcast about *ISV* sums up the feeling produced: "I saw the excitement in the eyes of kids and adults alike who felt seen in ways they rarely have in the past. I can tell you from personal experience that feeling seen represented is a very unreal feeling that makes you feel like you can be a hero yourself" (Olmedo, 2018). The depiction of an iconic superhero, even if animated, who physically and figuratively looks like how "we" desire to see ourselves reaffirms the existence of people of color into an optimistic and yet-to-be imagined future.

Continuing the Conversation

Studying contemporary media and popular culture reminds us of the continuing importance of the ideology, hegemony, difference, and representations, and it is why communication researchers must continue to heed Hall's call to marshal all that is within their critical power to study those complicated moments of humanity and self-recognition. Cultural studies concepts in communication studies remain central to explaining issues of difference, inequality, and power, and to exploring the ability of audiences to be playful and oppositional. It reminds us of why representation matters.

Given the emergence of nationalism linked to anti-immigration and anti-Black violence in the United States from 2000 to today, it is also critical that we recognize the limitations of some cultural studies approaches. Scholarship of mass media and popular culture without the historical, political, and economic contextualization that Hall called for voids its impact to study inequality and power. Similarly, ideological analysis that falls back on linear claims to false consciousness or beautifully written narrative readings hold limited connections to the lived conditions of those being represented. Indeed, theoretical approaches to media content and audiences grounded in social psychology and cognition make clear the limitations of ideological analysis. For example, during the Trump presidency, work on the troublesome effects of selective media exposure alongside economic and political factors document the potential for the increased dehumanization of Muslims, Latinas/os, and Black Americans by politically conservative publics. This research on cognition and difference affirms that representations do matters and so do the theoretical approaches we use to analyze it.

Summary

In summary, this chapter highlights the intellectual tradition of cultural studies and its significant impact on theorizing about mass-mediated experiences and people of the global majority. A discussion of Hall's key concepts and contributions—including his reconceptualization of the concepts of ideology, hegemony, and media audiences—demonstrated his influence on how difference and representation is centralized in the study of media and popular culture. Through three case studies, the chapter illustrate how Hall's ideas remain useful for understanding contemporary intersectional feminist media studies and ethnic studies media scholarship.

FOR FURTHER THOUGHT AND REFLECTION

1. Reflecting on a recent media or social media experience, how do the concepts of ideologies and hegemony help you make sense of content? What do you think the message says about cultural, economic, or political values?

2. Think about a film or television show where you and another person held opposing opinions about it. Reflect on why you disagreed and the role that class, gender, race, and ethnic differences might have played in the disagreement.

3. How does this chapter help you understand the importance of studying the media, popular culture, and representation to the social or political?

STORIED REFLECTION
Searching for Stuart Hall

Catherine R. Squires
University of Minnesota

My foray into communication theory began with a name.

"You need to go work with Stuart Hall," my English professor declared with all due certainty. I was starting my first solo research project, a comparison of news coverage of the trial of the men who lynched Emmett Till and the police who beat Rodney King. I was vexed by the dissonant media coverage of the Los Angeles Uprising. I was a sophomore in college. I witnessed the upheaval and anguish after the Simi Valley jury acquitted the five police officers. I couldn't wrap my head around the verdict, let alone the media coverage that seemed to blame the Black community for everything. The officers had been caught on video beating a Black man with a savagery and brutality few had witnessed, and he lived to tell the tale.

Seeing was clearly not believing.

I needed to understand what was driving these disparate narratives of what had happened, who was to blame. I was hurting. My friends were hurting. The city was burning.

"Stuart Hall?" I hadn't heard the name. My small college at the time had no media studies courses, but Professor Berg was a cultural studies proponent.

"Yes. When you go to England, work with Stuart Hall."

I nodded. I wrote the name in my idea journal, which I kept in my bag and took everywhere. I spent the summer commuting to libraries in Chicago, tracing Black newspaper coverage of the Till case. I was awed by the beauty of the Newberry Library's interior and the fierce pride of the staff at the Carter G. Woodson Regional Library who taught me better techniques for using indexes and microfiche, guiding me to the venerable *Pittsburgh Courier* and a bevy of Black newspapers I'd never seen.

I got curious: *Why, given the legacy of so many talented Black journalists and editors, are there not more Black journalists in so-called mainstream media?*

I rode the L train home, imagining how I would find Stuart Hall.

It turns out I never got to Birmingham, where Hall taught—I attended the University of East Anglia, many miles east—but I was assigned Hall's essays to read. I took a train to London to celebrate Malcolm X's birthday and heard Lola Young speak about transatlantic Black liberation movements. I broadened my sense of how race, class, and gender mattered in media and other systems.

My trip across the ocean connected me with theories that nourished me. Theory helped me unpack the dissonances I experienced not only when reading and watching the news about the police acquitted for beating Rodney King but also when I was put on the spot as the only Black person in my class to "explain" Black reactions to the verdict.

Theory was no longer abstract: it was integral to life, not just predicting narrow ranges of behavior or opinion.

Theory became a friend.

During graduate school, friendships deepened my relationship to theory. I crossed disciplinary boundaries to gain access to the thinkers who were explaining racism, sexism, and xenophobia. My Black, Indigenous, or People of Color (BIPOC) friends in sociology, anthropology, performance studies, and political science enticed me with course descriptions and reading lists that drew me into the orbit of thinkers like Kimberlé Crenshaw, Aldon Morris, and the Combahee River Collective. Conversations with friends about their engagements with theory brought me joy and a broader sense of possibility. I was lucky to have an advisor who likewise believed that interdisciplinary study enriches communication theory.

I was likewise lucky she identified my work as theory.

"That's your contribution, right there," she tapped on my final paper for her political communication class.

"Really?" I was friends with Theory, but I didn't think of myself as a Theorist.

"Yes. Build your dissertation around this model."

My mind fizzed. *I created a theory?*

What I thought I had done before that moment was "just explain" why a particular way of thinking about public spheres and media didn't fit Black media history. I wove together the work of public sphere theorists, race, and social movement theorists, and highlighted the absence of Black-owned media from current analyses of media and public opinion. That's all.

I realized that I still viewed theory-building as something more accomplished scholars did.

Theory tapped me on my shoulder to remind me: defining myself as not-a-Theorist is explained by theories of race and gender.

When I teach public sphere theory, I tell my students this story to remind them that they are exactly where they should be: in conversation, in awe and joy of how Theory can be a friend of our minds, a helpful lookout, and most of all a way to broaden "the horizon of possibilities," as Stuart Hall wrote not so long ago.

CHAPTER 18

(Counter)Public Sphere Theory

Catherine R. Squires

University of Minnesota

Mark P. Orbe

Western Michigan University

T his chapter features a description of public sphere theorizing, a body of work that is most often associated with works by European and U.S. thinkers such as Jürgen Habermas, John Dewey, and Walter Lippmann. Their conceptualizations of the public sphere as an area of social life where individuals assemble to engage sociopolitical issues and utilize their engagement as a springboard to action gained renewed interest in the aftermath of the fall of the Soviet Union. The focus of the chapter is on extensions and critiques of Euroamerican public sphere theory, specifically that which highlights the importance of considering social inequality and the copresence and prevalence of counterpublics, including Black public spheres, which are operationally different than dominant public spheres. We present several current examples of counterpublic spheres to highlight the relevancy of the theory in today's world. We conclude with a summary and brief discussion of implications for future research and practice.

Intellectual Tradition of Public Sphere Theory

The important contribution of public sphere theory, as it relates to communication theory, is its intentional focus on institutions, forms, and modes of communication in regards to political and public life. Accordingly, public sphere has influenced the study of public discourse, political communication, democratic deliberations, and the role of media. While different scholars in the 19th and 20th centuries, like John Stuart Mill and Hannah Arendt, contributed to the foundation of the concept, the translation of Jürgen Habermas's (1989) *The Structural Transformation of the Public Sphere* sparked renewed attention and reexamination of public sphere theory as a means to understand the roles of citizens, deliberation, culture, and power in existing and emerging democratic societies.

Habermas's (1989) model delineates the rise of the bourgeois public sphere in Europe in the 18th and 19th centuries. Newly wealthy merchants and other individuals with leisure time engaged in critical public debate on issues of common interest in places such as coffeehouses and literary salons. Ideally, the public sphere is characterized by a number of features, including: open access to all citizens irrespective of status; unrestricted debate about issues of common interest; absence of undue influence from established power structures through the economy and state; and the formation and articulation of public opinion as a foundation for action. Ongoing public debates occur both in communal spaces, such as a salon or coffeehouse, and mediated spaces, such as the editorial page or a viral tweet. The core idea of public sphere theory is that legitimate governance should be informed by critical public engagement, a hallmark of participatory democracy.

The work of Habermas and the public sphere represents an epicenter for communication scholars interested in citizen deliberation, civil engagement, media, and the state (e.g. Asen & Brouwer, 2001). The writings of Habermas rejuvenated interest in public sphere theory; yet his initial articulation that envisioned citizen participants who disregard their particular sociocultural identities was critiqued as idealizing and normalizing the role that bourgeois society played in maintaining democratic societies. Moreover, the emergence of the European bourgeois class is intertwined with the violence of colonialism, slavery, and extractive capitalism, which positioned Africans, Asians, and Indigenous peoples as lesser or sub-humans, incapable of reasoned debate and self-governance. Thus, critics centered new conceptualizations of the public sphere on the experiences of marginalized and oppressed groups, including African Americans and/or women (e.g., the Black Public Sphere Collective, 1995). Their criticisms and subsequent theorizing generated an important extension to public sphere theory, namely those associated with the existence of subaltern counterpublics (Fraser, 1992).

Theorizing the existence, manifestation, and relevancy of counterpublics is informed by the intellectual traditions of feminist and critical race theorists who critique "universal" theories that centralize dominant group perspectives and understandings without consideration of salient issues of culture and power. Squires (2002, p. 456) offers a productive set of questions to critically engage public sphere theory:

1. Who makes up the different collectives from which public spheres emerge?
2. What is the range of opinions and interests among these publics?
3. How much overlap is there between these publics in terms of interests and opinions?
4. Are many of these publics currently working in concert, or are they pursuing separate strategies to define and address their interests?

5.   How does each public interact with other public spheres and the state?

These questions help to generate insight into the relationship between public sphere and the state; differential access to political, economic, and social power; the diversity of the public sphere itself; and the prevalence of various counterpublics. The next section provides a detailed articulation of how marginalized groups, like people of color, are excluded from a universal public sphere and, consequently, form their own counterpublic spheres.

Main Goals and Features of Public Sphere Theory

According to Fraser (1992), in any given society, certain marginalized groups are excluded from a "universal" public sphere, something that is in actuality dominated by a specific social group. Fraser critiqued public sphere theory's ideals as simply shifting political power from the state (ruling by power) to the majority ideology (ruling through hegemony). Through her work, she offers two basic types of public spheres that coexist: a dominant public sphere and subaltern counterpublics created and maintained by historically marginalized group members.

By definition, subaltern counterpublics are "parallel discursive arenas where members of subordinated groups invent and circulate counterdiscourses, which in turn permit them to formulate oppositional interpretations of their identities, interests, and needs" (Fraser, 1992, p. 67). In other words, counterpublics exist outside of state-sanctioned or mainstream spaces and reflect opposing perspectives from dominant public spheres. Many contemporary theorists embraced Fraser's ideas and described multiple public spheres that exist based on various marginalized group identities like those associated with race/ethnicity, gender, sexuality, and nationality. Other theorists, like Warner (2002), noted that counterpublics have a critical relation to power and exist in tension with the larger public. Given this, dominant publics typically silence, disregard, or react to counterpublic discourse with hostility. Such dynamics highlight the importance of having safe, separate spaces where cocultural groups can discuss their interests without interference or undue influence of dominant groups. Counterpublics also are crucial for marginalized persons to critique dominant society without having their own identities and interests muted or invalidated.

According to Asen and Brouwer (2001), various counterpublics have emerged through the articulation of demands by historically marginalized groups seeking greater political and economic rights, responsibilities, and agency. Sociocultural groups (e.g., women, people of color, LGBTQ+ community, and the working poor) have utilized different counterpublic spheres in order to engage one another as a means toward redeeming the core promises of a democratic nation. In addition to legitimizing and sustaining minoritized peoples, counterpublic discourse also works to challenge dominant perspectives and knowledge, which oftentimes is situated as general knowledge universally accepted as true for all. While geared primarily for individuals who share a minoritized identity, counterpublics can also attract diverse coalitions—including individuals whose identity may provide easy access to the dominant public sphere—which are defined by a common ideology. In the next section, we focus on Black public spheres as a particular point of emphasis to highlight these ideas.

Focus on Black Public Spheres

Existing scholarship on Black public spheres is grounded within the conceptualization of counterpublics (e.g., Fraser, 1992). Within this body of theorizing, the Black public sphere operates as a counterpublic defined through the tension with dominant (white) publics. Where the dominant public sphere exists through privilege, property ownership, and economic liberty, such is not the case for Black public spheres whose existence emerged to: oppose and resist systemic oppression; maintain and foster cultural forms; preserve linguistic heritage; and nurture the perseverance of unique cultural expression and signification (Gittens, 2021). According to Baker (1995), the Black public sphere is distinct from the dominant public sphere because, rather than denying identity and culture to "normalize" oneself, it relies on aesthetic consciousness that reimagines and transposes the hegemonic forces of dominant society. Formulated outside of dominant societal structures and traditional modes of the public sphere, Black public spheres function in a multitude of ways.

Dawson (1995) was one of the first, and most influential, scholars to focus specifically on the diversity of Black public spheres. His work highlights the success of independent Black media, Black churches, sociocultural organizations, and popular music in fostering conversations regarding communal interests, rights, and strategies to resist white supremacist rule. Of significant importance is how Dawson highlights the prevalence of different ideologies within Black public spheres and counters the assumption of a unidimensional, monolithic Black community. Multiple examples of Black public spheres existing simultaneously, and sometimes in contrast with one another, are noted; these include those in the early 20th century when different ideologies informed the perspectives and discourse of Booker T. Washington, W. E. B. Du Bois, and Marcus Garvey.

According to Asen and Brouwer (2001), public spheres are not necessarily exclusive as individuals may participate in various spaces as reflective of their identities, interests, and ideas. This consideration is crucial to resist essentialist notions of various racial and ethnic groups, especially those that focus on differences between such groups with little recognition of the diversity within. As Squires (2002) notes, multiple Black publics exist and membership is not exclusive; she also notes that heterogeneous publics are likely to emerge, including non-Black people who engage in Black public spheres. This point of consideration, again, highlights the diversity within and between counterpublics.

At the core of public sphere theorizing as it pertains to nondominant communities is an articulation of different responses outside of dominant publics. Within this advancement, Squires (2002) contributes theoretical clarity by outlining similarities and differences between the (1) enclave, (2) counterpublic, and (3) satellite. This typology, informed through historical analysis of Black media institutions and social movements emerging from Black public spheres, should not be understood as rigid in its distinctions; instead, each type is conceptualizied to represent a range of responses that emerge from a public sphere based on larger political context, internal concerns, available resources, institutions, and cultural norms.

Among the responses marginalized communication might produce is an *enclave*, necessitated by societal norms that deny access, or meaningful participation, in public spaces created and maintained by dominant groups (Squires, 2002). Within this type of public sphere, a public produces lively debate, engagement, and planning while doing so in a manner largely hidden from dominant groups. Such a public sphere fosters counter-hegemonic ideas and strategies to be engaged without censorship, sanctions, or penalty. Enclave public sphere requires maintaining a separate and safe space for minoritized groups to produce discourse that works out issues amongst themselves. While interactions between dominant and enclave public spheres exist, it typically is highly scripted and lacking the passion, fervor, spirit, and dialogic honesty within the enclave itself. Part of the function of an enclave is to foster "oppositional consciousness," which is crucial to maintain cultural and group memory, important considerations in resisting oppression from dominant groups (Mansbridge & Morris, 2001). Even when opportunities for greater participation in public spheres have emerged, enclaves remain important in fostering pride and building community connections. They also represent an independent space where traditionally marginalized voices can be heard without interference from the dominant group. Examples of Black public enclaves can be seen within independent media, local artist collectives, community-based and faith-based organizations, as well as through social media venues such as Black Twitter.

According to Squires (2002), a second option for traditionally marginalized groups is to create a *counterpublic*. While some theorists use this term in a more broad, generic sense, within this typology, it is defined in more specific ways. A counterpublic, as defined by Squires, is created so that individuals can both exchange ideas internally and strategically engage other public spheres through social protests such as petitions, boycotts, rallies, and other acts of civil disobedience. While the enclave is typically deployed as a response to intense oppression and insurmountable political and economic conditions, the counterpublic emerges when Black publics have resources more readily available or perceive strategic opportunities for an action alliance. The defining feature of the counterpublic is increased public communication—through face-to-face, organizational, and mediated forms—between marginalized and dominant public spheres. Counterpublics reject the performance of more acceptable "public transcripts" (Scott, 1985) and instead articulate messages previously only heard within the enclave. As such, counterpublic discourse works to articulate group interests on their own terms, as they resist and change dominant group perspectives and seek solidarity with other marginalized groups. Examples of Black counterpublics include a variety of civil rights organizations over the years. While some might regard counterpublics as an optimal choice for minoritized groups, Squires (2002) reminds readers that much depends on larger sociopolitical contexts. While counterpublics may be possible as resources and opportunities increase, interpublic sphere discussions are still contained by macro-level structures that are largely controlled by dominant groups.

A third, and final, type within Squires's (2002) conceptualization of Black public spheres is the *satellite*. In contrast with other public spheres, the satellite deliberately seeks separation for reasons other than oppression. The explicit goal is to create and maintain a solid collective group identity within independent institutional spaces, one that can also engage in wider public discourses in a more equitable fashion. The preference for separation is motivated by a desire to resist cultural assimilation, remain true to communal identity and goals, and commit to group ideals. For some, the satellite may provide a space where self-segregated groups can retain a sense of superiority over other publics and selectively engage in larger debates when deemed necessary. For instance, satellite publics may engage in wider interpublic discourse when there is clear convergence of common interests with other publics, when their particular institutional practices cause friction or controversies with wider publics, or if their own independent manner of existence is threatened. This is to be expected given that satellite publics do not exist within a vacuum nor wholly independent of other publics or the state. Examples of Black satellite spheres, in Squires's (2002) work, include the Nation of Islam.

In summary, the enclave, counterpublic, and satellite exist as a reaction to oppression from the state and/or dominant public spheres as well as in a larger context of sociopolitical power dynamics and access to material and cultural resources (Squires, 2002). This theoretical extension is essential as the workings of Black public spheres largely have been "misidentified, overlooked, and misrepresented in scholarly and lay texts" (Squires, 2002, p. 455). The typology should not be viewed as a developmental or linear model, as each type is viable and appropriate in a given context. In fact, the diversity across and within marginalized public spheres is evident as they may take on different forms over time.

Research and Practical Applications of Public Sphere Theory

Within this section, we highlight three contemporary applications of public sphere theory, each of which highlights the unique positioning of counterpublics. The first focuses on the "hijacking" of a public relations campaign (#myNYPD) by the New York City Police Department in 2014 (Jackson & Welles, 2015). When the Twitter account for the NYPD invited the public to post photographs of officers with citizens throughout the community, thousands of citizens repurposed the #myNYPD hashtag to highlight instances of racial profiling, racism, and police brutality. In short, this case study demonstrates how citizen activists, especially minoritized peoples, can reframe dominant narratives of the dominant group and, in doing so, create and sustain counterpublics and social movements. It also highlights the utility of social media platforms, like Twitter, in creating networked counterpublics—as a means to democratize citizen activists in the age of new social media—that force dominant public spheres "to take note and respond" (Jackson & Welles, 2015, p. 24).

Gittens's (2021) article on rapper 2 Chainz's Pink Trap House in Atlanta, Georgia, is a second application of the power and diversity of counterpublic spheres, including those that exist as aesthetic communities. In the summer of 2017, the Pink Trap House became an Atlanta landmark, attracting thousands of local, national, and global hip-hop enthusiasts. In doing so, it emerged as a symbolic representation of drug-infested neighborhoods—in essence, disrupting the white spaces of suburban living. According to Gittens, the Pink Trap House represents a Black aesthetic counterpublic that materialized due to a lack of hidden space required to form an enclave and the reduction of satellites that have been converted into state-sponsored institutions. Best understood through a decoding of its name, album, color, events, and other functional features, this artistic expression functions as a political statement performed within a public sphere "under the gaze of the bourgeois public sphere" (Gittens, 2021, p. 437). By disrupting spaces and relationships created through white supremacy, the Pink Trap House reflects a counterpublic sphere produced through culturally centered aesthetic form. In addition, it provides a space where intersectional minoritized identities exist outside of dominant authority—representing a sense of freedom, albeit for a limited time.

The third research application of counterpublics assumes a broad conceptualization of the concept. Larson and McHendry (2019) analyze the recent surge and mainstreamed rhetoric of white nationalists within the United States and abroad. Their focus specifically was on "Swarmfront," a white nationalist collective that works to insert racist propaganda into everyday discussions via various digital forms, including comment sections. Larson and McHendry argue that such discourse reflects a different type of counterpublic sphere—one that feeds off oppressive conditions within the dominant public sphere and, in doing so, safeguards dominant public discourse against counter-discursive challenges. As such, they characterize these nonmainstream publics spheres as "parasitic publics." The primary argument that these scholars make is that white nationalist organizations, while holding a symbiotic relationship with dominant public spheres, are not embraced publicly within those very spheres. Instead, they exist within a particular space: outside, and in support of, the public sphere. They draw from Warner's (2002) definition of counterpublics, which highlights a subordinate status amidst some tension with the larger dominant collective. In short, this research highlights an interesting point of critical reflection, one that further develops a nuanced understanding of the complexities of race, nation, and counterpublic spheres.

Continuing the Conversation

Public sphere theory has proven itself invaluable for understanding the central role of communication as citizens participate in democratic discourse. It situates the public realm as the site of dialogue, politics, action, and freedom. While the work of Habermas and others has provided a useful foundation for studying participatory public discourse, scholars of color have extended the theory to reflect the lived experiences of traditionally marginalized people like African Americans. Motivated by the critique that a universal public sphere exists, these scholars have demonstrated the ways in which multiple counterpublics exist in any given society. In the words of Squires (2002, p. 465), "by allowing for these response-types to exist simultaneously not only across publics but within public spheres, we can retain the flexibility necessary to describe the fluid nature of public spheres."

Further analysis is needed to cultivate deeper understanding of the complexities of public spheres and the role they play in political and economic structures. As demonstrated within the chapter, this includes the power generated through networked counterpublics (Jackson & Welles, 2015) and a broadening of the conceptualization of public spheres to include aesthetic communities (Gittens, 2021) and those that have complex relationships with the existing power structures (Larson & McHendry, 2019). Further development in descriptions of various public spheres, including those created and maintained by those marginalized in dominant societal structures, will provide additional insight into how multiple spheres coexist simultaneously.

An especially fruitful area for further study is how computer-mediated communication channels work to create the type of public sphere discourse envisioned by Habermas and others. The important role that social media has played in various social movements has been well documented; however, additional analysis is warranted regarding the increasing important role that new media plays within dominant, marginal, and other public spheres. For instance, new research is needed that explores the communication processes, potential, and pitfalls of the virtual public sphere, especially in contrast to the emphasis of face-to-face interactions of traditional research. Concepts like Charles Mills's white ignorance, Cedric Robinson's racial capitalism, Katherine McKittrick's meditations on Black geographies, and the Black/Land Project's exploration of how we relate to the land/place that supports the space of the public sphere all suggest generative pathways for public sphere theorists. As we witness retrenchment of supremacist thinking, denial of histories, environmental crisis, and calls for reparations, public sphere theorists would do well to continue generative conversations with decolonial theory, grounded theory, Black feminist thought, and other bodies of work that help us imagine public spheres based not in commerce but on care and repair.

Summary

Public sphere theory, as conceptualized by Habermas, believes that democracy is maximized when private citizens and engaged thinkers can utilize egalitarian spaces—such as coffeehouses, table societies, salons, organizations, the media, and the like—to express, exchange, and develop ideas. While his ideas were important in creating a foundation for study, critics have been quick to point out the limitations of his initial ideas in that they reflected a privileged perspective based on race, gender, and class. Recognizing the existence of multiple public spheres, including counterpublics like those created by traditionally underrepresented groups, is crucial in understanding the diverse ways in which individuals participate in democratic deliberations. As demonstrated through this chapter, public sphere theory remains a highly relevant frame to study contemporary public discourse especially that which is facilitated through various mass-mediated platforms.

FOR FURTHER THOUGHT AND REFLECTION

1. Is cyberspace an ideal public sphere? Does it promote multiple public spheres that each function as an "echo chamber?" What evidence, in the form of specific examples, can you provide to support and/or refute your answers to these questions?

2. What current examples can you provide for Black enclaves, counterpublics, and satellites, as described by Squires (2002)? How would you characterize #BlackLivesMatter now compared to when it was created in 2013?

3. Consider how the idea of counterpublics can be extended to marginalized racial and ethnic groups featured through this book. What examples can you generate for Latinx, Indigenous, Asian American, and multiracial communities?

4. How would you describe the Proud Boys organization in the United States—as an example of a dominant public sphere and/or parasitic public (as described by Larson and McHendry, 2019)? Do you see the organization's discourse as complimentary, supportive, and/or counter to the status quo in the United States?

The public sphere is a spatial metaphor, but rarely do we talk about the actual lands upon which publics gather or garner resources to support media making and distribution. What would a public sphere theory centered on the role of the land look like?

STORIED REFLECTION
The (Mis)Education of Race

David Stamps
Bentley University

I recall sitting in a graduate student seminar and listening to group discussions and lectures concerning research on racial identities in general and my race in particular. According to the conversations, Black individuals exist in a precarious space where deficit and disfunction are foundational. I remember thinking that the narratives and a great deal of the published communication research presented in my courses about race did not reflect my lived experience. The conversations about Black people did not exemplify what I know: the communities' many favorable characteristics. The negative and demeaning examples that everyone nonchalantly discussed were not first-hand experiences and did not illustrate the attributes of the folks I know and who exist in social settings where we laugh, love, and build coalitions.

I noticed that some influential media scholars who publish research about race often do not belong to the racial groups referenced in their work. These scholars rarely acknowledge the lens through which they examine other racial groups is limited due to the lack of direct contact with the groups represented. Well-intentioned individuals can and should investigate any group they like, even if they do not represent that group, but the keyword is *well-intentioned*. What is alarming is that many individuals dismiss what Feagin (2020) calls the "white racial frame." The white racial frame is a person's assumption that the social world is shaped by social dominance, individualism, and hierarchy. According to Feagin (2020), individuals—white and nonwhite—decide the values, behaviors, and stereotypes that are desirable or undesirable. These decisions often extend to conventional emotions, images, behaviors, language, style of dress, and cultural practices. My takeaway from these conversations and the framing of racial groups in media scholarship highlights the importance of the researchers' role in producing and disseminating literature about race and media and the socialization of novice learners in accepting literature as absolute truth.

I have never attempted to speak for another individual or group. I feel uncomfortable claiming to possess the knowledge, skill set, or social capacities of groups I do not represent. I have yet to feel confident suggesting that I know what is suitable for entire communities. There are numerous identities that I do not occupy. I am cisgender, and although I grew up in a working-class household that missed some meals and skipped a few holidays, I am currently comfortably middle class. These are only a few of many identities I hold, but even from this reference point, I cannot speak for the transgender community; I cannot speak to the day-to-day engagement of upper-class, wealthy individuals. I may think about these groups, but my opinion does not carry weight and to assume as much is a problem. With the realization that researchers could be cavalier when examining the dynamics of racial groups, I began a research program that considered race, media, and the social implications of both from a standpoint that interrogations of racial groups dynamics should be approached fairly and without presumption. However, I have learned that the freedom to speak for someone else and tell their story requires privilege and can easily become an abuse of power.

To assume that your experience, attitudes, or beliefs are generalizable, normative, and the standard-bearer is not afforded to many individuals. Individuals lacking privilege often belong to racial groups with minimal representation and influence. Underrepresented racial groups are constantly scrutinized, erased, and deprived in influential spaces (e.g., academic journals, classrooms, politics). Interestingly, underrepresented racial groups represent the numerical majority globally. These populations include diverse Asian peoples that constitute two-thirds

of the global populace and an additional one-fifth of people that comprise the African continent. Regarding scholarship on media and race, we are doing something wrong.

Scholars note that research, textbooks, and syllabi favor Western, educated, industrialized,
rich, and democratic (WEIRD) groups' narratives (Bates, 2020). The default of examining
WEIRD populations minimizes discourse on diverse cultures, socialization practices, and distinct behaviors among non-WEIRD people. WEIRD groups are not representative of the global
population, and their comprehensions are not generalizable. Nevertheless, research often
relies on sampling from WEIRD people. Scholars often ignore the issue of biased sampling
and produce countless studies that feature unrepresentative samples, and this "knowledge
creation" lacks inclusion. We must be intentional and thoughtful when examining racialized
groups. This includes but is not limited to considering the application of distinct theories that
center race, citing racially diverse theorists and scholars, and for researchers to acknowledge
their positionality. If literature is to become more representative of society, critical and inclusive dialogue about race must be prominent.

CHAPTER 19

Critical Media Effects

Srividya "Srivi" Ramasubramanian

Syracuse University

S itting near the *chota* canteen of Mudra Institute of Communications Ahmedabad (now simply known as MICA), South Asia's premier institute for communication, I was studying for my mass communication theory exam. I felt fortunate to have laid my hands on Denis McQuail's (1994) latest edition of *Mass Communication Theory*. The volume explains what the "mass" means and what the "communication" means; it discusses structuralism, behaviorism, semiotics, functionalism, liberal-pluralism, and market economy; it covers the four models of communication—transmission, ritual, publicity, and encoding/decoding; and it goes over the models of Claude Shannon and Warren Weaver, Wilbur Schramm, Marshall McLuhan, Harold Lasswell, the Frankfurt School, and Everett Rogers. It was all very fascinating—scientists, scholars, terms, concepts, theories, models, and frameworks. Yet, in those approximately 400 pages, I didn't see myself or my lived experiences reflected in any meaningful way.

The idea for the critical media effects framework was born from the realization that traditional mass communication theories taught in classrooms around the world hardly ever include the perspectives and voices of scholars of color, immigrants, and other marginalized groups (Chakravartty et al., 2018). While much of the research on critical cultural communication did incorporate minoritized perspectives, "mainstream" theorizing within mass communication was largely situated within dominant ideologies of social sciences. Only a few of us in the mass communication area were looking into issues of sexism, racism, xenophobia, and other forms of intersecting oppressions within the larger context of studying journalism, advertising, public relations, broadcast journalism, and film studies. At best, cultural differences were discussed as special case studies when considering topics such as foreign films produced outside of the United States or the occasional reference to a multinational brand's advertising campaign.

As my fellow scholars and I looked around in our institutions and disciplines, we realized that Black and Brown voices did not matter within communication theories. Very few perspectives from the margins are reflected on, listened to, cited, or valued as communication scholarship, including within our subfield of media effects and mass communication theory. Black, Indigenous, and women of Color (BIWOC) scholars are underrepresented in the communication discipline, and even when they are present, we are hardly seen as innovators, theorizers, thought leaders, and knowledge producers. The unstated implication was that BIWOC faculty were mainly present to serve and assist others but are not "serious" scholars. Finding that much of the theorizing did not speak to our lived experiences as women immigrant scholar-moms of color in the U.S. academe, we decided to write our own within our subfield: *Critical media effects*. We created this framework for our fellow social scientists of color as an invitation to center our voices and experiences within their subfields in communication.

Intellectual Tradition of Critical Media Effects Theory

Jennings Bryant and Dolf Zillmann (1994) are often considered the founders of media effects research. Indeed, their *Media Effects: Advances in Theory and Research* continues to be the most important and classical "canon" within the subfield. Media effects theories were almost explicitly shaped by white male scholars from elite U.S. universities, and they were the only ones who theorized about media effects and mass communication at the time. These included cultivation theory by George Gerbner and colleagues, social cognitive theory by Albert Bandura, agenda-setting by Maxwell McCombs, uses and gratifications by Alan Rubin, diffusion of innovation by Everett Rogers, and entertainment theory by Bryant and Zillmann. As the feminist movement gained momentum, white women scholars such as Joanne Cantor, Jane Brown, Patricia Aufderheide, Sharon Strover, and Kathleen Jamieson contributed tremendously to the study of topics such as media and children as well as political communication. However, topics such as race and media were still being largely studied only by white men such as Robert Entman, Brad Greenberg, and Joe Feagin in the 1980s. In the late 1990s, the work of scholars such as Mary Beth Oliver, Sut Jhally, Dana Mastro, Travis Dixon, Shanto Iyengar, Erica Scharrer, Amy Jordan, Dave Ewoldsen, and Jake Harwood on topics of gender and race within media effects, intergroup processes, and children's media began to make significant contributions to theorizing about discrimination, representations, and stereotyping processes.

Over coffees and meals at professional organizations and conferences in the last couple decades, I have chatted with many women scholars of color about the absence of our voices within media effects and mass communication scholarship. In the beginning, we wondered what it would look like to center our BIWOC voices as leaders in theorizing about social scientific scholarship within the communication discipline. One such conversation was with my colleague Omotayo Banjo at the University of Cincinnati. We often found ourselves as outsiders within mass communication scholarship, where questions of critical communication and social justice were not central to the conversations. I drew courage from the solidarity from fellow scholar-activists such as Bernadette Calafell, Mohan Dutta, Walid Afifi, Robin Means Coleman, Ralina Joseph, Dana Cloud, Bryan McCann, Karma Chávez, Mary Beth Oliver, Lisa Corrigan, Aisha Durham, and Devika Chawla apart from numerous other junior scholars and graduate students who showed me through their lived example what it meant to fight the system for greater justice. I gain confidence by co-organizing with scholar-activists as part of the #CommunicationSoWhite and related movements both inside and outside the academe (Chakravartty et al., 2018). I also drew inspiration and guidance from academic foreparents who laid the foundation for this framework. These scholars, often from marginalized groups themselves as people of color, LGBTQ+ individuals, or immigrants, have been working on bringing in critical perspectives into quantitative empirical communication scholarship over the decades across various subfields. They have shown us that it is not just possible, but crucial, to engage with questions of voice, agency, inclusion, and social justice within social scientific aspects of communication.

Against the backdrop of global challenges, such as COVID-19, fascism, white supremacy, and xenophobia, the framework we have created highlights media effects research that incorporates critical consciousness about inclusion, inequalities, intersectionality, power, and privilege. In fact, our framework was published around the same time that COVID-19 was declared a pandemic by the World Health Organization in 2020. The global #BlackLivesMatter uprising in the summer of 2020 after George Floyd's murder led to further considerations, questioning, and reflections on the whiteness of academe and within the field of communication. The framework was published in the *Journal of Communication* (Ramasubramanian & Banjo, 2020) even as we were observing #ShutDownSTEM in response to exclusions and marginalization of scholars of color in STEM fields and engaging with hashtag activism through forums such as #BlackintheIvory started by Shardé Davis and Joy Melody Woods, two Black women scholars from the field of communication.

Apart from the lack of diverse perspectives and voices in theorizing about media effects scholarship, another main drawback was that the theories that were dominant within intergroup communication and media effects did not consider a critical perspective. For instance, the social identity theory, which formed the foundation for mediated intergroup communication, did not seriously consider power relations. All media processes and effects were assumed to be "neutral" and identical. Media effects were equated with psychological processes at the individual level without considering a more ecological approach that examined meso- and macro-level factors in terms of institutional, structural, and systemic factors that lead to differential media effects. Even among media effects scholars who were studying identities such as gender and race, which was just a handful of scholars, we had not considered issues such as intersectionality or structural discrimination.

Historically speaking, the state of communication theorizing is largely characterized with methodological polarization and theoretical divides about ontological and epistemological differences. These silences, siloed thinking, and serious gaps between various subfields of communication are a serious shortcoming. It is detrimental in meaningful theorizing about contemporary communication contexts and also limits researchers from having "real-world impact." Within media studies, these silos or divisions across areas mean that there aren't many theories that relate to the emerging and new media technologies. More importantly, many of these theories do not adequately address sociopolitical contexts within which media users select, use, and are influenced by media. They, therefore, do not engage typically with issues of social justice, cultural differences, contextual factors, power relationships, intersecting systems of oppression, or dynamic cultural contexts.

Critical media effects, which is a new approach that we advocate for, promotes a multimethods and multiperspectival approach to examining media effects. Specifically, we argue for a *quantitative criticalist approach* that uses empirical and data-driven approaches to understand, explain, and transform social inequalities shaped by and within mediated contexts. Just as we advocate strongly for the use of the critical paradigm within social scientific approaches to media effects and mass communication, we simultaneously make a case for critical communication scholars to incorporate empirical and evidence-based approaches to helping test their theories and make sense of nuanced theoretical mechanisms driving the effects of media on individuals, communities, and society as a whole.

Main Goals and Features of Critical Media Effects Theory

The critical media effects (CME) framework offers a new approach to theorizing about media effects scholarship, which is our home territory within communication, although our work now spans multiple subfields of communication (Ramasubramanian & Banjo, 2020). We discuss ways that media effects scholarship can be more inclusive of intersectional social identities, engage questions of social justice, and take a more user-centered approach to understand audiences in a contemporary hyper-digital media landscape. CME explores the crossroads of media effects research and social justice scholarship. It highlights media effects research that incorporates critical consciousness about inclusion, inequalities, intersectionality, power, and privilege to address important and timely social issues relating to inequalities, discrimination, and intergroup relations. It can be applied to media effects research across multiple media formats, sociopolitical contexts, and intersecting identities such as gender, race, ethnicity, sexual orientation, religion, and class.

The CME framework advocates for a more nuanced, multiperspectival approach to media effects scholarship that centers on issues of inclusion and social justice to address pressing contemporary global issues. It challenges notions that our existing theories are "color-blind," "neutral," and "universally valid." It advocates for considering broader social impact, community engagement, and integration of various subfields to stay relevant and meaningful. It addresses important and timely social issues by focusing on topics such as antidiscrimination, prejudice reduction, inclusive communication, and favorable intergroup relations. It strives to include perspectives and voices of those from historically marginalized groups.

The CME framework argues for the interrogation of inclusions and exclusions within media effects scholarship as well as media spaces overall. It grapples with questions of objectivity and validity of media processes and effects, considering that much of the theorizing has been based on limited samples from largely white U.S.-centric student populations based on studies conducted in research universities. It calls for a nuanced intersectional approach to studying identity and inclusion, which are driven by the community rather than the researchers. It brings to light the need to go beyond traditional college-based samples and Western, educated, industrial, rich, and democratic (WEIRD) samples and contexts in theorizing about media effects (Alper et al., 2016; Henrich et al., 2010). Furthermore, it incorporates structural hierarchies, institutional discrimination, and power relations into intergroup relations. Overall, the framework examines systemic, structural, and institutional inequalities that play an important role in shaping the role of media content, research, theorizing, and outcomes.

The CME framework bridges critical cultural communication with media effects scholarship through four central pillars of *power, intersectionality, context,* and *agency.* The dynamics of *power* are fundamental to any critical approach to communication studies. It challenges the power differences and inequalities within media effects research by bringing it to the forefront of theorizing. Some ways in which power operates within media effects scholarship is through erasure. Voices of minoritized groups are often erased in the formation of research questions, methods, theories, and initiatives relating to the media. In terms of structural inequalities, CME considers the impact or power status of institutionally disenfranchised persons by connecting individual media behaviors with macro-level systemic inequalities. CME considers power structures at the global, national, and local levels by challenging prevailing structures of domination that shape various discourses of resistance (Crenshaw, 1991). It amplifies the voices of communities that are marginalized within mainstream media.

The second pillar of the CME framework is *intersectionality.* Mono-categorical theorizing is a big issue within the communication discipline. Intersectionality asks more than just demographic questions. It addresses various dimensions of experiences such as discrimination, stress, media access, and media representation that are informed by multiple identities and power hierarchies. CME suggests that research questions, methods, and analyses examine how multiple identities intersect in influencing mediated processes and effects. One way in which the framework recommends moving forward is to go beyond the observed data to consider the broader structural inequalities and sociohistorical context within which the data emerge.

This leads us to the next pillar of the CME framework, which is *context*. Context could mean a variety of things such as social, cultural, political, and technological contexts that shape media effects scholarship. CME considers the social and cultural location with respect to power relations that influences media use as a shared social experience. It examines the broader political economic contexts and issues such as media imperialism to understand the ways in which media content and narratives shape their effects at the individual, societal, and global levels. CME situates media effects in ecologically valid ways that account for the sociocultural political contexts of individuals' media experiences and use.

The final pillar of the CME framework is *agency*. The CME approach goes beyond the active-passive binary to emphasize media users' agency to create meaning and counter the hegemonic nature of mainstream dominant discourses. One point that we raise in the framework is the importance of asset-based framing of media users rather than the usual deficit-based framing. Typically, difference is framed as a deficit rather than as an asset within communication scholarship, including in media effects research. For instance, terms and concepts within the media effects scholarship such as risky media use, media or internet addiction, abnormal media use, harmful media effects, inoculation approach, and so on frame media users, especially those from marginalized groups, often in terms of the dominant cultural perspective. CME moves away from such deficit framing to examine marginalized groups within their own cultural contexts without having to compare them to dominant group norms. For instance, the literature talks about "high versus low culture" soap operas and reality shows as "trashy media" or "sleaze TV" (Jenkins et al., 2002). The questions we would like to pose are: How are negativity and positivity defined and conceptualized within the subfield of media effects? How do marginalized users "talk back" or use creative and collective ways to disrupt inequalities within existing media systems?

Research and Practical Applications of Critical Media Effects Theory

CME is one of the youngest theories in this book, having been introduced as recently as 2020. Despite its infancy, it is already shaping the research conversations within media effects and social sciences in important ways. If you have worked on a research study, you likely know that typically it takes at least two years from conception to publication for most research studies. Even as this "newborn" theory is trying to find its place in the world, it has already been cited a dozen times and has been presented at conferences around the world.

I am excited to share the details of some research projects that are underway that apply CME. Along with Julius Riles and Elizabeth Behm-Morawitz from the University of Missouri, I am currently working on a paper on how exactly intersectionality can be conceptualized and measured using media selectivity, use, and effects of stereotypical media content. David Stamps from Bentley University is working on an experimental study applying CME to examine how portrayals of trans women of color in a scripted series influence attitudes and support for this group. Muniba Saleem from the University of California at Santa Barbara is applying CME to bicultural identities of Muslim American youth. Satveer Kaur-Gill from the National University of Singapore and I are working on a content analysis of Sikh Americans in U.S. mainstream news, which examines the intersections of religion, race, and gender by highlighting how turbaned Sikh men are portrayed as a threat to U.S. culture.

Minjie Li (2021) from the University of Miami has recently published an article that applies CME to experimental research. In this study, news stories of trans people are examined through the lens of power relations to understand effects on dehumanization. Critics have pointed out that the media overwhelmingly features powerful trans people in the news reports on trans policies/rights, while everyday trans people are mainly seen in tragic news (e.g., hate crimes). Li's study experimentally investigates how the power exemplification of marginalized outgroup members in the news redirects viewers' intergroup responses. The findings suggest that power exemplification of trans people functions with audience gender to influence attitudes towards trans issues, dehumanization of trans folks, and aggression towards them.

The CME framework offers the opportunity to reflect on the ways in which quantitative methods and media effects theories can be used to address critical issues in the emerging sociopolitical and mediated contexts. In fact, we use CME as one of the foundational theories in our new textbook, *Quantitative Research Methods in Communication: The Power of Numbers for Social Justice* (Scharrer & Ramasubramanian, 2021). In this book, we argue that not just media effects but social scientific theories in general can and should use a critical paradigm rather than the traditional postpositivist framework to examine the world around us. We give CME as an example of a theory within communication and media studies that fits with "quantitative criticalism" and is a set of theories that incorporate questions of power, agency, and structure while using quantitative methods.

Although CME is a very new theory, there is a lot of scope to further expand, elaborate, build, and refine it. The scholars highlighted in this section and many others beyond them are using CME to call on fellow social scientists to consider issues of power, inequalities, access, and social justice within our social scientific theorizing, especially within quantitative research. At the very least, we believe that social scientists within communication studies need to reflect on whether and how their research and theorizing might be complicit in reinforcing dominant ideologies and unspoken Eurocentrism within the discipline. As a starting point, we need to diversify our samples beyond predominantly white participants to incorporate a range of different perspectives on media effects.

Continuing the Conversation

We argue that taking a critical approach to our research process not only provides valuable and socially relevant nuance to our research questions but also examines the empowering utility of communication technology. Given the increasing interconnectedness of our everyday lives with media systems, media effects research has the potential to explain and respond to global systemic issues and equip people to use their voices through various media platforms. As we grapple with pandemic inequalities, white supremacy, anti-Black racism, rising fascism, and increasing xenophobia around the world, CME explores how media researchers and practitioners can use the power of media for prejudice reduction, inclusive communication, and favorable intergroup relations. It is important to go beyond narrow silos and disciplinary boundaries that limit collaborative possibilities to engage seriously with systemic inequalities.

The main goal of creating this framework is to start meaningful conversations as well as theoretical and methodological deliberations about our next steps as a field in these dynamic and evolving times. CME provides an opportunity to reexamine our curricula, theories, methods, and merit structures that currently are situated within Eurocentric imperial white logic. This approach calls for redefining merit and impact beyond h-indices, citations, and metrics to consider the practical implications of research on the lives of everyday people from marginalized groups, including communities of color. It has implications for the ways in which social scientific theorizing needs to incorporate critical perspectives in research, theories, pedagogy, and curriculum development.

Summary

In summary, the hope is that the CME framework will generate much-needed conversations regarding media research, theorizing, and praxis. In addition, it can lead to discussions related to the hiring, retention, and advancement of scholars of color within media and communication studies. This is an issue that also points to the need for mentoring, leadership, and community engagement within media effects and communication more broadly. We need to continuously ask whose perspectives and experiences are being privileged, how resources are being allocated, and how priorities are set in terms of disciplinary directions and institutional support. Furthermore, we need more scholars of color to be included and valued within the "canonical" texts within media effects scholarship rather than seen as peripheral, incidental, and "also-rans" within media effects and communication scholarship more generally.

FOR FURTHER THOUGHT AND REFLECTION

1. Conduct a critical inventory of your own media consumption over the years. How might your media experiences impact your perceptions of different racial and ethnic groups?

2. How do the main pillars of CME relate to key tenets of other theories featured in the book? How does each pillar help to centralize racially diverse and inclusive perspectives in meaningful ways?

3. What research projects might be a good fit for critical media effects? How might a CME approach provide a productive lens for a research project that you are interested in?

4. How can social scientific approaches to communication become more inclusive in the ways in which they study different media effects? What are some specific ideas that you can recommend?

STORIED REFLECTION
Theory as Liberation

Elizabeth M. Lozano
Loyola University Chicago

I grew up in Bogotá, Colombia, in a very difficult home environment. From childhood, I had a desperate need to make sense of things that made no sense. Things that hurt me. Because I could not ask anyone for help, I turned inwardly, and I became a *theoretician*. Lived experience was my data, and my own self (body, mind, and spirit) was the puzzle that needed answers.

The main role of theory is to name and explain or explicate reality. I did that empirically. Probably every child does. I would produce "grounded theory" that came from experience and observation. I would name phenomena and wonder how they came to be. In so doing, I could take distance from things that hurt and try to understand them, thereby reducing their malignant power over me. In this way, I believe *theory saved my life* at least twice. No matter how bad things got (and they got very bad), I could always return to them a little later and investigate them with curiosity. Doing so allowed me to overcome despair. The way I see it, there is something fundamentally uplifting and life-affirming about theory-making. It is always about understanding (well, sometimes controlling) an environment so that it can be altered, accepted, or affirmed. This is why I tell my students that there is nothing more practical than theory. It is a master key that opens a thousand doors.

At the time, I attended an all-girl Catholic school. The Dominican nuns wanted us to memorize, repeat, and obey. Those actions didn't allow me to understand the world, because that requires an active mind that is encouraged to question and explore. But all that would change unexpectedly. Two weeks after my 15th birthday, a family member tried to strangle me.

I ran away to Cali, where my estranged father lived. He rented a room for me, and I lived alone. My father seemed to believe that at age 15, I was perfectly capable of raising myself in any regard—except schooling. To that matter, he gave considerable thought and enrolled me in a one-of-a-kind school. It was a cooperative founded by professors—affordable, progressive, and experimental. I used to joke that the school was Marxist. There I met communists, socialists, and anarchists; Maoists; Trotskyites; and Castroists. There was also the occasional infiltrated paramilitary (armed far-right) or guerilla (armed far-left) among students and teachers. We would learn of their existence years later.

Contrary to what one may have expected from such a sudden and traumatic uprooting, I went from being a mediocre student in Bogotá to standing at the top of the class with the lefties. I was fascinated. In literature class, we read Latin American fiction critically. In theater, I practiced Brechtian acting, which confronts the audience rather than seducing it. In history, we studied Colombian social movements rather than heroes. In philosophy, we analyzed original texts from Descartes, Lenin, and Foucault. And in civics, we became acquainted with the antipsychiatry movement of Italy and Freud's texts on culture. I fell in love with ideas. I felt heard and seen.

There was very little speaking "down" to us. Thrillingly, we were challenged and exposed to theories that were complex and revolutionary. I was introduced to Brazilian Paulo Freire, a founder of critical pedagogy, and to his critique of the "banking system" of education. His seminal book *Pedagogia do Oprimido,* published in 1968, is still influential in Latin America and the United States. Finally, I understood why I had felt so bored and alienated with the nuns. It was not the religious element but rather the banking attitude. That is, their presumption that we all were empty slots on which they deposited information "value." We were supposed to lay there inert and ignorant, and passively receive their knowledge.

Schooling became liberating. The theoretical common thread that seemed to run through all these classes, from history to literature to philosophy, could have been summarized in three principles: Suspect the state, question order, and disrupt the status quo. The point was to deconstruct our dominant "order of things," question its logic, and resist oppression, consumerism, and imperialism. Given all my life experiences, these principles resonated. They would be challenged and complicated later; but their relevance has not diminished with the years. And, as it should be with any good theory, I applied these same principles to the lefty school itself. I questioned the school's administrative hierarchy, resisted pointless rules, and together with my classmates, we disrupted the order forming our own assembly. In doing so, I became quite well prepared for what would become my dream life next: A communication studies college degree and a Fulbright scholarship to the United States.

CHAPTER 20

Theory of Hyper(in)visibility

Amber Johnson

Saint Louis University

Jade Petermon

Georgia State University

Identity research has long confirmed that identities are messy, nuanced, and complex. Identities are constituted by an amalgamation of entities both sought and rejected, loved and hated, desired and deplorable. As we move through the world growing, learning, bending, and becoming, so do our identities. Despite the complexity of identity, mediated representations flatten identities into stereotypical formations that have real implications for lived experience. We created the theory of hyper(in) visibility to account for the physical, discursive, economic, political, and legislative violence targeting Black and Brown bodies, fat bodies, gender-expansive bodies, and the like in everyday, face-to-face interactions due to the lasting and damaging effects of hyper-visible stereotypes.

The story of how we came to hyper(in)visibility illuminates the profound endurance required to withstand stereotypes but also what happens when alignment exists. In 2012, Amber began working on a manuscript with Dr. Robin Boylorn about the YouTube series *Between Women*. They had an epiphany about how stereotypes are so pervasive, even when marginalized people have the chance to rewrite narratives, we often fall victim to stereotypical representation. They wondered why that was so and how to combat master narratives that never served marginalized populations.

Around the same time, Jade was working on her dissertation research about neoliberal media, Black bodies, and the idea that Black people are more visible in mediated texts than we have ever been, yet those representations lack subjectivity. Black bodies often fill the hallowed spaces of media without any reference to our nuanced and complex lived experience. In short, we are simultaneously visible and invisible. After both the article and dissertation were published, we found each other when Amber was searching for similar work to help guide their master's thesis advisee who wanted to use the theory as a theoretical framework. Amber reached out to Jade, and we were both awestruck by the distinct parallels and overlaps. We were both experiencing similar epiphanies at the same time despite never having learned of each other's research. In that moment, we decided to partner to continue developing the theory, and that brings us to this culminating work.

In this definitive essay, we define the theory of hyper(in)visibility, attend to the short history of visibility politics, explore the tenets of hyper(in)visibility, and offer two applications of the theory. We end by offering ideas for future research. For clarity, we both spell hyper(in)visibility differently. Jade uses the spelling *hyper(in)visibility* because the interpolation of *(in)* highlights how invisibility moves inside and around the hypervisibility of Blackness and Black bodies. Amber used *hyper/in/visibility* for similar reasons. For the sake of consistency, we will use hyper(in)visibility throughout the text; however, for scholars looking to explore the theory in more depth, use of the following spelling will generate the most results: *hyper(in)visibility, hyperinvisibility, hyper/in/visibility,* and *hyper-invisibility.*

Intellectual Traditions of Theory of Hyper(in)visibility

In the current pandemic atmosphere, it is hard to imagine a time when we had to share physical space to see others. We live in a quickly evolving world of mediated seeing (Thompson, 2005), where history, culture, politics, and personal experience dictate how we understand texts, people, and context. Visibility politics refers to the power constructs connected to ways of seeing. What we see, how we see, and the frequency with which we see something impacts power structures. Who we see, how we see them, and how often we see them guide how we interpret artifacts and come to know the identities of the people being seen, which leads to invisibility, visibility, hypervisibility, and hyper(in)visibility. *Invisibility* signifies a lack of mediated representation where groups are missing from narratives en masse (Johnson & Boylorn, 2015). *Visibility* signifies frequent and complex representation in media that leads to a fuller understanding of the human experience and results in fewer stereotypes (Johnson & Boylorn, 2015).

Hypervisibility is a more complex notion. It occurs when the body is stereotyped so heavily in media that the stereotypes become more visible and believable than refuting information (Johnson & Boylorn, 2015; Petermon, 2014). For instance, when media programming includes images of Blackness and Black bodies, they usually do so as flat, one-dimensional archetypes/stereotypes or as dichotomous emblems of struggle/progress. Both modes of representation obscure the multifarious nature of Blackness and Black people. One of the most notable examples of this is the circulation of photos of Emmett Till at his funeral. Till was a Chicago youth who, while on vacation in Mississippi in 1955, was brutally murdered by two white men after being falsely accused of whistling at a white women—Carolyn Bryant. The circulation of the funeral photos, which depict Till as a mass of flesh—bloated and disfigured—is meant to do political and racial work. The pictures, which ran in *Jet* and later *Time* magazine, make very clear the risk of being a joyful Black boy in the Deep South in 1955. What they obscure is the true humanity and subjectivity of Till himself. Constituted in the photos are two things: (1) the danger of Blackness in a white world; and (2) the invisibility of a Black boy who lost his life on summer vacation.

Despite the potential harm posed by hypervisibility, it can be curbed with interpersonal interaction. When a person who believed hypervisible stereotypes interact with different others at the personal level, they can forgo mass-mediated images and see people for the complex individuals that they are. Unfortunately, individual interactions do little to sway a person's negative feelings towards an entire group, and oftentimes that single, befriended individual ends up feeling tokenized. Hyper(in)visibility creates a much deeper and deadly problem.

Hyper(in)visibility

We define *hyper(in)visibility* as a state where a person chooses to cause another person harm and feels justified because they only associate their victim with a deeply sedimented stereotype. In essence, a person consumes enough stereotypical and mediated images about a group of people that they begin treating them differently during interpersonal interactions. Several moments in history help exemplify hyper(in)visibility. After 9/11, stereotypes of Muslims became so hypervisible, that Americans began treating Muslims, Arabic-speaking people, and/or people who could potentially be identified as Muslims in discriminatory ways (Yomtoob, 2013). Americans failed to see Muslims as anything other than terrorists, resulting in systemic oppression, dehumanization, and exclusion. Another example is the case of Michael Brown and Darren Wilson. Instead of a human with complex emotions, behaviors, needs, and desires within a system of power, Brown became hyper(in)visible and Wilson felt justified in shooting a "villainous monster" according to his account. Wilson assumed Brown to be a superhuman, dangerous thug; thus, Brown's body was both present (in the flesh) and absent, due to mediated representations of Black masculinity, resulting in Wilson only seeing the stereotype (Johnson, 2017).

Michael Brown's death is a jarring example of how the Black body itself is hyper(in)visible. The relational meanings of Black and white create excess for Black bodies. The normative white body is devoid of color, while the Black body contains too much color. The history and memory of the trans-Atlantic slave trade, chattel slavery, and colonialism materialize in the Black body. At the moment of visibility, Black skin (or Brown skin or fat or (dis)ability, etc.) stands in for one's subjectivity, and because of this, Black people, both individually and collectively, are hyper(in)invisible. Anytime a Black person is followed around a store or ignored at a restaurant, or stopped and frisked, they are experiencing hyper(in)visibility. Returning to the example of Emmett Till, while his images represent the destructive nature of hypervisibility, the way he was murdered illustrates the destructive nature of hyper(in)visibility. The same can be said for Michael Brown. The iconic image of him surfacing is a literal flattened narrative of his entire life summed up in the hashtags #MikeBrownForever, #Ferguson, #handsupdontshoot, and #BlackLivesMatter. His murder, however, reflects an act of hyper(in)visibility. Returning again to history, Frantz Fanon (2008, p. 112) sums up the tenuous relationship between being seen and unseen in *Black Skin, White Masks*. He describes this process as the experience of being identified as Black by being reduced to his skin and forced to be responsible for his body, his race, and his ancestors.

Hyper(in)visibility also illustrates the link between contemporary visual culture and neoliberal colorblindness. The rise of neoliberalism created a climate in which the visibility of Blackness itself is valuable yet rarely attends to the complexities and multiplicity of Black subjectivities. According to Stuart Hall, "Neoliberalism is grounded in the 'free, possessive individual,' with the state cast as tyrannical and oppressive" (Hall, 2011). As a result of neoliberalism's increased emphasis on the individual, moving away from societal concerns about race (and class, and gender, and sexuality) is an important step for the neoliberal state because these are group concerns. The upsurge in the visibility of Black people across the media helps portray the United States as a place where race is no longer an important or pivotal issue. This situation created a state of hyper(in)visibility for Black people. Black people are more visible than they have ever been, and because of this hypervisibility across mediascapes, the possibilities for witnessing a multiplicity of Black subjectivities is often denied by neoliberal corporate structures in the film and other media industries. As a result, the true depth and breadth, not to mention the beauty and varied nature, of Blackness and Black people continues to be obscured in the cultural sphere while the glut of these hypervisible images seem to confirm the postracial utopia that many believe was ushered in by the election of the 44th president of the United States, Barack Obama. In the next section, we discuss the tenets of hyper(in)visibility as a theoretical framework.

Main Goals and Features of Theory of Hyper(in)visibility

If one wanted to use hyper(in)visibility as a theoretical framework to analyze a text, interaction, narrative, or experience, the following list of concepts comprise the theoretical tenets. For the sake of clarity, we use the terms *characters* to refer to fictitious people and *stakeholders* to refer to actual people. After choosing an artifact to study (mediated or otherwise), the researcher should first look for evidence of the four layers of visibility. As they search for evidence, the researcher should keep track of the frequency and contextual details of each instance. For text-based analysis (narrative or interview transcripts, social media comments, etc.), we recommend using a color-coding scheme. For aural and/or visual artifacts (films, social media content, etc.), we recommend using a time-stamp method in a spreadsheet or table. The researcher should look for evidence of the four layers listed below and the following forms of violence (where applicable):

1. *Invisibility* signifies a lack of mediated representation. Look for context clues and historical connections that illuminate key stakeholders that were never mentioned or included. What is not visible or audible is also communicating messages.

2. *Visibility* signifies frequent and complex representation in media. Look for characters and/or stakeholders who are represented in holistic ways versus reductive ways. When witnessing a visible character and/or stakeholder, the audience will know them by name, be provided details about their life beyond the immediate and necessary experience, and will have a fuller understanding of the context of their situation.

3. *Hypervisibility* occurs when bodies are stereotyped so heavily in media that the stereotypes become more visible and believable than the truth. For this layer, researchers should search for stereotypical representations of people like Indigenous people masked as noble savages, hypersexual and aggressive Black men, angry Black women, Asian math wizzes, undesirable people with disabilities, and so on.

4. *Hyper(in)visibility* occurs when a person uses a stereotype to justify the harm they cause another person. The hypervisible stereotype leads to hyper(in)visible interactions. For this layer, researchers should look for moments where an individual is treated in violent ways because of the stereotypes attached to their bodies.

After researchers locate the various layers of visibility, the next step is documenting the violence connected to hyper(in)visibility. The specific types of violence the researchers should look for are listed below. This list was curated specifically to connect personal interactions to larger systems of power because representation has many consequences beyond viewer satisfaction.

1. *Discursive violence* is violence rooted in language. Name-calling, microaggressions, bad mouthing someone's character, libel, slander, and using derogatory terms are just some of the forms of discursive violence.

2. *Physical violence* manifests as direct harm to a person's body caused by assault or the unequal distribution of labor that results in premature death and suffering. The researcher should look for any form of assault, murder, or inequitable divisions of labor that result in suffering.

3. *Legislative violence* refers to laws meant to oppress one group while creating opportunities for other groups. Laws like stop and frisk, racial profiling, and the repealing of Deferred Action for Childhood Arrivals (DACA) constitute legislative violence. Researchers should look for evidence of any laws, policies, or repeals that are germane to understanding the context of the situation.

4. *Political violence* refers to any political situation that causes harm to a person or individual. Political violence might erupt as a staged coup at the White House to disrupt democratic practice, dishonest claims of voter fraud to steal an election, or voter suppression.

5. *Economic violence* occurs when those in power prey on those in poverty and/or create conditions for people to lose money, resources, opportunities, and/or class mobility. Redlining, outsourcing, targeted unemployment, and fraudulent mortgage-lending comprise some examples.

One thing of note is that not all types of violence will apply to any single text. Researchers should look for all applicable types of violence and be clear in their research write-ups why certain types were included and others omitted. The following section highlights two recent studies that utilize hyper(in)visibility as a theoretical framework across two artifacts: the movie *Straight Outta Compton* and Shonda Rhimes's television programming company, Shondaland.

Research and Practical Applications of Theory of Hyper(in)visibility

Straight Outta Erasure

In her essay "Straight Outta Erasure: Black Girl Magic Claps Back to the Hyperinvisibility of Black Women in *Straight Outta Compton*," Johnson (2018) uses visibility politics and the rhetorical power of nostalgia as theoretical frameworks to code the film for visibility, violence, and Black womanhood. Their results indicate that nostalgia serves as a conveyor belt for not only erasing Black women's narratives but also replacing them with service positions that cater to male dominance, resulting in a cycle of hyper(in)visibility. Specific to the theory of hyper(in)visibility, the author's results point to the following instances of visibility politics:

- Seven partially visible characters, or characters who enact agency but only in ways connected to the male characters in the film—that take up less than 10 minutes of total screen time.

- Fifteen moments of hypervisibility throughout the film where women populate spaces that are stereotypically oversexualized and undervalued.

- Nine key moments of invisibility where complete narratives are missing from the story.

- Twenty-nine moments of hyper(in)visibility like name-calling or speaking of women or the feminine form using foul language that use physical violence to cause harm and/or death to characters.

By pinpointing the direct link between the stereotype and the ensuing violence, Johnson (2018) is able to point to the political, personal, institutional, and systemic impact of stereotypes and not just the individual experiences. Critics often ignore larger systems when evaluating a message for representation, resulting in a framing of these issues as whining, lacking rigor, or unimportant in the greater landscape of liberation and freedom. However, by connecting the personal to the political via the various forms of violence, we see that representation matters and has deep level impact for our ability to survive and thrive in a world never meant for us to exist wholly and healthy.

After coding the film for visibility politics, Johnson (2018) used hip hop feminism as a lens to analyze counternarratives told by women of color via social media like Twitter, blogs, and even a full-length feature film by Michel'le. Johnson writes that these Black Girl Magic clap backs are alternate truths situated within lived experience that paint a fuller nostalgic gesture towards misogynoir and intersectional power. The author concludes that without the performative possibility of social media's rhetorical power, audiences would not be as privy to counternarratives, which ultimately serve to generate visibility, or nuanced representation couched in lived experience beyond simple and reductive stereotypes.

Shondaland

The late 1990s and early 2000s saw a plethora of culturally specific, Black television shows written and produced with Black audiences in mind. This includes shows like *The Bernie Mac Show* (Fox, 2001–2006), *My Wife and Kids* (ABC, 2001–2005), and *Everybody Hates Chris* (UPN/CW, 2005–2009). Today, primetime network television looks different. While shifts in culture have made all-white casts politically incorrect and most shows do attempt to achieve multicultural casting, this confluence of factors creates an environment ripe with hyper(in)visibility. In the analysis "Race (Lost and Found) in Shondaland," Petermon (2018) uses hyper(in)visibility as a framework to highlight major shifts in representation and visibility on primetime network television through an examination of Shonda Rhimes's tenure at ABC.

Petermon argues that the simultaneous rise of multiculturalism and neoliberalism created an environment in which a specific kind of visibility was desirable. Thus, the rise in hypervisible Black characters created a rise in hyper(in)visibility on primetime network television. Petermon first charts changes in multicultural rhetoric in the political arena from Reagan to Obama. Her findings suggest that while each president uses racialized rhetoric, each presidency (regardless of political party) further cemented a rise in neoliberal colorblindness. Petermon then examines parallel changes on primetime network television, exposing the deeply enmeshed relationship between racialized political rhetoric and media industry practices. Finally, with this background as foundation, the analysis ends with a broad reading of Rhimes's work at ABC, arguing that while in her early days she championed colorblind casting and produced hyper(in)visible characters, as she gained power and influence in the industry, she attempted to complicate her characters to varying degrees of success. Rhimes aside, Petermon asserts, "the problem with multicultural colorblind television is that it reinforces the idea that race is no longer an important societal issue, further instantiates post-racialism, and floods the visual field with hyper(in)visible characters of color to the benefit of white society and the detriment of people of color" (Petermon, 2018, p. 116).

Continuing the Conversation

While both examples described in the previous section use television and film as artifacts, the theory of hyper(in)visibility has proven valuable for analysis of different mediated texts. As such, several scholars have used the theory to mark moments of hyper(in) visibility in contemporary real life. For instance, the theory was used to analyze how Facebook users relied on stereotypes to justify physical and discursive violence against Syrian refugees during the Syrian refugee crisis. The author coded Facebook comments under the first stories shared by the most popular news sites on social media and found recurring themes pointing to the direct justification of violence couched in stereotypes like "All Muslims are terrorists" (Gonzalez Noveiri, 2016). Another study employed hyper(in)visibility to address the tokenization that occurs during hiring practices in institutions (Johnson, 2017). The author uses the theory to address how hyper(in)visibility works in tandem with canonical prejudice to weed out qualified Black and Brown candidates as "undesirable" based on stereotypes and white supremacy.

While the theory has been used primarily to locate mediated representation rooted in stereotypes that promote different types of violence, we see this theory as having larger implications for future communication research beyond mediated representation. Hyper(in)visibility is a powerful theory because it brings the mediated into conversation with real-time violence. Since the coronavirus pandemic, we have seen a national rise in anti-Asian violence alongside the rise of institutions calling for naming racism as a public health crisis and a call for ending anti-Blackness. In March of 2021, two incidents highlight the need to address how hyper(in)visibility bolsters these issues. Hyper(in) visibility could be used to analyze the mass shooting in Atlanta, Georgia, that left eight people dead, among them six Asian American women, and how anti-Asian narratives rooted in sexual and cultural stereotypes created the perfect situation to absolve "white boys who had a bad day" from their domestic terrorism. This theory can also be used to address how conversations around reparations use hyper(in)visibility to diminish the impact of systemic racism on Black people and the importance of repairing the harms associated with American slavery.

Summary

Identity research has developed in unique and interesting ways over the course of the communication discipline. As we continue developing frameworks for understanding identity politics, it is imperative that we create clear, concise methods for connecting the personal to the political and illuminating how identity politics causes systemic oppression, not just personal problems. As we move through the world consuming content, creating content, and challenging content, we must attend to the political, social, economic, and legislative violence associated with that content. Hyper(in)visibility as a theoretical framework creates opportunities to connect the personal to the political and systemic in ways that matter and make visible how stereotypes promote violence beyond discursive representation.

FOR FURTHER THOUGHT AND REFLECTION

1. Review the list of specific types of violence that the authors identify with different layers of visibility. What examples can you provide for each type from your own experiences with how traditionally marginalized groups are represented in social media?

2. Track the controversy surrounding critical race theory, beginning with its inception and application in the late 20th century and continuing to present-day attempts to ban it from education curriculum. How can you associate the hyper(in)visibility of the theory to specific examples of violence against people of the global majority?

3. What are some current examples of specific media (e.g., #hashtages, viral memes, trending topics, etc.) that are best understood through hyper(in)visibility theory? Do similar dynamics exist for instances when majority group members are depicted in attempts to reduce violence against people of the global majority? For instance, how might memes of a "Karen" or a "Becky" be interpreted through this theoretical lens?

REFERENCES

Abrams, J., Hill, A., & Maxwell, M. (2019). Underneath the mask of the strong Black woman schema: Disentangling influences of strength and self-silencing on depressive symptoms among U.S. Black women. *Sex Roles, 80*(4), 1–10. https://doi:10.1007/s11199-018-0956-y

Abrego, L. J., & Negrón-Gonzales, G. (Eds.). (2020). *We are not dreamers: Undocumented scholars theorize undocumented life in the United States.* Duke University Press.

Adorno, T. W., & J. M. Bernstein. (2001). *The culture industry: Selected essays on mass culture.* Routledge.

Aguilar, C. (2019). Undocumented critical theory. *Cultural Studies ↔ Critical Methodologies, 19*(3), 152–160. https://doi.org/10.1177/1532708618817911

Allen, B. J. (1996). Feminist standpoint theory: A Black woman's (re)view of organizational socialization. *Communication Studies, 47*(4), 257–271.

Allen, B. J. (2011). *Difference matters: Communicating social identity* (2nd ed.). Waveland Press.

Alper, M., Katz, V. S., & Clark, L. S. (2016). Researching children, intersectionality, and diversity in the digital age. *Journal of Children and Media, 10*(1), 107–114. doi.org/10.1080/17482798.2015.1121886

Alvarez, W. (2013). Finding "home" in/through Latinidad ethnography: Experiencing community in the field with "my people." *Liminalities: A Journal of Performance Studies, 9*(2), 49–58.

Anderson, J. (1996). *Communication theory: Epistemological foundations.* Guilford Press.

Anderson, P., Sims, J. D., Shuff, J., Neese, S., & Sims, A. (2015). A price-based approach to the dialectics in African American female entrepreneur experiences. *Journal of Business Diversity, 15*(2), 46–59.

Anzaldúa, G. (1999). *Borderlands = La frontera* (2nd ed.). Aunt Lute Books.

Aristotle (1932). *The rhetoric of Aristotle* (L. Cooper, Trans.). Appleton-Century Company.

Asen, R., & Brouwer, D. C. (2001). *Counterpublics and the state.* SUNY Press.

Bailey, V. (2018). Stronger: An examination of the effects of the Strong Black Woman narrative through the lifespan of African American women. Dissertation retrieved from https://scholarworks.gsu.edu/communication_theses/119/

Baker, H. (1995). Critical memory and the Black public sphere. In Black Public Sphere Collective (Eds.), *The Black public sphere: A public culture book* (pp. 199–228). University of Chicago Press.

Bakhtin, M. M. (1981). *The dialogic imagination: Four essays* (M. Holquist & C. Emerson, Trans.). University of Texas Press.

Ball-Rokeach, S. J., & DeFleur, M. L. (1976). A dependency model of mass media effects. *Communication Research, 3*(1), 3–21. doi.org/10.1177/009365027600300101

Bates, B. R. (2020). Making communication scholarship less WEIRD. *Southern Communication Journal, 86*(1), 1–4. http://doi.org/10.1080/1041794X.2020.1861078

Baxter, L. A. (2004). A tale of two voices: Relational dialectics theory. *Journal of Family Communication, 4*(3–4), 181–192.

Baxter, L. A., & Montgomery, B. M. (1996). *Relating: Dialogues and dialectics*. Guilford.

Berger, C. R. & Calabrese, R. J. (1975). Some explorations in initial interaction and beyond: Toward a developmental theory of interpersonal communication. *Human Communication Research, 1*(2), 99–112.

Bitzer, L. F. (1968). The rhetorical situation. *Philosophy and Rhetoric, 1*(1), 1–14.

Black Lives Matter. (2021). About Black Lives Matter. https://blacklivesmatter.com/about/

Black Public Sphere Collective (Eds.). (1995). *The Black public sphere: A public culture book*. University of Chicago Press.

Braithwaite, E. K. (1974). *Contradictory omens: Cultural diversity and integration in the Caribbean*. Savacou Publications.

Brayboy, B. M. J. (2005). Toward a Tribal critical race theory in education. *Urban Review, 37*(5), 425–446. https://doi.org/10.1007/s11256-005-0018-y

Brown, P., & Levinson, S. (1987). *Politeness: Some universals in language usage*. Cambridge University Press.

Bryant, J., & Zillmann, D. (1994). *Media effects: Advances in theory and research*. Lawrence Erlbaum Associates.

Buller, D. B., & Burgoon, J. K. (1996). Another look at information management: A rejoinder to McCornack, Levine, Morrison, and Lapinski. *Communication Monographs, 63*(1), 92–98. https://doi.org/10.1080/03637759609376377

Burgoon, J. K. (1978). A communication model of personal space violations: Explication and an initial test. *Human Communication Research, 4*(2), 129–142. https://doi.org/10.1111/j.1468-2958.1978.tb00603.x

Burgoon, J. K., Buller, D. B., Guerrero, L. K., Afifi, W. A., & Feldman, C. M. (1996). Interpersonal deception: XII. Information management dimensions underlying deceptive and truthful messages. *Communication Monographs, 63*(1), 50–69. https://doi.org/10.1080/03637759609376374

Burke, K. (1966). *Language as symbolic action*. University of California Press.

Burke, K. (1969a). *A grammar of motives* (California ed.). University of California Press.

Burke, K. (1969b). *A rhetoric of motives* (California ed.). University of California Press.

Burt, R. S. (1987). Social contagion and innovation: Cohesion versus structural equivalence. *American Journal of Sociology, 92*(6), 1287–1335. https://doi.org/10.1086/228667

Cabrera, N. L. (2018). Where is the racial theory in critical race theory?: A constructive criticism of the Crits. *Review of Higher Education, 42*(1), 209–233. https://doi.org/10.1353/rhe.2018.0038

Cabrera, N. L. (2019). Critical race theory v. deficit models. *Equity & Excellence in Education, 52*(1), 47–54. https://doi.org/10.1080/10665684.2019.1630342

Cacho, L. (2012). *Social death: Racialized rightlessness and the criminalization of the unprotected*. New York University Press.

Canary, D. J., Cody, M. J., & Manusov, V. L. (2008). *Interpersonal communication: A goals-based approach*. Bedford/St. Martin's.

Carbaugh, D. (2007). Commentary: Six basic principles in the communication of social identities: The special case of discourses and illness. *Communication and Medicine, 4*(1), 111–115. doi:10.1515/CAM.2007.011

Cardwell, M. E., & Soliz, J. (2020). Examining the role of sibling interaction in multiethnic-racial identity development in the United States. *Identity*, 20(1), 58–72. https://doi.org/10.1080/15283 488.2019.1707678

Cardwell, M. E., Soliz, J., Crockett, L. J., & Bergquist, G. L. (2020). Critical incidents in the development of (multi)ethnic-racial identity: Experiences of individuals with mixed ethnic-racial backgrounds in the U.S. *Journal of Social and Personal Relationships*, 37(5), 1653–1672. https://doi.org/10.1177/0265407520906256

Castle Bell, G. (2019). "There's a difference between Black people and N******": A cultural contracts exploration of interracial communication barriers. *Communication Quarterly*, 67(3), 243–270. doi.org/10.1080/01463373.2019.11573744

Castle Bell, G., Hopson, M. C., Weathers, M. R., & Ross, K. A. (2015). From "laying the foundations" to building the house: Extending Orbe's (1998) co-cultural theory to include "rationalization" as a formal strategy. *Communication Studies*, 66(1), 1–26. https://doi.org/10.1080/10510974.2013 .858053

Chaffee, S. H. (1991). *Explication*. SAGE.

Chakravartty, P., Kuo, R., Grubbs, V., & McIlwain, C. (2018). #CommunicationSoWhite. *Journal of Communication*, 68(2), 254–266. doi.org/10.1093/joc/jqy003

Chávez, K. R. (2015). Beyond inclusion: Rethinking rhetoric's historical narrative. *Quarterly Journal of Speech*, 101(1), 162–172. https://doi.org/10.1080/00335630.2015.994908

Chen, Y.-W., & Lawless, B. (2018). "Oh my god! You have become so Americanized": Paradoxes of adaptation and strategic ambiguity among female immigrant faculty. *Journal of International and Intercultural Communication*, 11(1), 1–20.

Chin, J. L., & Trimble, J. E. (2015). *Diversity and leadership*. SAGE.

Chin, J. L., Trimble, J. E., & Garcia, J. E. (Eds.). (2018). *Global and culturally diverse leaders and leadership: New dimensions and challenges for business, education and society*. Emerald.

Cole, J. B., & Guy-Sheftall, B. (2003). *Gender talk: The struggle for women's equality in African American communities*. Ballantine.

Collins, P. H. (2000). *Black feminist thought: Knowledge, consciousness, and the politics of empowerment* (2nd ed.). Routledge.

Combs, G. M. (2003). The duality of race and gender for managerial African American women: Implications of informal social networks on career advancement. *Human Resource Development Review*, 2(4), 385–405. https://doi.org/10.1177/1534484303257949

Cooper, A. J. (1892). *A voice from the south*. Aldine Press House.

Cornwell, E. Y., & Cornwell, B. (2008). Access to expertise as a form of social capital: An examination of race- and class-based disparities in network ties to experts. *Sociological Perspectives*, 51(4), 853–876. https://doi.org/10.1525/sop.2008.51.4.853

Crenshaw, K. (1991). Mapping the margins: Intersectionality, identity politics, and violence against women of color. *Stanford Law Review*, 43(6), 1241–1299. https://doi.org/10.2307/1229039

Crapanzano, V. (1985). *Waiting: The whites of South Africa*. Random House.

Crotty, M. J. (1998). *The foundations of social research: Meaning and perspective in the research process*. SAGE.

Crowder, S. B. (2016). *When Momma speaks: The Bible and motherhood from a womanist perspective*. Westminster John Knox Press.

Cuevas, S. (2019). "Con mucho sacrificio, we give them everything we can": The strategic day-to-day sacrifices of undocumented Latina/o parents. *Harvard Educational Review*, 89(3), 473–496. https://doi.org/10.17763/1943-5045-89.3.473

Daniel, J., & Daniel, J. (1999). African-American childrearing: The context of the hot stove. In T. Socha & R. Diggs (Eds.), *Communication, race, and family: Exploring communication in Black, White and biracial families* (pp. 27–48). Lawrence Erlbaum Associates.

Danquah, M. N. (1998). *Willow weep for me: A Black woman's journey through depression*. One World.

Davis, A. Y. (2011). *Women, race, & class*. Vintage.

Davis, O. I. (1998). A Black woman as rhetorical critic: Validating self and violating the space of otherness. *Women's Studies in Communication, 21*(1), 77–90. https://doi.org/10.1080/07491409.1998.10162414

Davis, S. (2015). The "strong Black Woman Collective": A developing theoretical framework for understanding collective communication practices of Black women. *Women's Studies in Communication, 38*(1), 20–35. https://doi.org/10.1080/07491409.2014.953714

Davis, S. (2019). When sistahs support sistahs: A process of supportive communication about microaggressions among Black women. *Communication Monographs, 89*(2), 133–157. https://doi.org/10.1080/03637751.2018.1548769

Davis, S., & Jones, M. (2020). Black women at war: A comprehensive framework for research on the strong Black woman. *Women's Studies in Communication 44*(3), 301–322. https://doi.org/10.1080/07491409.2020.1838020

Dawson, M. (1995). A Black counterpublic?: Economic earthquakes, racial agenda(s), and Black politics. In Black Public Sphere Collective (Eds.), *The Black public sphere: A public culture book* (pp. 199–227). University of Chicago Press.

De Fulviis, A. (2020, May 31). Black female writers who changed feminist theory. *CR Fashion Book.* https://www.crfashionbook.com/culture/g30982388/influential-black-feminist-writers-history/?slide=7

De La Garza, A. T. (2015). A critical eulogy for Joaquin Luna: Mindful racial realism as an intervention to end racial battle fatigue. In J. L. Martin (Ed.), *Racial battle fatigue: Insights from the front lines of social justice advocacy* (pp. 177–189). ABC-CLIO.

De La Garza, A. T. (2019). A eulogy for Roxsana Hernández: Tracing the relationship between border rhetoric and queer debility. *QED: A Journal in GLBTQ Worldmaking, 6*(3), 94–99.

De La Garza, A. T., & Ono, K. A. (2015). Retheorizing adaptation: Differential adaptation and critical intercultural communication. *Journal of International and Intercultural Communication, 8*(4), 269–289.

Deetz, S. (2005). Critical theory. In S. May & D. Mumby (Eds.), *Engaging organizational communication theory & research: Multiple perspectives* (pp. 85–111). SAGE.

Delgado, R., & Stefancic, J. (2017). *Critical race theory: An introduction* (Vol. 20). New York University Press.

Dillard, J. P., & Pfau, M. (Eds.) (2002). *The persuasion handbook: Developments in theory and practice* (2nd ed.). SAGE.

Drummond, D. K., & Orbe, M. P. (2009). "Who are you trying to be?:" Identity gaps within intraracial encounters. *Qualitative Research Reports in Communication, 10*(1), 81–87. doi.org/10.1080/17459430903236098

Dubin, R. (1969). *Theory building.* Free Press.

Dutta, M. J. (2004). The unheard voices of Santalis: Communicating about health from the margins of India. *Communication Theory, 14*(3), 237–263.

Dutta, M. J. (2008). *Communicating health: A culture-centered approach.* Polity.

Dutta, M. J. (2011). *Communicating social change: Structure, culture, and agency.* Routledge.

Dutta, M. J. (2018). Culture-centered approach in addressing health disparities: Communication infrastructures for subaltern voices. *Communication Methods and Measures, 12*(4), 239–259. http://doi.org/10.1080/19312458.2018.1453057

Dutta, M. J. (2020). *Communication, culture and social change: Meaning, co-option and resistance.* Palgrave Macmillan.

Dutta, M., Pandi, A. R., Zapata, D., Mahtani, R., Falnikar, A., Tan, N., Thaker, J., Pitaloka, D., Dutta, U., Luk, P., & Sun, K. (2019). Critical health communication method as embodied practice of resistance: Culturally centering structural transformation through struggle for voice. *Frontiers in Communication, 4,* 1–14. https://doi.org/10.3389/fcomm.2019.00067

Dutta, M., Sastry, S., Dillard, S., Kumar, R., Anaele, A., Collins, W., Roberson, C., Dutta, U., Jones, C., Gillespie, T., & Spinetta, C. (2017). Narratives of stress in health meanings of African

Americans in Lake County, Indiana. *Health Communication*, 32(10), 1241–1251. https://doi.org/1
0.1080/10410236.2016.1204583

Dutta, M. J., & Thaker, J. (2020). Sustainability, ecology, and agriculture in women farmers' voices:
Culture-centering gender and development. *Communication Theory*, 30(2), 126–148. https://doi.
org/10.1093/ct/qtz029

Dura, L., & Singhal, A. (2009). Utilizing a positive deviance approach to reduce girls' trafficking
in Indonesia: Asset-based communicative acts that make a difference. *Journal of Creative
Communications*, 4(1), 1–17. http://doi.org/10.1177/097325861000400101

Dyer, W. W. (1976). *Your erroneous zones*. Funk & Wagnalls.

Elers, C., Jayan, P., Elers, P., & Dutta, M. J. (2021). Negotiating health amidst COVID-19 lockdown
in low-income communities in Aotearoa New Zealand. *Health Communication*, 36(1), 109–115.
https://doi.org/10.1080/10410236.2020.1848082

Epstein, R., & Herndon, A. (6 January 2021). The 10-year Stacey Abrams project to flip Georgia
has come to fruition. *New York Times*. https://www.nytimes.com/2021/01/05/us/politics/stac-
ey-abrams-georgia.html

Erroneous. (2021). *Dictionary.com*. https://www.dictionary.com

Fadiman, A. (1997). *The spirit catches you and you fall down: A Hmong child, her American doctors, and
the collision of two cultures*. Farrar, Straus and Giroux.

Fanon, F. (2008). *Black skin, white masks*. Grove Press.

Feagin, J. R. (2020). *The white racial frame: Centuries of racial framing and counter-framing*.
Routledge.

Fenton, S. (2010). *Ethnicity* (2nd ed.). Polity Press.

Flaherty, C. (2019, June 13). When white scholars pick white scholars. Inside
Higher Education. https://www.insidehighered.com/news/2019/06/13/
communication-scholars-debate-how-fields-distinguished-scholars-should-be-picked

Floyd-Thomas, S. M. (2006). *Deeper shades of purple: Womanism in religion and society*. New York
University Press.

Foss, S. K., & Griffin, C. L. (1995). Beyond persuasion: A proposal for an invitational rhetoric.
Communication Monographs, 62, 2–18. https://doi.org/10.1080/03637759509376345

Foster, B. A., Aquino, C. A., Mejia, S., Turner, B. J., & Singhal, A. (2018). Identification and characterization of families that are positively deviant for childhood obesity in a Latino population: A
case-control study. *Journal of Obesity*.

Fraser, N. (1992). Rethinking the public sphere: A contribution to the critique of actually existing
democracy. In C. Calhoun (Ed.), *Habermas and the public sphere* (pp. 109–142). MIT Press.

Freire, P. (2014). *Pedagogy of the oppressed* (30th anniv. ed.). Bloomsbury Publishing.

Gass, R. H., & Seiter, J. S. (2003). *Persuasion, social influence, and compliance gaining* (2nd ed.). Allyn
and Bacon.

Gastil, J. (2008). *Political communication and deliberation*. SAGE.

Gearhart, S. M. (1979). The womanization of rhetoric. *Women's Studies International Quarterly*, 2(2),
195–201. https://doi.org/10.1016/S0148-0685(79)91809-8

Geertz, C., & Pacanowsky, M. (1988). Cultural approach to organizations. In J. A. Anderson,
Communication Yearbook 11 (pp. 356–379). Routledge.

George, B. (2004). *Authentic leadership: Rediscovering the secrets to creating lasting value*.
Jossey-Bass.

Gerbner, G. (1983). The importance of being critical—in one's own fashion. *Journal of
Communication*, 33(3), 355–362.

Gerbner, G. (1998). Cultivation analysis: An overview. *Mass Communication and Society*, 1(3–4), 175–
194. doi.org/10.1080/15205436.1998.9677855

Giddens, A. (1984). *The constitution of society: Outline of the theory of structuration*. Polity Press.

Giles, H., Coupland, J., & Coupland, N. (1991). *Contexts of accommodation: Developments in applied
sociolinguistics*. Cambridge University Press.

Gittens, R. A. (2021). Atlanta's pink trap house: Reimagining the Black public sphere as an aesthetic community. *Theory & Event, 24*(2), 434–455. doi.org/10.1353/tae.2021.0021

Goffman, E. (1955). On face-work: An analysis of ritual elements in social interaction. *Psychiatry: Interpersonal and Biological Processes, 18*(3), 213–231. http://doi.org/10.1080/00332747.1955.11023008

Goffman, E. (1959). *The presentation of self in everyday life.* Doubleday.

Golden, J., & Rieke, R. (1971). *The rhetoric of black Americans.* Charles E. Merrill Publishing.

Goldsmith, D. J. (2001). A normative approach to the study of uncertainty and communication. *Journal of Communication, 51*(3), 514–533. https://doi.org/10.1111/j.1460-2466.2001.tb02894.x

Gonzalez Noveiri, S. (2016). "You don't fool me; I know who you are": Facebook users' construction of Syrian refugees as hyperinvisible. Unpublished Master's Thesis. Saint Louis University.

González, A. (1997). My back pages: Confessions of a fugitive interculturalist. In J. Trent (Ed.), *Communication: Views from the helm for the 21st century* (pp. 380–384). Allyn and Bacon.

González, A., & Chen, Y.-W. (Eds.) (2016). *Our voices: Essays in culture, ethnicity and communication* (6th ed.). Oxford University Press.

González, A., & Makay, J. J. (1983). Rhetorical ascription and the gospel according to Dylan. *Quarterly Journal of Speech, 69*(1), 1–14.

Graen, G. B., & Uhl-Bien, M. (1995). Relationship-based approach to leadership: Development of leader-member exchange (LMX) theory of leadership over 25 years: Applying a multi-level multi-domain perspective. *Leadership Quarterly, 6*(2), 219–247.

Greenfield-Sanders, T. (director & producer) (2016). *The trans list* [Film]. HBO.

Greenleaf, R. (1977). *Servant leadership: A journey into the nature of legitimate power and greatness.* Paulist Press.

Gresson, A. (1995). *The recovery of race in America.* University of Minnesota Press.

Gresson, A. (1997). Minority epistemology and the rhetoric of creation. *Philosophy & Rhetoric, 10*(4), 244–262.

Gresson, A. (2015). *America's atonement: Racial pain, recovery rhetoric, and the pedagogy of healing.* Peter Lang.

Grice, P. C. (1989). *Studies in the ways of words.* Harvard University Press.

Gudykunst, W. B. (1995). Anxiety/uncertainty management (AUM) theory: Current status. In R. Wiseman (Ed.), *Intercultural communication theory* (pp. 8–58). SAGE.

Habermas, J. (1989). *The structural transformation of the public sphere: An inquiry into a category of bourgeois society* (T. Burger, Trans.). MIT Press.

Hackman, M. & Johnson, C. (1991). *Leadership.* Waveland Press.

Hall, S. (1991). Encoding, decoding. In S. During (Ed), *The cultural studies reader* (pp. 90–103). Routledge.

Hall, S. (1985). Signification, representation, ideology: Althusser and the post-structuralist debates. *Critical Studies in Mass Communication, 2*(2), 91–114. doi.org/10.1080/15295038509360070

Hall, S. (1986). Gramsci's relevance for the study of race and ethnicity. *Journal of Communication Inquiry, 10*(2), 5–27. doi.org/10.1177/019685998601000202

Hall, S. (1992). Race, culture, and communications: Looking backward and forward at cultural studies. *Rethinking Marxism, 5*(1), 10–18. doi.org/10.1080/08935699208657998

Hall, S. (2011, September 12). The march of the neoliberals. *The Guardian.* http://www.theguardian.com/politics/2011/sep/12/march-of-the-neoliberals

Hamlet, J. D. (2000). Assessing womanist thought: The rhetoric of Susan L. Taylor. *Communication Quarterly, 48*(4), 420–436. https://doi.org/10.1080/01463370009385607

Harding, S. (Ed.) (2004). *The feminist standpoint theory reader: Intellectual and political controversies.* Routledge.

Hassan, H., & Blackwood, L. (2021). (Mis)recognition in the therapeutic alliance: The experience of mental health interpreters working with refugees in U.K. clinical settings. *Qualitative Health Research, 31*(2), 399–410. https://doi.org/10.1177/1049732320966586

Heath, R. L. (2020). *Management of corporate communication: From interpersonal contacts to external affairs*. Routledge.

Hecht, M., Warren, J. R., Jung, E., & Krieger, J. (2005). A communication theory of identity: Development, theoretical perspective, and future directions. In W. B. Gudykunst (Ed.), *Theorizing about intercultural communication* (pp. 257–278). SAGE.

Heifetz, R. (1994). *Leadership without easy answers*. Harvard University Press.

Henrich, J., Heine, S. J., & Norenzayan, A. (2010). The weirdest people in the world? *Behavioral and Brain Sciences, 33*(2–3), 61–83. doi.org/10.1017/s0140525x0999152x

Homans, G. C. (1958). Social behavior as exchange. *American Journal of Sociology, 63*(6), 597–606.

hooks, b. (1990). *Yearning: Race, gender, and cultural politics*. South End Press.

hooks, b. (1991). Theory as liberatory practice. *Yale Journal of Law and Feminism, 4*(1), 1–12.

hooks, b. (2014). *Ain't I a woman: Black women and feminism*. Routledge.

Hopson, M. C. (2011). *Notes from the talking drum: Exploring Black communication and critical memory in intercultural communication contexts*. Hampton Press.

Hsieh, E. (2006). Conflicts in how interpreters manage their roles in provider-patient interactions. *Social Science & Medicine, 62*(3), 721–730. https://doi.org/10.1016/j.socscimed.2005.06.029

Hsieh, E. (2008). "I am not a robot!" Interpreters' views of their roles in health care settings. *Qualitative Health Research, 18*(10), 1367–1383. https://doi.org/10.1177/1049732308323840

Hsieh, E. (2010). Provider-interpreter collaboration in bilingual health care: Competitions of control over interpreter-mediated interactions. *Patient Education and Counseling, 78*(2), 154–159. https://doi.org/10.1016/j.pec.2009.02.017

Hsieh, E. (2016). *Bilingual health communication: Working with interpreters in cross-cultural care*. Routledge.

Hsieh, E., & Kramer, E. M. (2021). *Rethinking culture in health communication: Social interactions as intercultural encounters*. Wiley.

Hu, H. C. (1944). The Chinese concepts of "face." *American Anthropologist, 46*(1), 45–64. https://doi.org/10.1525/aa.1944.46.1.02a00040

Hughes, D. L., Watford, J. A., & Del Toro, J. (2016). A transactional/ecological perspective on ethnic-racial identity, socialization, and discrimination. In S. S. Horn, M. D. Ruck, & L. S. Liben (Eds.), *Advances in Child Development and Behavior* (Vol. 51, pp. 1–41). Elsevier. https://doi.org/10.1016/bs.acdb.2016.05.001

Hughes, D., Rodriguez, J., Smith, E. P., Johnson, D. J., Stevenson, H. C., & Spicer, P. (2006). Parents' ethnic-racial socialization practices: A review of research and directions for future study. *Developmental Psychology, 42*(5), 747–770. https://doi.org/10.1037/0012-1649.42.5.747

Hull, G. T., Scott, P. B., & Smith, B., Eds. (1982). *All the women are white, all the Blacks are men, but some of us are brave*. Feminist Press.

Jackson, R. L. (2002). Cultural contracts theory: Toward an understanding of identity negotiation. *Communication Quarterly, 50*(3–4), 359–367. doi:10.1080/01463370209385672

Jackson, R. L. (2006). *Scripting the Black, masculine body: Identity, discourse, and racial politics in popular media*. SUNY Press.

Jackson, R. L., II, & Crawley, R. L. (2003). White student confessions about a Black male professor: A cultural contracts theory approach to intimate conversations about race and worldview. *Journal of Men's Studies, 12*(1), 25–41. doi:10.3149/jms.1201.25

Jackson, R. L., Johnson, A., Hecht, M. L., & Ribeau, S. A. (2020). *African American communication: Exploring identity and culture* (3e). Routledge.

Jackson, S. J., & Welles, B. F. (2015). Hijacking #myNYPD: Social media dissent and networked counterpublics. *Journal of Communication, 65*(6), 932–952. doi:10.1111/jcom.12185

Jenkins, H., McPherson, T., & Shattuc, J. (2002). Defining popular culture. In H. Jenkins, T. McPherson, & J. Shattuc (Eds.), *Hop on Pop: The politics and pleasures of popular culture* (pp. 26–42). Duke University Press. doi.org/10.2307/j.ctv11g96r2.5

Johnson, A. (2017). From academe, to the theatre, to the streets: My autocritography of aesthetic cleansing and canonical exception in the wake of Ferguson. *Qualitative Inquiry* 24(2), 1–13. doi.org/10.1177/1077800416684869

Johnson, A. (2018). Straight outta erasure: Black girl magic claps back to the hyperinvisibility of Black women in Straight Outta Compton. *National Political Science Review*, 19(2), 34–49.

Johnson, A., & Boylorn, R. (2015). Digital media and the politics of intersectional queer hyper/in/visibility in *Between Women*. *Liminalities: A Journal of Performance Studies*, 11(1), 1–26.

Jones, M., Harris, K., & Reynolds, A. (2021). In their own words: The meaning of the strong Black woman schema among Black U.S. college women. *Sex Roles*, 84, 347–359. https://doi.org/10.1007/s11199-020-01170-w

Kaplan, A. (1964). *The conduct of inquiry*. Chandler.

Katz, E., Blumler, J. G., & Gurevitch, M. (1973). Uses and gratifications research. *Public Opinion Quarterly*, 37(4), 509–523. doi.org/10.1086/268109

Knapp, M. L. (1978). *Social intercourse: From greeting to goodbye*. Allyn & Bacon.

Kramarae, C. (1981). *Women and men speaking: Frameworks for analysis*. Newbury House.

Larson, K. R., & McHendry, G. F., Jr. (2019). *Parasitic publics*. Rhetoric Society Quarterly, 49(5), 517–541. doi:10.1080/02773945.2019.1671986

Lazarsfeld, P. F., Berelson, B., & Gaudet, H. (1944). *The people's choice: How the voter makes up his mind in a presidential campaign*. Columbia University Press.

Lee, S. K. (2014). The impact of social capital in ethnic religious communication networks on Korean immigrant's intercultural development. *International Journal of Intercultural Relations*, 43, 289–303. https://doi.org/10.1016/j.ijintrel.2014.10.001

Li, M. (2021). Exemplifying power matters: The impact of power exemplification of transgender people in the news on issue attribution, dehumanization, and aggression tendencies. *Journalism Practice*. doi.org/10.1080/17512786.2021.1930104

Liu, W. (2020). Disaster communication ecology in multiethnic communities: Understanding disaster coping and community resilience from a communication resource approach. *Journal of International and Intercultural Communication*, 1–24. https://doi.org/10.1080/17513057.2020.1854329

Liu, W., Lai, C. H., & Xu, W. W. (2018). Tweeting about emergency: A semantic network analysis of government organizations' social media messaging during Hurricane Harvey. *Public Relations Review*, 44(5), 807–819. https://doi.org/10.1016/j.pubrev.2018.10.009

Mackintosh, U., Marsh, D., & Schroeder, D. (2002). Sustained positive deviant child care practices and their effects on child growth in Viet Nam, *Food and Nutrition Bulletin*, 23(4 supplement) 18–27.

Mansbridge J., & Morris, A. (Eds.). (2001). *Oppositional consciousness: The subjective roots of social protest*. University of Chicago Press.

Martin, J. N., & Nakayama, T. K. (1999). Thinking dialectically about culture and communication. *Communication Theory*, 9(1), 1–25.

Martinez, A. R. (2017). Intersectionality, voz, and agency: A culture-centered approach to understanding U.S.-born Mexican Americans' depression experiences. *Southern Communication Journal*, 82(5), 278–297.

Matsunaga, M., & Torigoe, C. (2008). Looking at the Japan-residing Korean identities through the eyes of the "outsiders within": Application and extension of co-cultural theory. *Western Journal of Communication*, 72(4), 349–373. https://doi.org/10.1080/10570310802446007

McCombs, M., & Shaw, D. (1972). The agenda-setting function of mass media. *Public Opinion Quarterly*, 36(2), 176–187. doi.org/10.1086/267990

McCornack, S. A. (1992). Information manipulation theory. *Communication Monographs*, 59(1), 1–16. https://doi.org/10.1080/03637759209376245

McGuire, W. J. (1961). The effectiveness of supportive and refutational defenses in immunizing and restoring beliefs against persuasion. *Sociometry, 24*(2), 184–197. https://doi.org/10.2307/2786067

McGuire, W. J. (1962). Persistence of the resistance to persuasion induced by various types of prior belief defenses. *Journal of Abnormal and Social Psychology, 64*(4), 241–248. https://doi.org/10.1037/h0044167

McLuhan, M., & Fiore, Q. (2005). *The medium is the massage*. Gingko Press.

McPhail, M. (1994). *Zen in the art of rhetoric: An inquiry into coherence*. SUNY Press.

McPhail, M. (2004). *The rhetoric of racism revisited: Reparations or separation?* Rowman & Littlefield.

McPhail, M. (2018). Complicity theory. In Y. Y. Kim (Ed.), *The international encyclopedia of intercultural communication*. John Wiley & Sons. https://doi.org/10.1002/9781118783665.ieicc0202

McQuail, D. (1994). *Mass communication theory: An introduction*. SAGE.

Mead, G. H. (1934). *Mind, self, and society: From the standpoint of a social behaviorist*. University of Chicago Press.

Melamed, J. (2011). *Represent and Destroy: Rationalizing violence in the new racial capitalism*. University of Minnesota Press.

Memmi, A. (1965). *The colonizer and the colonized*. Beacon Press.

Memmi, A. (1984). *Dependence: A sketch for a portrait of the dependent*. Beacon Press.

Miller, G. R. (2002). On being persuaded: Some basic distinctions. In J. P. Dillard & M. Pfau (Eds.), *The persuasion handbook: Developments in theory and practice* (pp. 3–16). SAGE.

Mills, C. (1997). *The racial contract*. Cornell University Press.

Mills, C. (2007). White ignorance. In S. Sullivan & N. Tuana (Eds.), *Race and epistemologies of ignorance* (pp. 11–38). SUNY Press.

Minniear, M. (2020). *Ethnic-racial socialization mapping in ethnic-racial minority populations: Exploring the efficacy of an intervention to increase well-being and secure ethnic-racial identity* [Doctoral Dissertation, University of Nebraska]. https://digitalcommons.unl.edu/commstuddiss/48/

Minniear, M., & Soliz, J. (2019). Family communication and messages about race and identity in Black families in the United States. *Journal of Family Communication, 19*(4), 329–347. https://doi.org/10.1080/15267431.2019.1593170

Moemeka, A. (1997). Communalistic societies: Community and self-respect as African values. In C. Christians & M. Traber (Eds.), *Communication ethics and universal values* (pp. 170–193). SAGE.

Mohanty, C. (1984). Under Western eyes: Feminist scholarship and colonial discourses. *Boundary, 2*(12/13), 333–358. doi:10.2307/302821

Molina-Guzmán, I. (2010). *Dangerous curves: Latina bodies in the media*. New York University Press.

Molina-Guzmán, I. (2021). Into the Spider-Verse and the commodified (re)imagining of Afro-Rican visibility. In S. Dagbovie-Mullins & E. Berlatsky (Eds.), *Mixed-race superheroes* (pp. 229–247). Rutgers University Press.

Montoya, M. (2019, April). Movement lawyering: Origins, developments, and future. Paper presented at the Harvard Law School Critical Race Theory Conference, Cambridge, MA.

Neblett, E. W., Jr., White, R. L., Ford, K. R., Philip, C. L., Nguyên, H. X., & Sellers, R. M. (2008). Patterns of racial socialization and psychological adjustment: Can parental communications about race reduce the impact of racial discrimination? *Journal of Research on Adolescence, 18*(3), 477–515. https://doi.org/10.1111/j.1532-7795.2008.00568.x

Nelson, T., Cardemil, E., & Adeoye, C. (2016). Rethinking strength: Black women's perceptions of the "Strong Black Woman" role. *Psychology of Women Quarterly, 40*(4), 551–563. https://doi.org/10.1177/0361684316646716

Nkomo, S. M., & Cox, T., Jr. (1996). Diverse identities in organizations. In S. R. Clegg, C. Hardy, & W. R. Nords (Eds.), *Handbook of organization studies* (pp. 338–356). SAGE.

Northouse, P. G. (2016). *Leadership, theory and practice* (7th ed.). SAGE.

Norton, R. (1983). *Communicator style: Theory, applications, and measures.* SAGE.

Oetzel, J. G., & Ting-Toomey, S. (2003). Face concerns in interpersonal conflict: A cross-cultural empirical test of the face negotiation theory. *Communication Research, 30*(6) 599–624. https://doi.org/10.1177%2F0093650203257841

Offen, K. (1988). Defining feminism: A comparative historical approach. *Signs: Journal of Women in Culture and Society, 14*(1), 119–157.

Ogunyemi, C. O. (1985). Womanism: The dynamics of the contemporary Black female novel in English. *Signs: Journal of Women in Culture and Society, 11*(1), 63–80.

Olmedo, C. (2018, October 10). Miles Morales: Our Afro-Latino Spider-Man, https://butwhythopodcast/2018/10/10/miles-morlaes-our-afro-latino-spider-man/

Onuzulike, U. (2014). Ethnic and transnational identities in the diaspora: A phenomenological study of second-generation Igbo-American young adults (Doctoral dissertation, Howard University).

Onuzulike, U. (2018). The Igbo communication style: Conceptualizing ethnic communication theory. In K. Langmia (Ed.), *Black/Africana communication theory* (pp. 41–59). Palgrave Macmillan.

Onuzulike, U. (2021). Ethnicity and belonging among young Igbo in the United States: Explicating coculturation and ethnic communication theory. *Howard Journal of Communications 32*(2), 1–15.

Orbe, M. (1996). Laying the foundation for co-cultural communication theory: An inductive approach to studying "non-dominant" communication strategies and the factors that influence them. *Communication Studies, 47*(3), 157–176. https://doi.org/10.1080/10510979609368473

Orbe, M. P. (1998). *Constructing co-cultural theory: An explication of culture, power, and communication.* SAGE. http://dx.doi.org/10.4135/9781483345321

Orbe, M. P., & Bruess, C. J. (2005). *Contemporary issues in interpersonal communication.* Oxford University Press.

Orbe, M. P., & Roberts, T. L. (2012). Co-cultural theorizing: Foundations, applications & extensions. *The Howard Journal of Communications, 23*(4), 293–311. https://doi.org/10.1080/10646175.2012.722838.

Padilla, A. M. (2006). Bicultural social development. *Hispanic Journal of Behavioral Sciences, 28*(4), 467–497.

Parker, P. S. (2005). *Race, gender, and leadership: Re-envisioning organizational leadership from the perspectives of African American women executives.* Lawrence Erlbaum Associates.

Parker, P. S., & Grimes, D. S. (2009). "Race" and management communication. In F. Bargiela-Chiappini, *The handbook of business discourse* (pp. 292–304). Edinburgh University Press.

Pascale, R. T., Sternin, J., & Sternin, M. (2010). *The power of positive deviance: How unlikely innovators solve the world's toughest problems.* Harvard University Press.

Pearce, W. B., & Cronen, V. E. (1980). *Communication, action, and meaning: The creation of social realities.* Praeger.

Perry, R. (2007). *"Race" and racism: The development of modern racism in America.* Palgrave MacMillan.

Petermon, J. D. (2014). Hyper (in)visibility: Reading race and representation in the neoliberal era. [Doctoral dissertation, University of Santa Barbara.] Open Access Dissertations, Alexandria. https://www.alexandria.ucsb.edu/lib/ark:/48907/f3ccoxvc

Petermon, J. D. (2018). Race (lost and found) in Shondaland: The rise of multiculturalism in prime-time network television. In R. Griffin & M. Meyer (Eds.), *Adventures in Shondaland: Identity politics and the power of representation* (pp. 101–119). Rutgers University Press.

Petty, R. E., & Cacioppo, J. T. (1986). *Communication and persuasion: Central and peripheral routes to attitude change*. Springer-Verlag.

Pfau, M. (1992). The potential of inoculation in promoting resistance to the effectiveness of comparative advertising messages. *Communication Quarterly, 40*(1), 26–44. https://doi.org/10.1080/01463379209369818

Pfau, M., Tusing, K. J., Lee, W., Godbold, L. C., Koerner, A., Penaloza, L. J., Hong, Y., & Yang, V. S. (1997). Nuances in inoculation: The role of inoculation approach, ego-involvement, and message processing disposition in resistance. *Communication Quarterly, 45*(4), 461–481. https://doi.org/10.1080/01463379709370077

Pindi, G., & De La Garza, A. (2019). "The colonial Jesus": Deconstructing white Christianity. In D. McIntosh, D. Moon, & T. Nakayama. *Interrogating the communicative power of whiteness* (pp. 218–238). Routledge.

Poussaint, A. (1999). "They hate, they kill. Are they insane?" *The New York Times*, August, A21.

Ramasubramanian, S., & Banjo, O. (2020). Critical media effects framework: Bridging critical cultural communication and media effects through power, intersectionality, context, and agency. *Journal of Communication, 70*(3), 379–400. doi.org/10.1093/joc/jqaa014

Razzante, R. J. (2018). Intersectional agencies: Navigating predominantly white institutions as an administrator of color. *Journal of International and Intercultural Communication, 11*(4) 339–357. http://doi:10.1080/17513057

Razzante, R. J., & Orbe, M. P. (2018). Two sides of the same coin: Conceptualizing dominant group theory in the context of co-cultural theory. *Communication Theory, 28*(5), 354375. https://doi.org/10.1093/ct/qtx008

Redfield, R., Linton, R., & Herskovits, M. J. (1936). Memorandum for the study of acculturation. *American Anthropologist, 38*(1), 149–152.

Rogers, E. M. (1994). *A history of communication study: A biological approach*. Free Press.

Rosas, R. O. (2020). "Paradise … They make you feel at home": A case study on understanding the role of an undocumented student resource center and its influence on the college journey of undocumented students. California State University–San Bernardino.

Salabarría-Peña, Y., Trout, P., Gill, J., Morisky, D., Muralles, A., & Ebin, V. (2001). Effects of acculturation and psychosocial factors in Latino adolescents' TB-related behaviors. *Ethnicity & Disease, 11*(4), 661–675.

Santos, B. de S. (2006). *Renovar la teoría crítica y reinventar la emancipación social: Encuentros en Buenos Aires*. CLACSO: Universidad de Buenos Aires, Facultad de Ciencias Sociales, Instituto de Investigaciones Gino Germani.

Scharrer, E., & Ramasubramanian, S. (2021). *Quantitative research methods in communication: The power of numbers for social justice*. Routledge.

Schramm, W. (1983). The unique perspective of communication: A retrospective view. *Journal of Communication, 33*(3), 6–17.

Schramm, W. (1997). *The beginnings of communication study in America: A personal memoir* (S. H. Chaffee & E. M. Rogers, Eds.). SAGE.

Scott, J. (1991). *Social network analysis: A handbook*. SAGE.

Scott, J. C. (1985). *Weapons of the weak: Everyday forms of peasant resistance*. Yale University Press.

Shange, N. (2010). *For colored girls who have considered suicide/when the rainbow is enuf*. Simon and Schuster.

Shoemaker, P. J., Tankard, J. W., Jr., & Lasorsa, D. L. (2004). *How to build social science theories*. SAGE.

Sims, J. D. (2020). No gentlemen's agreement here: Higher education reflections on being womanist and the dialectics present in an African American woman's administrative journey. In J.

Cubbage (Ed.), *Developing women leaders in the academy through enhanced communication strategies* (pp. 175–190). Lexington Books.

Sims, J. D., Cunliff, E., Sims, A., & Robertson, K. (2018). Probing leadership from racio-ethnic perspectives in higher education: An emergent model of accelerating leader identity. In J. L. Chin, J. E. Trimble, & J. E. Garcia (Eds.), *Global and culturally diverse leaders and leadership: New dimensions and challenges for business, education, and society* (pp. 183–209). Emerald.

Singhal, A. (Ed.) (2021). *The art of positive deviance: A radically different way of solving the world's toughest problems*. Change Designers Press.

Singhal, A., & Kim, D. K. D. (2021). The role of the communication discipline to tackle COVID-19: Interrogating positive deviations and critical discourses. *Journal of Creative Communications*, 16(2), 135–138. https://doi.org/10.1177/09732586211002930

Singhal, A., & Sowards, S. (in press). *The craft of positive deviance: A new research paradigm for solving complex social problems*. Change Designers Press.

Singhal, A., & Svenkerud, P.J. (2018). Diffusion of evidence-based interventions or practice-based positive deviations. *Journal of Development Communication*, 29(2): 34–44.

Singhal, A., Buscell, P., & Lindberg, C. (2010). *Inviting everyone: Healing healthcare through positive deviance*. Plexus Press.

Singhal, A., Buscell, P., & Lindberg, C. (2014). *Inspiring change and saving lives: The positive deviance way*. Plexus Press.

Sims, J. D. (2011). A muted voice on holy ground: Reflections on the dialectics experienced as an African American female professor in a Christian university. In M. N. Niles and N. S. Gordon (Eds.), *Still searching for our mothers' gardens: Experiences of new, tenure-track women of color at "majority" institutions* (pp. 21–40). University Press of America.

Smitherman, G. (2000). *Black talk: Words and phrases from the hood to the amen corner*. Houghton Mifflin.

Soliz, J., Thorson, A. R., & Rittenour, C. E. (2009). Communicative correlates of satisfaction, family identity, and group salience in multiracial/ethnic families. *Journal of Marriage and Family*, 71(4), 819–832. DOI?

Squires, C. R. (2002). Rethinking the Black public sphere: An alternative vocabulary for multiple public spheres. *Communication Theory*, 12(4), 446–468. doi.org/10.1111/j.1468-2885.2002.tb00278.x

Sterling, D. (Ed.) (1984). *We are your sisters: Black women in the nineteenth century*. W. W. Norton.

Sue, D. (2004). Whiteness and ethnocentric monoculturalism: Making the "invisible" visible. *American Psychologist* 59(8), pp. 761–769.

Tajfel, H., & Turner, J. C. (1986). The social identity theory of inter-group behavior. In S. Worchel & W. G. Austin (Eds.), *Psychology of intergroup relations* (pp. 7–24). Nelson-Hall.

Tan, N., Kaur-Gill, S., Dutta, M. J., & Venkataraman, N. (2017). Food insecurity in Singapore: The communicative (dis)value of the lived experiences of the poor. *Health Communication*, 32(8), 954–962. https://doi.org/10.1080/10410236.2016.1196416

Terborg-Penn, R. (1978). Discrimination against Afro-American women in the woman's movement, 1830–1920. In S. Harley & R. Terborg-Penn (Eds.), *The Afro-American woman: Struggles and images* (pp. 17–27). Kennikat Press.

The "Migrant Protection Protocols." (2021, January 22). American Immigration Council. https://www.americanimmigrationcouncil.org/research/migrant-protection-protocols

Thomas, A. J., & Blackmon, S. M. (2015). The influence of the Trayvon Martin shooting on racial socialization practices of African American parents. *Journal of Black Psychology*, 41(1), 75–89. https://doi.org/10.1177/0095798414563610

Thompson, J. B. (2005). The new visibility. *Theory, Culture & Society*, 22(6), 31–51. http://doi.org/10.1177/0263276405059413

Ting-Toomey, S. (1985). Toward a theory of conflict and culture. In W. B. Gudykunst, L. Stewart, & S. Ting-Toomey (Eds.), *Communication, culture, and organizational processes* (pp.71–86). SAGE.

Ting-Toomey, S. (1988). Intercultural conflict styles: A face-negotiation theory. In Y. Y. Kim & W. B. Gudykunst (Eds.), *Theories in intercultural communication* (pp. 213–235). SAGE.

Ting-Toomey, S. (2005). Identity negotiation theory: Crossing cultural boundaries. In W. B. Gudykunst (Ed.), *Theorizing about intercultural communication* (pp. 211–234). SAGE.

Ting Toomey, S. (2005). The matrix of face: An updated face-negotiation theory. In W. B. Gudykunst (Ed.), *Theorizing about intercultural communication* (pp. 71–92). SAGE.

Ting-Toomey, S. (2017). Conflict face-negotiation theory: Tracking its evolutionary journey. In X. Dia & G.-M. Chen (Eds.), *Conflict management and intercultural communication: The art of intercultural harmony* (pp. 123–143). Routledge.

Ting-Toomey, S., & Chung, L. C. (2022). *Understanding intercultural communication* (3rd ed.). Oxford University Press.

Ting-Toomey, S., & Dorjee, T. (2019). *Communicating across cultures* (2nd ed.). Guilford Press.

Ting-Toomey, S., & Kurogi, A. (1998). Facework competence in intercultural conflict: An updated face-negotiation theory. *International Journal of Intercultural Relations, 22*(2), 187–225. http://doi.org/10.1016/S0147-1767(98)00004-2

Ting-Toomey, S., & Oetzel, J. G. (2001). *Managing intercultural conflict effectively.* SAGE.

Umaña-Taylor, A. J., Quintana, S. M., Lee, R. M., Cross, W. E., Jr., Rivas-Drake, D., Schwartz, S. J., Syed, M., Yip, T., Seaton, E., & Ethnic and Racial Identity in the 21st Century Study Group. (2014). Ethnic and racial identity during adolescence and into young adulthood: An integrated conceptualization. *Child Development, 85*(1), 21–39. https://doi.org/10.1111/cdev.12196

Vertovec, S. (2001). Transnationalism and identity. *Journal of Ethnic and Migration Studies, 27*(4), 573–582.

Villegas, P. (2020). Writing in community at the Undocumented Student Success Center. *University Diversity Committee records.* https://scholarworks.lib.csusb.edu/udc/4

Walcott, D. (1987). Love after love. *In Collected Poems, 1948–1984* (pp. 328–329). Farrar, Straus and Giroux.

Walker, A. (1983). *In search of our mother's gardens: Womanist prose.* Harcourt Brace Jovanovich.

Wang, M.-T., Henry, D. A., Smith, L. V., Huguley, J. P., & Guo, J. (2020). Parental ethnic-racial socialization practices and children of color's psychosocial and behavioral adjustment: A systematic review and meta-analysis. *American Psychologist, 75*(1), 1–22. https://doi.org/10.1037/amp0000464

Warner, M. (2002). *Publics and counterpublics.* Zone Publishers.

Watson, N., & Hunter, C. (2015). "I had to be strong": Tensions in the strong Black woman schema. *Journal of Black Psychology, 42*(5), 424–452. https://doi.org/ 10.1177/0095798415597093

Weick, K. E., Sutcliffe, K. M., & Obstfeld, D. (2005). Organizing and the process of sensemaking. *Organization Science, 16*(4), 409–421.

Wellington, E. (2017, October 23). Tarana Burke: Me Too movement can't end with a hashtag. *The Philadelphia Inquirer.* https://www.inquirer.com/philly/columnists/elizabeth_wellington/philly-me-too-movement-founder-tarana-burke-20171023.html

West, C. (2001). *Race Matters.* Beacon Press.

Wilmot, W. W. (1995). *Relational communication.* McGraw-Hill.

Wolf, D. L. (2002). There's no place like "home": Emotional transnationalism and the struggles of second-generation Filipinos. In P. Levitt & M. C. Waters (Eds.), *The changing face of home: The transnational lives of the second generation* (pp. 255–294). Russell Sage Foundation.

Woods-Giscombé, C. (2010). Superwoman schema: African American women's views on stress, strength, and health. *Qualitative Health Research, 20*(5), 668–683. https://doi.org/10.1177/1049732310361892

World Health Organization (2015). Double burden of malnutrition. https://www.who.int/nutrition/double-burden-malnutrition/en/ Accessed on April 30, 2021.

Yin, J. (2018). Beyond postmodernism: A non-western perspective on identity. *Journal of Multicultural Discourses, 13*(3), 193–219. doi.org/10.1080/17447143.2018.1497640d

Yomtoob, D. (2013). Caught in code: Arab American identity, image, and lived reality. In R. Boylorn and M. Orbe (Eds.), *Critical autoethnography: Intersecting cultural identities in everyday life* (pp. 144–158). Left Coast Press.

Zeitlin, M., Ghassemi, H., & Mansour, M. (1990). *Positive deviance in child nutrition*. UN University.

ABOUT THE EDITORS

Jasmine T. Austin (Ph.D., University of Oklahoma) is an assistant professor of organizational communication in the Department of Communication Studies at Texas State University. Her research focuses on socialization efforts and the influence that communication about historically marginalized identities (e.g., race, gender, etc.) have on members' experiences and future communication. Known for being the lead organizer for the African American Communication and Culture #ScholarStrike Conference, she has published in top-tier journals, including *Management Communication Quarterly, Communication Studies,* and *Health Communication.*

Mark P. Orbe (Ph.D., Ohio University) is a professor of communication and diversity in the School of Communication at Western Michigan University, where he also is a Faculty Fellow in the Office of Institutional Equity. His teaching, research, and service interests focus on the inextricable relationship of culture, power, and communication as manifested in a variety of contexts.

Jeanetta D. Sims (Ph.D., University of Oklahoma) is a professor in the College of Business's Department of Marketing at the University of Central Oklahoma, where she serves as dean of the Jackson College of Graduate Studies and the University College. She is accredited in public relations. Along with leadership, her research focuses on persuasion/social influence, strategic communication, and diversity. She has coached and consulted with professionals and organizations on leadership, marketing communications, and diversity.

ABOUT THE CONTRIBUTORS

Carlos Aguilar (M.A., Harvard University) is a doctoral student in the Department of Sociology at the University of Pennsylvania. His current research seeks to explore the experiences and opportunities that undocumented immigrants encounter in historically racialized and marginalized contexts. As an undocumented immigrant and DACA recipient, Carlos's underlying emphasis is not to provide alternative concepts to what we know but rather to explore alternative ways of thinking about issues.

Fatima Albrehi (M.A., Western Michigan University) is a doctoral student in communication studies at Wayne State University. Her research is intercultural and interracial in nature and focuses on communication messages present through the ostracism of marginalized, nonwhite populations, hip hop culture as a tool for addressing and resisting inequality, and sexual misconduct in academia.

Gina Castle Bell (Ph.D., George Mason University) is an associate professor at St. John's University in New York City and a white ally. She explores how language reinforces the status quo and contributes to racism. She has authored one book and 25 manuscripts related to the study of prejudice, police brutality, active listening, facework, and interracial communication tensions in the U.S. cultural context.

Ed Cunliff (Ph.D., University of Oklahoma) is a professor of adult and higher education at the University of Central Oklahoma, where he served for several years as an assistant vice president in academic affairs. Along with leadership, his teaching and research focuses on transformative learning, authentic leadership, and MBE (mind, brain, education). He has consulted with a variety of organizations in the areas of planning and communications.

Shardé M. Davis (Ph.D., University of Iowa) is an assistant professor in communication at the University of Connecticut. She studies interpersonal communication with emphases in Black women's identity, intra/intergroup dynamics, and supportive communication, as well as resistance and resilience. She has published two theories and over 30 articles and book chapters and has received numerous awards, including the 2018 American Research Fellowship and 2019 Ford Foundation Postdoctoral Fellowship.

Antonio Tomas De La Garza (Ph.D., University of Utah) is an associate professor of communication at California State University, San Marcos. He is a member of the *Contra Viento y Marea* collective, which provides support to Tijuanas refugee and homeless population and the National Latino Research Center, under which he provides training on resilience and support for undocumented and mixed status students. His research includes "A Eulogy for Roxsana Hernández" in QED: *A Journal in GLBTQ Worldmaking.*

Mohan J. Dutta (Ph.D., University of Minnesota) is the Dean's Chair Professor of Communication and Director of the Center for Culture-Centered Approach to Research and Evaluation (CARE), where he directs community-led antiracist organizing for securing health in communities at the margins. From building community-owned health spaces to leading activist campaigns seeking transformations in capitalist and colonizing structures, his community-immersed everyday life shapes his approach to health communication.

Elaine Hsieh (Ph.D., University of Illinois at Urbana-Champaign; J.D., University of Oklahoma) is a professor of communication at the University of Oklahoma. Dr. Hsieh's work examines the intersections of culture, medicine, and health behaviors. Her latest book, *Rethinking Culture in Health Communication* (2021), coauthored with Eric M. Kramer, is an extension of this line of research by situating culture front and center in conceptualizing health theories and health policies.

Ronald L. Jackson II (Ph.D., Howard University) is past president and distinguished scholar of the National Communication Association, International Communication Association fellow, professor of communication, and former dean of the McMicken College of Arts & Sciences at the University of Cincinnati. He is an award-winning author of 16 books and more than 85 publications related to the study of masculinity, identity negotiation, race, and culture.

Amber Johnson (Ph.D., The Pennsylvania State University) is professor of communication and associate provost in the Office of Diversity and Community Engagement at St. Louis University. They are also the cofounder of the Institute for Healing Justice and Equity and founding director of the Justice Fleet.

Martinque K. Jones (Ph.D., University of Houston) is an assistant professor in psychology at the University of North Texas. She employs an intersectional lens to the study of Black women's identity, mental health, and counseling processes. She has published in feminist and race-specific journals, including *Journal of Black Psychology*, *Sex Roles*, and *Women Studies in Communication*. She earned the American Psychological Association 2019 Carolyn Patton Award for her research pertaining to the psychology of Black women.

Daniela Juarez (University of Texas at Dallas) is an undergraduate student in the Department of Sociology at the University of Texas at Dallas. Her current research interests seeks to explore and illustrate the obstacles that undocumented queer students face in higher education institutions. Daniela uses her own experiences of being queer and undocumented to guide and frame her research.

Wenlin Liu (Ph.D., University of Southern California) is an assistant professor of strategic communication at the Jack J. Valenti School of Communication, University of Houston. Liu's research focuses on interorganizational alliance building, multiethnic community, and social media–mediated disaster communication using a social network approach.

Mark Lawrence McPhail (Ph.D., University of Massachusetts) is a professor of communication at Indiana University Northwest. He is the author of *Zen in the Art of Rhetoric: An Inquiry into Coherence* and *The Rhetoric of Racism Revisited: Reparations or Separation*. His scholarship has been published in the *Quarterly Journal of Speech*, *Critical Studies in Mass Communication*, the *Howard Journal of Communications*, *Rhetoric and Public Affairs*, *Qualitative Inquiry*, and *Rhetoric Review*.

Mackensie Minniear (Ph.D., University of Nebraska Lincoln) is an assistant professor in the Department of Communication Studies at the University of Georgia. She studies ethnicity, race, and the family, to understand how families understand ethnicity and race as a social identity and as a social structure. Her work can be found in the *Journal of Family Communication*, the *Journal of Social and Personal Relationships*, and *Communication Reports*.

Isabel Molina-Guzmán (Ph.D., University of Pennsylvania) is a professor of communication and Latina/Latino studies with affiliations in gender and women Studies, Latin American and Caribbean studies, and the Institute of Communications Research at the University of Illinois Urbana-Champaign. Molina-Guzmán founded the Ethnicity Race in Communication Division of the International Communication Association in 2005 and currently serves as coeditor of the journal *Feminist Media Studies*.

Marnel Niles Goins (Ph.D., Howard University) is dean of the College of Sciences and Humanities and professor at Marymount University. She has a special interest in leadership, as well as gender and racial dynamics in organizational settings. Marnel has numerous publications, including serving as first editor of the recently published *Routledge Handbook of Gender and Communication*. She is also president of the Western States Communication Association and a past president of the Organization for Research on Women and Communication.

Uchenna Onuzulike (Ph.D., Howard University) is an assistant professor for the organizational communications graduate program in the Department of Communications at Bowie State University. His research foci lie in (critical) intercultural communication; ethnic and transnational identities; communication theories; organizational communication; transnational media and globalization; interrelationships of religion, culture, folk belief, and language; the second-generation Igbo; and Nollywood/film analysis and criticism.

Jade Petermon (Ph.D., University of California, Santa Barbara) is an assistant professor in the School of Film, Media, and Theater at Georgia State University. She is currently working on a manuscript that examines visibility of radicalized subjectivities across several media platforms during the Obama era. Dr. Petermon has taught courses on race, class, gender, and sexuality in women and gender studies, Black studies and film and media studies.

Srividya "Srivi" Ramasubramanian (Ph.D. Penn State University) was born and raised in South India and is currently Professor Newhouse School of Public Communications at Syracuse University. She is founding Director of CODE^SHIFT (Collaboratory for Data Equity, Social Healing, Inclusive Futures & Transformation), and Media Rise, a nonprofit media collective for social justice. Her research focuses on critical media effects, media literacy, antiracism, bias reduction, algorithmic justice, and data justice. You can read more about her at www.drsrivi.com.

Arvind Singhal (Ph.D., University of Southern California) is the Samuel Shirley and Edna Holt Marston Endowed Professor of Communication at the University of Texas at El Paso and appointed Professor 2, Inland School of Business and Social Sciences, Inland Norway University of Applied Sciences, Norway; William J. Clinton Distinguished Fellow at the Clinton School of Public Service, University of Arkansas at Little Rock; and Chancellor's Honorary Professor at Amity University, India. His teaching and research interests include the diffusion of innovations, the positive deviance approach, the entertainment-education communication strategy, and liberating interactional structures.

Catherine R. Squires (Ph.D., Northwestern University) is professor of communication studies at the University of Minnesota, Twin Cities. Her research and teaching interests involve intergenerational healing and storysharing, public spheres and public histories, and the politics of race, gender, and media.

Stella Ting-Toomey (Ph.D., University of Washington) is a professor of human communication studies at California State University, Fullerton. Her teaching passions include intercultural communication theory and interpersonal conflict management. She is the author or editor of 19 scholarly books. Her recent books include *Communicating across Cultures*, second edition (with Tenzin Dorjee; Guilford Press), and *Understanding Intercultural Communication*, third edition (with Leeva Chung; Oxford University Press). She has also published more than 130 articles and chapters in prestigious journals and handbooks.

Dianna Watkins-Dickerson (Ph.D., University of Memphis) specializes in rhetoric and media studies, foregrounding issues of womanist theory, politics, religion, and health. She is a veteran of Operation Enduring Freedom and Operation Inherent Resolve and an ordained itinerant elder in the African Methodist Episcopal Church.

INDEX